Anth
social experience – such as field be re... im language.
Social Experience and Anth asked f Knowledge focuses on this
paradox and on the actual processes leading from individual experiences in the field to the production of anthropological
knowledge.

The contributors emphasize the value of fieldwork in the process
of knowledge production. Against the background of recent
debates in anthropology on subjectivity, they challenge the distinction between subjectivity and objectivity, redefine what we should
mean by 'empirical', and demonstrate the complexity of present-
day epistemological problems by way of concrete examples. They
trace the route from the field experience to the analytical results,
showing how fieldwork enables the ethnographer to arrive at an
understanding, not only of 'culture' or 'society', but also of the
processes by which cultures and societies are transformed.

Social Experience and Anthropological Knowledge shows a clear
way out of the impasse created by postmodernism and its claim to
have dismantled science. By demystifying subjectivity in the ethnographic process and re-emphasizing the vital position of fieldwork, the book will do much to renew confidence in the
anthropological project of comprehending the world.

Kirsten Hastrup is Professor of Social Anthropology, and **Peter
Hervik** is Senior Research Fellow, both at the Institute of
Anthropology, University of Copenhagen.

EUROPEAN ASSOCIATION OF SOCIAL ANTHROPOLOGISTS

The European Association of Social Anthropologists (EASA) was inaugurated in January 1989, in response to a widely felt need for a professional association which would represent social anthropologists in Europe, and foster cooperation and interchange in teaching and research. As Europe transforms itself in the 1990s, the EASA is dedicated to the renewal of the distinctive European tradition in social anthropology.

Other titles in the series

Conceptualizing Society
Adam Kuper

Revitalizing European Rituals
Jeremy Boissevain

Other Histories
Kirsten Hastrup

Alcohol, Gender and Culture
Dimitra Gefou-Madianou

Understanding Rituals
Daniel de Coppet

Gendered Anthropology
Teresa del Valle

Syncretism/Anti-Syncretism
Charles Stewart and Rosalind Shaw

Fieldwork and Footnotes
Han F. Vermeulen and Arturo Alvarez Roldán

Social experience and anthropological knowledge

Edited by
Kirsten Hastrup and Peter Hervik

London and New York

First published 1994
by Routledge
11 New Fetter Lane, London EC4P 4EE

Simultaneously published in the USA and Canada
by Routledge
29 West 35th Street, New York, NY 10001

© 1994 Kirsten Hastrup and Peter Hervik, selection and editorial
material; the individual chapters, the contributors

Typeset in Times by Florencetype Ltd, Kewstoke, Avon
Printed and bound in Great Britain by Biddles Ltd, Guildford and
King's Lynn

British Library Cataloguing in Publication Data
A catalogue record for this book is available from the British Library

Library of Congress Cataloging in Publication Data
A catalog record for this book has been requested

ISBN 0–415–10657–5 (hbk)
ISBN 0–415–10658–3 (pbk)

Contents

Contributors

Karin Ask is Research Fellow at Chr. Michelsen's Institute, Bergen. She has done fieldwork in Pakistan, and applied studies in Bangladesh and Afghanistan. Her publications include 'Life-course, stress and diagnosis: the case of a Pakistani immigrant woman', in K. Ask, R. Grønhaug, A. Teslie and J. Chr. Knudsen, eds, *Health and International Lifecourses* (1986); and 'Ishq aur Mohabbatt: contrastive ideas on love and friendship in a northern Pakistani community', in T. Bleie, V. Broch-Due and I. Rudie, eds, *Carved Flesh/Cast Selves: Gendered Symbols and Social Practices* (1994).

Wojciech J. Burszta is Associate Professor at Adam Mickiewicz University, Poznan. His publications include *Jezyk a kultura w mysli etnologicznej* (Language and Culture in Ethnological Thought) (1986), *O zalozeniach interpretacji antropologicznej* (On Assumptions of Anthropological Interpretation), co-authored with Michal Buchowski (1992), *Wymiary antropologicznego poznania kultury* (Dimensions of Anthropological Cognition of Culture) (1992).

Francisco Cruces is Associate Fellow in the Department of Social Anthropology at the Universidad Nacional de Educación a Distancia in Madrid. He has done fieldwork in rural areas of Extremadura, and in the city of Madrid, on festivals, discourse and politics. Francisco Cruces has co-authored various publications with Angel Díaz de Rada, among them 'Public Celebrations in a Spanish Valley', in J. Boissevain, ed., *Revitalizing European Rituals* (1992).

John Davis is Professor of Social Anthropology at Oxford University. He has done fieldwork in Italy and Libya. His publications include *Libyan Politics: Tribe and Revolution* (1987), and *Exchange* (1992).

Angel Díaz de Rada is Assistant Professor in the Department of Social Anthropology at the Universidad Nacional de Educación a Distancia. He has carried out field research in Spain. His publications include *Rituales y proceso social. Un estudio comparativo en cinco zonas espanolas*, co-authored with Jose Luis García, Honorio Velasco *et al.* (1992).

Andre Gingrich is Senior Lecturer in Social Anthropology at the University of Vienna. He has done extensive fieldwork in Syria, Saudi-Arabia, and the Yemen. His publications include *Beiträge zur Ethnographie der Provinz Sa'da*, with Johann Heiss (1986), and *Studies in Oriental Culture and History* (1993).

Kirsten Hastrup is Professor of Anthropology at the University of Copenhagen. She has done fieldwork and historical research in Iceland. Her publications include *Nature and Policy in Iceland 1400–1800: An Anthropological Analysis of History and Mentality* (1990) and *Island of Anthropology: Studies in Icelandic Past and Present* (1990).

Peter Hervik is Research Fellow of the Institute of Anthropology at the University of Copenhagen. He has carried out fieldwork among the Yucatec Mayas of Mexico. His publications include 'Learning to be Indian: aspects of new ethnic and cultural identity of the Yucatec Maya', *Folk* (1992); 'Maya culture – beyond boundaries', *Ethnos* (1992).

Pavlos Kavouras is Lecturer Designate in the Department of Social Anthropology at the University of the Aegean, Mytilene, Greece. His publications include 'The Medea of Euripides: an anthropological perspective', *Dialectical Anthropology* (1989); and 'Dance at Olymbos, Karpathos: cultural change and political confrontations', *Ethnographica* (1992).

Marian Kempny is Assistant Professor in Culture Theory Unit, at the Institute of Philosophy and Sociology of the Polish Academy of Sciences. His publications include *Wymiana i społteczenstwo* (Exchange and Society) (1988); *Struktura, wymiana, władza* (Structure, Exchange, and Power), as co-author and co-editor (1993); *Kulturowy wymiar zmiany spotecznej* (The Cultural Dimension of Social Change), as co-author and co-editor (1993).

Tamara Kohn is Lecturer in Anthropology at the University of Durham. She has done extensive fieldwork both in the Inner Hebrides, Scotland, and in east Nepal. She is currently working on a monograph based on her Scottish research, entitled *Becoming Scottish: An Ethnograpic Study of Incomers*, and is co-author of J. Klama, ed., *Aggression: Conflict in Animals and Humans Reconsidered* (1988).

Judith Okely is Reader in Social Anthropology at the University of Edinburgh. She has carried out fieldwork in France and in England. Publications include *The Traveller-gypsies* (1983), *Simone de Beauvoir* (1986) and *Anthropology and Autobiography*, with Helen Callaway (1992).

Ingrid Rudie is Professor of Anthropology at the University of Oslo. She has done fieldwork in Norway and Malaysia. Her publications include 'A hall of mirrors: autonomy translated over time in Malaysia', in D. Bell, P. Caplan and W. K. Karim, eds, *Gendered Fields. Women, Men & Ethnography* (1993); and *Visible Women in East Coast Malay Society* (in press).

Thomas Widlok studied anthropology, philosophy, and theology at the Universities of Münster and Cologne before beginning postgraduate training in Social Anthropology at the London School of Economics and Political Science, University of London. He has completed one and a half years of field research with Hai‖om in northern Namibia (1990–2) as part of his Ph.D. project. Since 1992 he has been working with the Cognitive Anthropology Research Group in Nijmegen, Netherlands.

Introduction

Kirsten Hastrup and Peter Hervik

The aim of this volume is to elucidate the process from individual experiences in the field to the production of general anthropological knowledge.[1] In spite of its crucial position in our discipline, this process is far from clear. The lack of clarity is owed to several interrelated difficulties inherent in the specific nature of anthropological research, as based in fieldwork. First, processes are difficult to render in words, which by their nature punctuate and distort what they claim to represent. Further, the production of anthropological knowledge is not comprehensible solely in the traditional scientific terms of objectivity and rationality as something distinguishable from subjectivity and intuition. Together these two factors seem to have effectively blocked discussion of the route from ethnographic experience to analytical results.

Until recently, even the ethnographic experience was only reluctantly dealt with, as experience that is; what mattered were objective analytical results. They are still the core of anthropological knowledge, of course, but they are no longer seen as absolutely separate from subjective experiences in the field. Anthropology and autobiography merge in the process of knowledge production, as recently demonstrated in an important volume (Okely and Callaway 1992). Apart from this recent attempt at stock-taking in the busy backyard of the anthropological showrooms, the last one and a half decades have witnessed a number of experimental monographs and autobiographical works. If nothing else, these works have demonstrated a heightened awareness of the intricacies inherent in the process of acquiring information about people in the first place. 'Selves' and 'others' have been deconstructed as objective entities, and shown to be categories of thought.

The process from the experiences of the self to a valid

knowledge of the others has remained obscure, however. The present volume seeks to straddle the gap. While acknowledging the indubitable significance of autobiography and the situatedness of the anthropologist, the starting-point is not the self, but the field into which the ethnographer invests her powers of imagination. Through this investment, the ethnographer arrives at an understanding not only of 'culture' or 'society', but more importantly of the processes by which cultures and societies are reproduced and transformed.

Societies are conceptualized in a number of different ways, locally and analytically (Kuper 1992). What unites them is some sense of corporateness, however. The social body may be marked by dynamics and unclear boundaries; but this is still only ascertainable in relation to a concept of social integration beyond the individual, or within a particular tradition of knowledge (cf. Barth 1993a). For a time, it seemed that the 'new world' defied analysis, being too fragmented to deal with at all within an anthropology that some way or the other still saw itself as in many ways tied up with holism. Truly, 'our "present" appears to be substantially different from the "present" that our predecessors confronted, even just a short time ago' (Fox 1991: 1). The words used to indicate the qualities of our present have been words like decentred, fragmented, compressed and refracted, indicating a shift from their opposites. This is not only, maybe not even mainly, a substantial difference, but a difference in interest and in analytical focus: from structure to process, or from stability to change as an inherent feature of all social systems.

The focus on the process of knowledge creation within anthropological scholarship thus reflects a general shift in the conception of the anthropological object. Holism must be reinvented but not necessarily abandoned. The previous images of 'culture' (whether as a system of meanings or as a text) and 'social structure' (as a functional whole) are obsolete, even if still useful shorthands for those dynamic social spaces that anthropologists enter in the field and recollect ever after. The close, virtually self-confirming, relationship between the world and the science about it once again is strikingly revealed (cf. Hastrup 1987). The strategy of contextualization shifts: the whole studied or made manifest by anthropology is not a reifiable entity, but a space that embraces the process of knowledge production itself.

One of the targets of recent postmodernist criticisms of anthropological practice has been the idea of realism, as expressed in the sustained and often sophisticated discussion of representation. With realism gone, it seems that we can only speak of 'the empirical' in quotation marks, for ever distorted by our own concepts and subjective inclinations. One of the more ambitious aims of the present volume is to show that however much the anthropologist is part of the reality studied, it is still real. As a matter of course it is still a possible and legitimate object of investigation. Far from necessitating quotation marks that distantiate us from our object, the empirical needs direct confrontation as a first step towards a generalized knowledge that englobes ourselves and the processes of knowledge production. In short, while we have no intention of returning to old virtues of the lost paradise of Objectivism, we do want to demystify subjectivity in the ethnographic process and to call renewed attention to the vital position of fieldwork. By investigating the road from experience to knowledge we wish to contribute to a renewed confidence in the anthropological project of comprehending the world.

THE PRACTICE OF ANTHROPOLOGY

The shift of interest from structure to practice, or from pattern to process is a corollary also of the deconstruction of the the image of 'the others' as generalized objects for our professional curiosity. Anthropologists have been ingenious in extracting information on other worlds, and there is no need to belittle the efforts of our predecessors. There is a permanent need of considering the limits of the anthropological practice, however. One of the more pressing considerations concerns the fact that 'about large areas and important aspects of culture no one, not even the native, has information that can simply be called up and expressed in discursive statements' (Fabian 1990: 6). Such aspects are made present only in action. Far from devaluing the tradition of fieldwork as participant observation, it emphasizes its sustained value in the process of knowledge construction. As movingly demonstrated in Judith Okely's account of her use of vicarious and sensuous knowledge to understand the past and present of the rural French elderly, actual physical presence in their world is an absolute prerequisite to access to their lived experience. There is no way to substitute a phone call for fieldwork; most of the relevant information is non-verbal and cannot be 'called up', but has to be experienced as performed.

This is neither a return to old positivist notions of observation at the closest possible distance, nor is it an undue romanticization of participation in exotic worlds. There is always a limit to what one can actually share with other people, as succinctly shown by Tamara Kohn. It is simply a call for renewed reflection on the epistemological basis for our practice and thereby for expanding its field of significance. In this we disagree with a recent critic stating that 'academic disciplines do not create their fields of significance, they only legitimize particular organizations of meaning. They filter and rank – and in that sense they truly *discipline* – contested arguments and themes that often precede them' (Trouillot 1991: 17; emphasis original). The latter does not preclude the former, as far as we are concerned. While it is possibly true that anthropology inherited a field of significance, a 'savage slot', before it was properly formalized as a social science, we have higher notions of academia than to attribute to it mere mirroring or representation of preconceived notions and conceptual hierarchies. One of the more important contemporary insights is precisely this: that any science reflects back upon the reality studied and has a real historical impact. The causal connections are difficult to establish and they are far from even; yet to think of them exclusively in terms of temporal causation and unilinear determination seems to belie the insights generated within the anthropology of history (Hastrup 1992).

This inherently reflexive relationship between the world studied and the students of the world has a peculiar reality in anthropology, as shown by Peter Hervik. Reflexivity is not solely a matter of speculating about the mode of production of a particular text or other kind of scientific account; it is part of the human condition under which scholars must also abide. It is the fundamental mode of shared reasoning; and reasoning about the world *must* be shared. Meaning is a public feature: 'What no one can, in the nature of the case, figure out from the totality of the relevant evidence cannot be part of meaning' (Davidson 1984: 235). This is what 'authorizes' shared social experience in the field as the basis for anthropological knowledge.

This particular ethnographic authority has been vigorously questioned in the postmodern period (e.g. Clifford and Marcus 1986). Questioning the conditions for authority is certainly both legitimate and pertinent, but we are convinced that the ethnographic authority must be positively redeemed in view of the shift in the conception of the anthropological object. There is no way back to the summits of unchallenged authority on a particular culture by way of stating that 'I saw it myself'; but there is reason to maintain that one's own experience of the process of gradual understanding – and indeed of misunderstanding – in the field is still both the means to comprehension and the source of authority. This authority may not be 'on' a particular culture, but will certainly be on the performative context in which action and interaction in general take place and make sense.

The papers in the present volume contribute to a renewed sense of anthropological authority as grounded in fieldwork and expressed in a sophisticated scholarly discourse. The ethnographers were there alright, but that is not the only ground for listening to anthropologists. After all, the natives were there first and stayed longer. If our aim were solely to let the natives speak for themselves quantities of tape recorders would do the trick; no one would ever listen to them, of course, every one of us having enough voices in our immediate social space. As discussed by Francisco Cruces and Angel Díaz de Rada, even native speakers of a particular language may be surprised by their own words. The point is that there is a huge leap from the native voice to the anthropological vision; this is not a leap out of reality, since no discourse can exhaust reality anyway (Hastrup 1993). It is a shift from implicit knowing to explicit understanding. This shift is a precondition of scholarship. However many 'voices' speak in the ethnographic texts, they must be edited and reformulated through analysis and reflection if they are not to remain mere voices, speaking to no one in particular. Today, the editorial process includes a degree of anthropological self-reflexiveness, which adds to rather than detracts from the ethnographic authority, as abundantly demonstrated in this volume. The practice of anthropology is as vital and important as ever, even if the world we study seems to have changed to a point where the old notions on everybody's lips are gaining new significance.

WORLDS AND WORDS

The papers of this volume collectively and significantly contribute also to a redressal of the balance between worlds and words. As implied above, the ethnographic material is composed of so much more than words. While until relatively recently it could be maintained that 'fieldwork is significantly composed of language events' (Clifford 1988: 41), we have wanted to show that language events, or the eliciting of 'information', are but a fraction of what constitutes the material. That is one reason for emphasizing *experience* rather than *dialogue* as the starting-point for the route to anthropological knowledge.

In the field of linguistics itself, there has been a recent shift in focus from structure and grammar to practice and actual events (Lakoff 1987). It is stressed that there is no language without speakers; whenever we talk about the world in which humans live 'we are talking about the perceived world and not a metaphysical world without a knower' (Rosch 1978: 29). In both linguistics and anthropology, actor-centred research has had profound impacts on a number of longstanding theoretical issues. The relationship between cultural or linguistic models and actual behaviour has been recast. The individual is no longer seen as the passive enactor of culture, reflecting the so-called 'fax model of internalizing culture', which casts the person as a machine copying public messages into private psyches (Strauss and Quinn 1994). Instead, individual actors are seen as motivated human agents, whose activities constitute whatever 'culture' there is for anthropologists to study (cf. D'Andrade and Strauss 1992). One apt illustration of this is provided by Pavlos Kavouras in his discussion of the embodiment of moral judgment and social criticism in a particular person in Karpathos. This person acts on his or her own account but certainly contributes to traditional values – and vice versa of course.

Taking the perspective of the individual does not of necessity deconstruct the whole. As shown by recent studies of cultural models and motivation, there is an intricate connection between the individual actor and his/her interactive field (D'Andrade and Strauss 1993; Quinn and Strauss 1993). Actions are not at all random or just tactical, even if there is no longer any guarantee that they are 'grammatical'. The complexities of culture do not preclude regularities; cultural models are not of themselves directive, and evidently are not entities to be called forward for guidance. Notwithstanding, they are conceivable in terms of common resources that may or may not be used. As such they are no guarantee of systematicity in culture, but they are reflected in particular thematicities (Quinn and Holland 1987: 10).

Such thematicities are not primarily linguistic; they are embodied in action. Cultural models cannot be called forward in native language; they must be experienced. In other words, and as demonstrated by the papers in this volume, anthropology is now integrating categorical and textual approaches to culture within a more comprehensive study of practices and motivation. In Thomas Widlok's reassessment of the Kalahari debate this is a vital resource for his convincing recontextualization of the problem.

The interest in motivation also redirects the interest in internalization. What is internalized is not culture as a given text, which the anthropologist may then read over the native shoulders, as earlier interpretivists would have it (Geertz 1973: 452); nor is it a system of cognitive categories that forever restricts the conceptual world of people. Instead, internalization should be viewed as a holistic experience within the interpersonal realm, comprising thought, feelings and emotions. One is tempted to label it a 'total social experience', with a bow to a prominent ancestor of social anthropology. Internalization points to the locale of both cognized and embodied knowledge, while also stressing its link to the extrapersonal realm of the public world – towards which language reaches out.

The process of internalization, often named enculturation, is not governed by a systematic programming; no 'rules' are encoded in the brain. Learning culture is a process of gradual familiarization in practice. The cultural models, therefore, have no explanatory power of themselves, while they may still account 'for culturally informed interpretations of experience' (Holland 1992: 75), and thus for the experience of continuity in one's world. Whatever motivational force cultural models may have, it is conditioned by practice, not by some abstract code. A general point to be extracted from this is that any study of experience is also a study of values, emotions and motives.

These domains of experience are not easily captured in language, as we know: 'Every ethnographer is painfully aware of the discrepancy between the richness of the lived field experience and the paucity of the language used to characterize it' (Bruner 1984: 6). The apparent problem of turning this common pain into a telic demand for redressal is owed partly to the fact that, by contrast to pleasure, which is usually shared, pain is lonesome and considered an unnatural and temporary state of affairs (cf. Leder 1990). In the final chapter, Kirsten Hastrup discusses this in terms of the absent body – an absence which is also reflected in the lack of awareness of the degree to which experience and memory are embodied and not only (re-)cognized in language. Generally, she deals with some of the pressing epistemological problems which this volume implicitly addresses.

To conclude this section, we shall merely note that it is no longer possible to claim that language mirrors reality and that language, consequently, is a privileged entry into any culture. It is one entry among others, and a wide open one, but we should not let ourselves be deceived by the broad alley of words into society. If it seems to lead right to the heart of culture, this is largely an optical illusion based on the folk model of Western logocentrism. Most social experience lies beyond words (Hastrup, in press).

TIME AND EXPERIENCE

The focus on experience and action naturally leads also to a renewed awareness of time as a parameter of research. One of the pioneers in this field was Pierre Bourdieu (1977). His introduction of the notion of 'habitus' explicitly stressed both the patterns of regulated improvisation that were previously discussed in terms of 'culture', and the profound import of time in any activity of communication. Later, 'the work of time' was even more thoroughly analysed (Bourdieu 1990: 98ff.).

Life is a flow, and so is experience, even if it has been claimed that 'temporal succession cannot be experienced as such because the very observation of time fixes our attention and interrupts the flow of experience' (Bruner 1986: 8). Andre Gingrich's contribution to this volume is a timely modification of this ethnocentric view of time as having exclusively to do with fixation in chronology. Times are, indeed, experienced; they have their own textures, their own densities or emptinesses. Social experience cannot be studied without an awareness of the temporal vectors inherent in life, which do not necessarily frame it in a preconceived notion of an equidistant temporal scale. This is confirmed by other recent studies (e.g. Siverts, in press).

Experience has to be turned into expression to become part of ethnography, of course (Bruner 1986: 29). The trackless moments of inner experiences evade our curiosity, and leave us with a more limited set of manifestations or expressions to study. As so impressively shown by John Davis, the expression that we are left with, for instance in marriage documents, gives a clue only to a very limited set of those multitudes of experiences and actual choices made on the basis of lived experiences. Nevertheless, experiences are what we live by – not cultural expression (*pace* Bruner, ibid.).

Expressions are what we share, however. Phrased generally, 'what meaning there is for us depends in part on our powers of expression' (Taylor 1989: 22). It is far more difficult to claim that we share impressions, or experiences. It remains to be ascertained to what extent it is possible at all to speak of a *shared* social experience as the basis of ethnography. Even though one of the features that unites humanity is the fact that we are imaginable to one another, we can see from a variety of the perspectives offered in this volume that the question about who is actually sharing what remains open. Karin Ask poses the question fairly directly when she discusses the actual closeness to her female friends in purdah: however much she attempted to observe the practices herself, a veil remained between her and them, not least when they jumped stark naked into the river for any man to see – had he dared. Even if we are engaged in an apparently coherent conversation with people we cannot be sure that we share the understanding of the words.

A central methodological problem facing anthropology today is how to deal with the flow of intersubjective human experience without dehumanizing it, that is without deconstructing it *as experience* and transforming it into totalizing professional models of knowledge (cf. Kleinman 1992: 190). The epistemological magnitude of this problem again has to do with time: experience is always emergent, never preformed, while anthropological models often display a degree of finality (cf. ibid.). Ingrid Rudie, in her paper, is keenly aware of this feature of emergence, even if she does not use the word. In an important way, all experience is 'new', if not always absolutely unprecedented.

Again we are directed towards the problem of time; 'precedence' points to prior experience, not to preconceived cultural models. By consequence it stresses motivation rather than prescription, and opens the way for a discussion of changing values rather than fixed meanings. Focusing on experience rather than pattern thus firmly historicizes ethnography, while not debunking its generalizing potential.

One concept which may actually link the experiential inside of reality and the analytical outside is the concept of common sense, vigorously advocated by Marian Kempny and Wojciech J. Burszta in this volume. The concept of common sense in our view has the beauty also of ambiguity; the notions both of communality and of sense contain paradoxes of the kind that make us acutely aware of the epistemological problem inherent in the idea of representation.

We are now, we believe, in a position to rethink the critical anthropological strategy of defamiliarization (cf. Marcus and Fischer 1986: 137ff.). The traditional power of anthropology to grab attention by means of recreating exotic worlds can be brought a step forward to a truly epistemological critique.

The strength of ethnographic practice remains its focus on detail, and its unfailing respect for context in the making of any generalization, as well as the full recognition of persistent ambiguity (Marcus and Fischer 1986: 159). While the scope of anthropology lies beyond the retelling of local stories, these and their experiential grounding remain the foundation of anthropological knowledge. 'Any existential human problem will have found diverse solutions, which must be worth knowing about, thinking about, and comparing' (Barth 1994: 5). It is this respect for the diversity of solutions that may eventually dethrone our culture as the yardstick for others and expand the world in which we all live.

A necessary step towards the widening of the field of significance of anthropology, which we believe is impending, is a reassessment of professional standards of value and truth. We have to talk about the acceptable limits of failure, and the criteria we have for saying that this or that is an adequate expression of experience.[2] Along with such standards we would probably also profit from an ethics of inarticulacy, supplementing the quest for advocacy in anthropology. With this volume we hope to have opened the floor for further waltzing to the resounding rhythms of a long and important tradition of anthropology.

NOTES

1 The volume is the outcome of a session held at the Second Conference of the European Association of Social Anthropologists in Prague, August 1992. The session was convened by the editors of the volume. Apart from the papers included here, Iain Edgar contributed a stimulating paper on dreams and their interpretation, which is published elsewhere (Edgar, in press). Kirsten Hastrup's chapter was not given in Prague but is added as a comprehensive discussion of some of the more general themes that the session brought to the fore.

As editors we have, evidently, wanted to stress the unity of the concerns discussed in this volume. The approaches described and the solutions offered are by no means uniform, however. They reflect the diversity of European anthropology, while also – we believe – illustrating a shared concern with social theory and holism, solidly anchored in the European anthropological tradition.

The editors want to thank both the contributors and the audience in Prague for a memorable experience of a lively and constructive academic debate. For technical assistance in the preparation of the manuscript we want to thank Morten Dag Hellemose.

2 This point was raised by John Davis during the discussion at the Prague session.

REFERENCES

Barth, Fredrik (1993) 'Assessing anthropology', in Robert Borofsky, ed., *Assessing Developments in Anthropology*, New York: McGraw-Hill.

—— (1994) *Balinese Worlds*, Chicago: University of Chicago Press.

Bourdieu, Pierre (1977) *Towards a Theory of Practice*, Cambridge: Cambridge University Press.

—— (1990) *The Logic of Practice*, Cambridge: Polity Press.

Bruner, Edward M. (1984) 'The opening up of anthropology', in Edward M. Bruner, ed., *Text, Play and Story: The Construction and Reconstruction of Self and Society*, Washington, DC: American Ethnological Society.

—— (1986) 'Experience and its expressions', in Victor W. Turner and Edward M. Bruner, eds, *The Anthropology of Experience*, Urbana: University of Illinois Press.

Clifford, James (1988) *The Predicament of Culture*, Cambridge, Mass.: Harvard University Press.

Clifford, James, and Marcus, George, eds (1986) *Writing Culture: The Poetics and Politics of Ethnography*, Berkeley: University of California Press.

D'Andrade, Roy, and Strauss, Claudia, eds (1992) *Human Motives and Cultural Models*, Cambridge: Cambridge University Press.

Davidson, Donald (1984) *Inquiries into Truth and Interpretation*, Oxford: Clarendon Press.

Edgar, Iain (in press) 'Dream imagery becomes social experience: the cultural elucidation of dream interpretation', in A. Delux and S. Heald, eds, *Anthropology and Psychoanalysis: An Encounter through Culture*, London: Routledge.

Fabian, Johannes (1990) *Power and Performance: Ethnographic Explorations through Proverbial Wisdom and Theater in Shaba, Zaire*, Madison: University of Wisconsin Press.

Fox, Richard (1991) 'Introduction: working in the present', in Richard G. Fox, ed., *Recapturing Anthropology: Working in the Present*, Santa Fe, N. Mex., and Washington, DC: School of American Research.

Geertz, Clifford (1973) *The Interpretation of Culture*, New York: Basic Books.
Hastrup, Kirsten (1987) 'The reality of anthropology', *Ethnos* 52: 287–300.
—— ed. (1992) *Other Histories*, London: Routledge.
—— (1993) 'The native voice and the anthropological vision', *Social Anthropology/Anthropologie sociale* 1: 173–86.
—— (in press) 'Beyond words: on the limits of writing in anthropology', in Eduardo Archetti, ed., *The Multiplicity of Writing Social Anthropology*, Oslo: Oslo University Press.
Holland, Dorothy (1992) 'The woman who climbed up the house: some limitations of schema theory', in Theodore Schwartz, Geoffrey M. White and Catherine Lutz, eds, *New Directions in Psychological Anthropology*, Cambridge: Cambridge University Press.
Kleinman, Arthur (1992) 'Pain and resistance: the delegitimation and relegitimation of local worlds', in Mary-Jo Delvecchio Good, Paul E. Brodwin, Byron J. Good and Arthur Kleinman, eds, *Pain as Human Experience: An Anthropological Perspective*, Berkeley: University of California Press.
Kuper, Adam, ed. (1992) *Conceptualizing Society*, London: Routledge.
Lakoff, George (1987) *Women, Fire and Dangerous Things*, Chicago: University of Chicago Press.
Leder, Drew (1990) *The Absent Body*, Chicago: University of Chicago Press.
Marcus, George, and Fischer, Michael M.J. (1986) *Anthropology as Cultural Critique*, Chicago: University of Chicago Press.
Okely, Judith, and Callaway, Helen, eds (1992) *Anthropology and Autobiography* (ASA Monographs 29), London: Routledge.
Quinn, Naomi, and Holland, Dorothy, eds (1987) *Cultural Models in Language and Thought*, Cambridge: Cambridge University Press.
Quinn, Naomi, and Strauss, Claudia (1993) 'A cognitive framework for a unified theory of culture', *American Ethnologist* (in press).
Rosch, Eleanor (1978) 'Principles of categorization', in Eleanor Rosch and B.B. Lloyd, eds, *Cognition and Categorization*, Hillsdale, NJ: Lawrence Erlbaum.
Siverts, Henning (in press), 'Campesino time and space in Mesbilja', *Folk* 36.
Strauss, Claudia, and Quinn, Naomi (1994) 'A cognitive/cultural anthropology', in Robert Borofsky, ed., *Assessing Developments in Anthropology*, New York: McGraw-Hill.
Taylor, Charles (1989) *Sources of the Self: The Making of the Modern Identity*, Cambridge: Cambridge University Press.
Trouillot, Michel-Rolph (1991) 'Anthropology and the savage slot: the poetics and politics of otherness', in Richard G. Fox, ed., *Recapturing Anthropology: Working in the Present*, Santa Fe, N. Mex., and Washington, DC: School of American Research.

Chapter 1

Incomers and fieldworkers
A comparative study of social experience

Tamara Kohn

A decade ago, Malcolm Crick suggested that 'the knowledge we formulate about "the other" is bound to be refracted through the knowledge we have built to define ourselves' (1982: 293). In other words, 'we' are interpreters of cultures and can observe 'others' only through our own cultural and experiential lenses. The 'other' and the 'self', however one might define them, are frequently brought together in such statements to remind ourselves of the subjective, creative and relative nature of our craft, especially apparent in our writing. Yet anthropological discourses about 'others' (or even deeper probes into indigenous 'selfhoods') and reflexive discussions about fieldworking 'selves' are rarely seen as directly comparable in a larger experiential sense. I wish here to indulge in such a direct comparison.[1]

In this paper I share a few of my early fieldwork experiences amongst the Yakha (one of several Tibeto-Burman groups living in the middle hills of east Nepal),[2] and examine to what extent these experiences are comparable to those of women from other ethnic/linguistic groups who marry into Yakha households.

Anthropologists fairly new to the field, as well as non-Yakha incoming brides, spend most of their time in households where the language of everyday family interaction – the language of the society they are trying to enter – is incomprehensible. They absorb new sights, sounds, rhythms, silences, feelings and tastes amidst a backdrop of Yakha gibberish. But are the anthropologist's impressions and senses comparable to the bride's? Is it possible to talk about shared experiences that exist in the absence of and *preceding* local comprehension and use of a language? I would suggest that the very attempt to do so raises interesting theoretical and methodological questions about the anthropology of experience.

First, I must clarify what I mean by experience *in the absence of language*. I do not mean the experience of tiny children or of deaf-mutes who do not know how to sign. Both anthropologists and non-Yakha brides are linguistically experienced people. Their thoughts are communicated, and others' thoughts and commands are received, at least partially through language (e.g. in Nepali, the lingua franca of Nepal), but the talk which occurs in the natural flow of interaction around them is incomprehensible and, initially at least, they take no active part in it. They do and indeed *must* physically interact with people and will most likely partici-pate in a range of shared activities (e.g. fetching water and com-munal rice-planting). I would suggest, however, that it is in the course of this interaction, which takes place amidst the hum of an unlearned language, that they take a sensory inventory of the world around them in a way they may never do again. It is the accessibility of others' sensory experiences that I want to explore in this article.

From such queries about newcomers' earliest experiences, what-ever their comparability and accessibility, I ask a slightly different but related question. To what extent do early experiences, feel-ings, impressions, etc. set the scene for later knowledge? How do they allow us to move along the particular roads to knowledge that we end up traversing? Is it feasible that early experiences, which take place in a frustrated haze of linguistic incompetence (and which, for most anthropologists, are seen as ill-informed, impres-sionistic and thus dispensable to all but the reflexive introductions of final drafts), are in large degree responsible for the material that ends up being seen as important or 'ethnographically rich'?

THE INCOMING BRIDE AND ANTHROPOLOGIST

People who call themselves Yakha are found scattered throughout the hills of east Nepal, with the greatest number concentrated in settlements in southern Sankhuwasabha and northern Dhankuta districts. One such community is called Tamaphok, and this is where the bulk of my fieldwork was conducted. There are about 10,000 Yakha in total, although this figure might be higher were Yakha who have migrated to northeast Indian hill states and beyond to be taken into account.

Inter-ethnic marriages amongst the Yakha are quite common (approximately 30 per cent). The vast majority of these are to members of other 'Kiranti' (Rai and Limbu) groups in east Nepal. These are all Tibeto-Burman peoples, and from an outside (e.g. Western scholarly) perspective the Kiranti have not generally been seen as different enough to count as 'inter-ethnic' (Kohn 1992). I, however, categorize them as such because the Yakha and their spouses do – the different languages the 'Kiranti' speak are mutually unintelligible, and cultural differences between the groups are locally writ large. We might ask, then, how Yakha identity is defined or, more specifically, what are Yakha ideas about the relationship of 'culture' and 'language', and do incomers, be they non-Yakha brides or anthropologists, share these ideas?

My own preconceptions about the relationship of 'culture' and 'language' were largely based on my schooling. At the University of Pennsylvania I was convinced by Ward Goodenough's assertion that one must learn a people's language before one can learn its culture, and that 'culture' is learned – 'the things one needs to know in order to meet the standards of others' (1981: 50). If one could learn local 'emic' categories and their meanings (and note here the direct and popular adaptation of the linguistic 'phoneme' to the analysis of culture), then one had access to local culture. Goodenough allowed his model to encompass all 'experience' and insisted that the 'human approach to experience is categorical . . . there are color categories, shape categories, taste categories, and so on' (ibid.: 63).[3]

It thus follows that once I was in the field and able to communicate in Nepali I was eager to move on to learn Yakha words for things. My early notes and letters were full of my own sensory discoveries and the deep frustration of not understanding words. Very early on I wrote:

> I am moved by the minuscule – things that are mere common sense – that make people human – the chhhh . . . ptiu sound of hacking and spitting, the bitter gritty feel of millet beer sliding down the throat, the howl of jackals piercing the black night. But this isn't what I need to know – I need to understand the animated chatter in the tea shops and kitchens and porches and paddy fields. Like watching a play in a foreign language, I constantly guess at meanings.

You can see that I would shape my fieldwork on the basis that language is the key to culture – 'the best mirror of the human mind' (Chomsky 1986). My later notes had little time for my own thoughts, for I was too busy translating words and grammars to get at local thoughts and meanings. However, the following inter-action at a Yakha wedding which took place well into our first year somewhat knocked the wind out of my sails:

> About eight rather inebriated young women clustered at my elbow as we chewed on some unidentifiable buffalo bits served on leaf plates. Kamala had told Chandra Kumari that we knew a Yakha *paalam* (rhyming verse), and she must have told the others. Giggling and grinning behind hands, they pestered us to perform, 'Come on, sister, brother, tell us, tell us.' 'OK, OK.' We got their silent attention and then recited, '*Makkaiga caamaa, chi'waaga kiu, chaabaak ta lakhti, ango-tengma jiu*' ('Maize porridge, nettle stew, dance the rice dance, dear *angotengma*').[4] After we finished performing, I took out my notebook and asked them to teach us more Yakha verses. They recited about fifteen as I scribbled them down in phonetic script. 'But these are all in Nepali language – what about some Yakha verses.' 'Sister, these are the ones we know – the usual ones.' 'But I would really like to have a few Yakha ones too.' There was a short silence and then one said, 'Sister, the verses we gave you are in Nepali language . . . but Yakha thought.'

Nepali language but Yakha thought. How could that be? What imbues the verses with Yakha thought I will never know for sure, but that language was seen as immaterial through Yakha eyes was very interesting.

This would be confirmed over and over. It was evident in the very existence of a large Yakha community across the valley in Madi Mulkarka where the language had virtually died and most communicated in Nepali. One did not have to speak Yakha to be Yakha and to think Yakha thoughts. Later, as my fieldwork focus turned to looking at incomers who married into the Yakha community from other ethnic and linguistic groups, I became interested in the ways in which the women were drawn into Yakha households. I knew many who never learned Yakha but had no problem fitting into the community and were not seen by others as being any less integrated than women who did learn the language. Let us turn back to fieldnotes to hear how incoming women who did speak Yakha felt about the process of learning to belong:

> Chandra Maya brought us millet beer and perched on the bench opposite while we drank. She runs the household and lives with her two children, daughter-in-law and grandchildren. I said, 'You are Mareki, but you speak Yakha with your children. How did you learn it?' 'By living, I suppose. Yakha takes about ten to twelve years to learn – after one has learned Yakha ways of doing things. I've even forgotten Marek language now after all these years.' She disappeared into the kitchen and we could hear her blowing on the fire. Then the sharp sizzling noise of meat hitting hot oil. We looked at each other, knowing that we'd have to ready ourselves for yet more meat, something so missed most of the year and so over-indulged in at Dasain-time.[5] She brought us the plates of spicy pig meat and fat with some pounded rice flakes on the side. 'Delicious! What good meat!' we exclaimed in a mix of Yakha and Nepali. She said, 'You are learning to like our food, then? And you learn our language too!' 'Well, slowly, slowly', I replied and then asked, 'How was it for you at first here in Tamaphok?' She said, 'Difficult, sister, difficult. Another country, another house. After I had my first daughter I had to work and others were not so helpful to an unknown person. What could they say to me?'

Chandra Maya was not the first to tell us that the process of 'learning Yakha ways of doing things' is not just separate from, but *precedes* the learning of the local language. What could this slow, difficult socialization consist of? Learning to cook food the right way, or in our case even learning to like it? Budhu Maya, a Limbu woman also married a long time in Tamaphok, told me that for her learning Yakha was easy. It just took time, but one also had to learn new customs right from the beginning – different wedding rituals, different offerings to different household gods. She paused a long time then and said, 'Sister, it's hard to say – I learned by seeing and hearing, maybe.'

Learning how to do the right thing at the right time – performing well, behaving appropriately – is part of the early socialization Chandra Maya and Budhu Maya talked about which preceded language learning. It is also part of the experience of the early

fieldworker setting out to be a 'participant observer'. Both we in
our conversations and notes, and they in their attempt to share
their experiences, are locked in language and the things language
describes best, such as actions – the things we *do* and *see* done
from day to day. The early fieldworker and the incoming bride
strive, perhaps for entirely separate purposes, towards what
Bourdieu has aptly called 'practical mastery' (1977). They both
wish to read the right signals and arrive at some sort of synchrony
of action – they wish to 'do' things without sticking out like a sore
thumb. This type of knowledge is not in itself 'language-like', but
nevertheless we attempt to describe it with words.

But Chandra Maya and Budhu Maya hinted that some things
are past description – are 'hard to say'. I would suggest that this
unknown something, this quality of culture that we may un-
wittingly access before anything else, comes alive through senses
other than visual observation or linguistic comprehension and
expression. Furthermore, this knowledge is larger than just 'the
study of the way we learn practical, everyday tasks' (Bloch 1991:
186). It is hidden beneath action in the subtlest of senses that we
are only able to detect or react to because, as human beings, we
are all deeply engaged with one another (Carrithers 1992).
Anthropological knowledge depends not merely on translating the
verbal part of culture, but on tapping this engagedness.

For most Yakha women and men we spoke to, the Yakha
language was only one means of communication. Language did
not carry with it all the romantic conceptual baggage which in the
West has given it authority as a primary means of learning and
sharing culture. To the Yakha and Yakha-to-be, and perhaps now
for this anthropologist, language is not necessarily the crux or
foundation of culture. It can be *made* to be so by certain political
rhetoric. For instance, after the successful campaign for the
'democracy' of a multi-party state which took place in Nepal
during our stay, one Yakha schoolteacher asked to borrow our
Limbu grammar (van Driem, 1987) which had charts illustrating
locally unknown Kiranti scripts. He said: 'The king made us teach
only Nepali in the school, but the Communist party says we should
now try to teach our own languages in the schools. Maybe this
script is good for that?' However, the politicized Bhim Bahadur
was voicing an exceptional stance that may only serve to prove
the rule.

So, what are the senses beyond language that can be felt but perhaps never wholly expressed? In Paul Stoller's recent book *The Taste of Ethnographic Things*, we learn that the Songhay of Niger 'taste kinship, smell witches, and hear the ancestors' (1989: 5), and Stoller writes convincingly about the vibrance and meaningfulness of these senses. The bulk of his material comes from understanding the subtleties of Songhay language/innuendo as well as through his own gradual training of senses to taste good and bad sauces and to feel and hear the sounds of possession. In one example, a woman served Stoller and other guests a particularly nasty-tasting sauce, and the meaning behind this carefully premeditated affront was discovered by the ethnographer through lengthy conversations and observations over time. Stoller gives us impressively rich narratives, but I am still left to wonder about the experiences of culture which thrive before narration – the tastes, smells and feelings of ethnographic things before they are explained, qualified and classified away.

This, it seems, is where our comparison of the early fieldworker and the incoming bride has its strength. The incomer and the anthropologist both experience first impressions in their new abodes – both select things that strike them as unfamiliar. While their ears are muted to the meanings of words, their other senses go into high gear. The anthropologist struggles to capture some of these in fieldnotes and letters, the bride perhaps goes home to her *maaiti ghar* (parents' home) to share her pent-up impressions and feelings with her kin. For both bride and anthropologist, it is very hard to find words that do justice to those new things that are not visible, like tastes and sounds. For both, this is a period of discovery. A heightened awareness is not just a privilege of the observant traveller or anthropologist; it is a feature of 'incomerness', 'intermarriage', the meeting of 'others'.

THE PSEUDO-SHARED EXPERIENCE

The *situation* the anthropologist and the bride find themselves in may be comparable, but the *substance* of their experiences most certainly is not. The roles and positions of power held by the two are different – the anthropologist is led out and about to meet leaders and shamans, attend ceremonies, teach English to students and interview a huge range of people. The bride spends most of her time in her new home, where she is expected to work with her husband's family. In a sense, the bride who works together with her new family day in and day out is locked into the very centre of human life, while the busy anthropologist who delights in sampling more variety over a relatively short time-span is kept dancing on the periphery of the experience. The differences between them in terms of setting and accessibility will affect what they sense around them. And, of course, the cultural differences between the Yakha and most incoming brides are much less profound than those between the Yakha and the American anthropologist.

Even if the anthropologist and the bride were in the position to taste the same bowl of rice, it would be impossible to know to what extent they have *shared* any experience. The 'other's' sensory experience, whether or not there is a vocabulary to describe it, can never be completely shared, only imagined (cf. Hastrup 1993). That imagination, however, is powerfully influential in our descriptions of others. In one origin myth told by a Yakha shaman, we heard that men were made from chicken shit: 'Well, if you rub yourself and sniff', he said, 'it smells like chicken shit.' I can sniff with my own nostrils, but not with his. I can likewise taste Yakha *raksi* (distilled rice liquor), and have, over time, learned to identify what Yakha generally call 'good' *raksi* as opposed to 'bad' *raksi*, but never with a Yakha's tastebuds – even with my own I have a hard time describing the difference with words. I can pick up on a certain sense of space in a Yakha kitchen and have interpreted how Yakha social organization is reflected in its use (cf. Ardener 1981), but I can only approximate, through a number of verbal and non-verbal cues, how others feel within it. I can go out and spend full days working in the paddy fields with Yakha women and can experience what their work feels like to *me*, but I will never literally experience what it is like to do that work, barefoot, almost every day of one's life.

The 'shared experience' is the stuff of art, poetry and imagination, but it is often too literally associated with participant observation. It makes a good punchline for the joke, 'How many Californians does it take to screw in a light bulb?',[6] but it is also used to describe how the participant observer playing poker, 'as an *insider* . . . felt some of the same emotions during the course of the game that the ordinary participants felt' (Spradley 1980: 57). Surely, the participant observer cannot feel other people's emotions. To say he does replaces the requisite notion of 'being there' with 'being in their shoes' – something he can never be.

We can give two experiences the same name – 'the taste of

Yakha pickles', 'anger', 'embarrassment', etc. – but they are not entirely shared. To acknowledge this is to understand the tremendous gulf between experience and the part of it which we might code or classify with language. *This is not to say that we cannot learn deeply about other cultures and other selves.* As Michael Carrithers has suggested:

> Yes, anthropological research is based on personal experience, and indeed on personal capacities. Those capacities are the same ones which allow people to engage in social life, to learn aesthetic standards in the first place as children, or to learn, or create, new aesthetic standards or forms of life in adulthood. Just as immigrants can learn their way around their host society, and just as converts can take part in the institutions of a new religion, so can anthropologists learn to understand a new way of life.
>
> (1992: 149)

The content of culture, which we learn about through our experiences with others, is much more than what we can confine to texts – our learning is much more than a textual interpretation. Clifford Geertz has written that we 'cannot live other people's lives, and it is a piece of bad faith to try' (1986: 373). Fair enough. But then he goes on to say that we 'can but listen to what, in words, in images, in actions, they say about their lives . . . it is with expressions – representations, objectifications, discourses, performances, whatever – that we traffic' (ibid.). What this implies is that the experiences which precede or indeed defy textual representation cannot be part of what we 'traffic'. It implies that things we do and feel in other cultures are lost if the 'natives' have failed to tell us about them. But surely this is a reduction of our enterprise.

Renato Rosaldo gives us a brilliant example of how he came to understand the intensity of rage felt by Ilongot men upon bereavement – rage which they could only vent by beheading an unknown victim. His early attempts to elicit words that would give meaning to the connection between rage, bereavement and headhunting were futile, because to the Ilongot the connection was 'so powerful . . . as to be self-evident beyond explication' (1984: 178). Rosaldo was only able to imagine such a rage when he subsequently experienced the tragic loss of his wife. He did not experience the *same* anger, but he could come closer to a lived understanding about the 'the cultural force of emotions' (ibid.: 188, 193). Anthony Cohen uses the same paper by Rosaldo to illustrate how experiences that lie outside of our fieldnotes but within our 'mental notebook' may be useful or indeed more authentic than anything we could hope to capture with our pens in the field (1992). If Cohen is interested in 'post-fieldwork fieldwork' and the learning that we do through our experiences and 'headnotes' after the fact, I have been looking at 'early-fieldwork fieldwork' – at the senses that are enlivened through a lack of words and an intensity of newness.

THE IMPRESSIONS SHAPE THE QUESTIONS

Ultimately, when I did fieldwork in Tamaphok, I only *felt* my *own* experiences, but these were essential elements in all cultural descriptions and interpretations I have attempted since. After the glamorous poetic intensity of the early phase of fieldwork wore off, and I was busy translating conversations, conducting interviews and compiling Yakha word-lists, I believe that the questions I asked and the notes I took were still shaped by my early field experiences. Let me give an example by comparing a letter I wrote early on about my first personal confrontation with caste conflict and my later observations:

> A few days ago we visited Bimala, a lovely woman of the blacksmith, 'untouchable' caste. She insisted we have food and it was delicious – eggs, rice flakes, and tall glasses full of thick sweet yogurt. We never mentioned this to our Yakha family, but then yesterday we returned to Bimala's to get some yogurt in a jar. Bimala said we should hide the jar of yogurt in our bag, because our Yakha family would not let it into their house. Then she insisted we return the following morning for some hot milk. So today when Kamala [our Yakha sister] asked where we were going we said we were going to the Gajamer's for a chat. There was a whispered debate that ensued in the kitchen between Ama and Kamala in Yakha, and the vibes that filtered through to us were of disagreement, perhaps displeasure. Then Kamala gave a long intense lecture in Nepali about how it would be fine to talk, but that we must not eat or drink at their house or pass over the threshold between the porch and the house interior or else we could not come inside their house again. I had thought we'd be exempt from all that, but we're not. Nor, obviously, are 'tribal' people in Nepal as relaxed

about caste pollution as previous researchers have led us to believe. Our lecture wasn't given in an angry tone that would be a giveaway for exaggeration. It's all matter of fact and was said without the shame or defensiveness of the bigot or racist – said with an outrageous confidence. And the rub: in order to stay here and work and live with Yakha we must comply. In our compliance we are on this front 'honorary Yakha', but on the fronts in which we wish to belong (language, cultural knowledge, etc.) we never will! If I can never learn to feel or believe in caste pollution, can I ever really understand it?

Although the scenario here was set by means of language – our stated destination and 'our family's' verbal warnings – the focus of the text was on my interpretation of tones of voice and on the frustrations and anxieties I felt about cultural things that were never made explicit. In the following excerpt from notes taken fifteen months later, it is illustrated how that early experience shaped my later observations and analyses:

We went over to visit Bimala's this morning, as surreptitiously as possible. After a snack of meat, rice flakes and *raksi* which, as usual, was beautifully prepared by Bimala, we sat in the inner porch where Lok Bahadur [her husband] told us about his first marriage, which had been arranged when he was only nine years old. Imagine our surprise when Sharada [a female Brahmin schoolteacher] showed up with her boy, Suresh, and a great sack of unhusked rice and started pounding it in Bimala's *Dhikii* [a big wooden rice pounder] across the yard! Sharada looked a bit surprised to see us there too, I think. Bimala and I went out to help her, leaving the men on the porch. I swept the straying rice back into the bowl-like impression under the pounding wood while the women took turns pedalling. At one stage, Bimala offered Suresh a drink of fresh milk and he drank it in the courtyard and put the cup just inside the porch. We spoke about all the recent political changes and how they have affected Tamaphok. Sharada made a comment about how easy it is to talk about changing the system at public meetings, but that one must teach by example. She was alluding, of course, to her presence there today – of all *Dhikii*s in Tamaphok to use, she chose the most polluting. Her action was an intentional and powerful statement denying the principle of caste pollution. It was so effective because unlike statements of commitment

made by political activists at home, which can later be criticized
as having been put on for show, overtly breaking caste rules
requires a change of heart that is very real indeed.

The point I want to draw from this example is that I was
only able to imagine the depth of meaning implied by Sharada's
actions and words because I had had the much earlier, and very
emotionally stirring, confrontation with Kamala and Ama over
caste. If I had not had the earlier experience, I probably would not
have attributed the same intensity of meaning to the later scenario.

This process is further illustrated in Nancy Scheper-Hughes's
new book *Death without Weeping: The Violence of Everyday Life
in Brazil* (1992). The author's early traumatic experiences as a
Peace Corps volunteer confronting the frequent and often un-
necessary deaths of babies at a Brazilian health post *informed* her
subsequent narrative chronicles of 'the routinization of suffering'
and local ideas of the normality of death (ibid.: 16). The resultant
book is successful partly because a reflexivity about early experiences which were felt but not entirely expressible in words allowed
the author to select effective narratives which speak to their
audiences. In most ethnographies, however, early fieldwork experiences which are felt and tasted tend to be forgotten or at best
confined to reflexive introductions. Likewise, anthropologists
searching for cultural 'cores' have searched out indigenes, and
have left out the incomers – the likes of my non-Yakha brides.
Neither of these sources should be ignored if part of our concern is
to know about the processes by which culture is experienced and
learned.

CAN METHOD OBLIGE?

In this chapter, a question has been raised about the comparability
of two very different types of newcomer to Yakha culture – the
anthropologist and the non-Yakha bride. Their ideas about the
relationship between language and culture have made us look
beyond language at the fragile, impressionistic and remarkably
'sensual' period between the newcomer's arrival and her relative
linguistic competence in the Yakha community. Early experiences
were found to illuminate the anthropologist's later observations
and analyses. A methodological question of accessibility, however, remains in question. How can the anthropologist make her

experiences of the 'other' accessible if words do not do justice to them? Charles Seeger, an American forefather in the field of ethnomusicology, has suggested that we should be wary about using words to express music – that as modes of communication speech and music are incompatible. Instead, we should be *music- ing* about music (1977: 179), whatever that might consist of. Likewise, perhaps, tastes should not just be approximated with words, they should be tasted. I will never forget a course I took at Berkeley on South American ethnography with Brent Berlin – one day he brought in a pot full of boiled manioc so that the whole class could have a taste – 'Aha! So that's what it tastes like', we all probably said, each having had our own personal opinion of the root. Recently Kamala, our 'sister' in Tamaphok, sent us a long letter that positively reeked of Yakha kitchen fires. The envelope was passed around the room in a recent seminar as a supplement to visual aids – the smell could not evoke in the audience the memories it did for us, but with the aid of a descriptive text, perhaps, the smell may have enriched the audience's experience of the other.

No matter what tricks are played, we are stuck knowing that we are working with second-hand experiences – the experiences *we* have of other places, plus whatever we can elicit from our subjects through their narratives that will help us to attribute some local meanings to things. We have the ability to imagine our informants' pains, joys and first impressions because we are often painfully aware of our own, even if we cannot find words that fully describe them. What we are left with is a collage in which the very proxim- ity of different media speaks beyond the scenario set with words.

So, what can we do about it as ethnographers – chroniclers of culture? We are truly caught in a bind if we wish to translate the feelings of members of other cultures with a pen. Literary theorists call our predicament 'the intentional fallacy' – one can never know what an artist intended by looking at the art, and it is the wrong pursuit of the critic to try to do so. Anthropologists should know that we do not share other cultures so much as imagine them *in situ*.

NOTES

1 I was able to attend the Prague EASA conference, where I gave an earlier draft of this article, with the support of a grant from the

Bamborough Fund at Linacre College, Oxford and with funds from the Oxford Polytechnic (now Oxford Brookes University). I am grateful for helpful suggestions and comments made by friends and colleagues, in particular Elvira Belaunde, Sandra Bell, Michael Carrithers, Robert Layton, Dan Rose, Bob Simpson, Kay Tillyer, Jackie Waldren, Sean Williams and my husband, Andrew Russell.

2 Most conversations translated in this text were conducted in Nepali and took place in Tamaphok, where Andrew and I lived for nearly two years. The 'we' in the fieldnotes refers to times when we were both present.

3 Goodenough, the father of the American ethno-science movement, was only one small voice in the debate about the linguistic categorization of culture. See Ardener (1971) for an excellent overview.

4 *Angotengma* means 'the sisters of one's brothers- and sisters-in-law'.

5 *Dasain* is a major Hindu festival that takes place in the month of *Asoj* (the end of September or beginning of October). In worship to the goddess *Durga* at *Dasain* there are many animal sacrifices and slaughters, and meat is plentiful.

6 The punchline is 'Ten. One to screw it in, and nine to share the experience.'

REFERENCES

Ardener, E. (1971) 'Introduction', in E. Ardener, ed., *Social Anthropology and Language* (ASA Monographs 10), London: Tavistock.

Ardener, S. (1981) 'Ground rules and social maps for women: an introduction', in S. Ardener, ed., *Women and Space: Ground Rules and Social Maps*, London: Croom Helm.

Bloch, M. (1991) 'Language, anthropology and cognitive science', *Man* 26, 2: 183–98.

Bourdieu, P. (1977) *Outline of a Theory of Practice*, Cambridge: Cambridge University Press.

Carrithers, M. (1992) *Why Humans Have Cultures: Explaining Anthropology and Social Diversity*, Oxford: Oxford University Press.

Chomsky, N. (1986) *Knowledge of Language: Its Nature, Origin and Use*, New York: Praeger.

Cohen, A.P. (1992) 'Post-fieldwork fieldwork', *Journal of Anthropological Research* 48: 339–54.

Crick, M.R. (1982) 'Anthropology of knowledge', *Annual Review of Anthropology* 11: 287–313.

Geertz, C. (1986) 'Making experiences, authoring selves', in V.W. Turner and E.M. Bruner, eds, *The Anthropology of Experience*, Urbana: University of Illinois Press.

Goodenough, W.H. (1981) *Culture, Language, and Society*, 2nd edn, Menlo Park, Calif.: Benjamin/Cummings Publishing Co.

Hastrup, K. (1993) 'Hunger and the hardness of facts', *Man* 28, 4: 727–39

Kohn, T. (1992) 'Guns and garlands: cultural and linguistic migration through marriage', *Himalayan Research Bulletin* 12 (in press).

Rosaldo, R.I. (1984) 'Grief and a headhunter's rage: on the cultural force of emotions', in E.M. Bruner, ed., *Text, Play and Story: The Construction and Reconstruction of Self and Society*, Washington: American Anthropological Association.

Scheper-Hughes, N. (1992) *Death without Weeping: The Violence of Everyday Life in Brazil*, Berkeley: University of California Press.

Seeger, C.L. (1977) *Studies in Musicology 1935–1975*, Berkeley: University of California Press.

Spradley, J.P. (1980) *Participant Observation*, New York: Holt, Rinehart & Winston.

Stoller, P. (1989) *The Taste of Ethnographic Things*, Philadelphia: University of Pennsylvania Press.

van Driem, G. (1987) *A Grammar of Limbu*, Berlin: Mouton de Gruyter.

Chapter 2

Making sense of new experience

Ingrid Rudie

The dominance of participant observation as methodological credo in anthropology has been founded on an idea that we can understand another culture through sharing the experience of the practitioners themselves as far as possible. More specifically, this implies that it is important to get at what people *do* because there is so much cultural practice that is never *verbalized*. The anthropologist infers 'culture' from a number of other representations besides and underneath speech and writing. These representations take several forms – as bits of practice, symbolic and ritual expressions in the widest sense. Just as the polysemy of words is filtered through the context of the sentence (Ricoeur 1981: 12), we assume that the polysemy of acts and sub-linguistic representations is solved through the context of the situation, a notion introduced by Bronislaw Malinowski (1923), and internalized and elaborated on by later generations of anthropologists.

In anthropology, however, contextualization goes beyond the unfolding situation; context is also determined by the experiential luggage of the participants including the participant-observer, and the way in which such learned disposition intersects with new experience. Our experiential luggage consists of events that have already been mentally processed and internalized so that they fall in familiar patterns or at least create an illusion of patterns. Every day we face a series of events, most of which are compatible with these patterns and therefore do not challenge our understanding. Some events, however, are truly unprecedented in the sense that they call for new explications.

My discussion departs from this point. I will be concerned with the problem of making sense, but instead of seeing it as a matter of synchronic contextualization I shall be concerned with it as a process, and I build my discussion on the assumption that human actors have a universal drive towards making sense, which implies an ongoing transformation *from* experience *to* knowledge. New experiences are screened against the experiential luggage, and if they make sense they are added to a stock of knowledge, skills and recipes for action. My ambition is to try to sensitize our attention to some of this information-processing, through which anthropologists as well as informants appropriate experience and make sense of it. In doing this I depart from two assumptions that I give axiomatic status.

One assumption is that informant and anthropologist make sense in essentially similar ways. The anthropologist and the 'other' operate their experience along parallel lines: both balance on the edge between *doxa* and *opinion*, between practical understandings that are never brought to the level of explicit discussion, and those that are explicitly verbalized and discussed (Bourdieu 1977) in the management of their own lives. Anthropologists and informants act as catalysts to each other's efforts to make sense. The anthropologist's keen interest in what, to the informants, may be only everyday trivia has the potential of speeding up the informants' own reflections, which, in their turn, become subject to the anthropologist's analysis. In other words, anthropological analysis is not only concerned with acts and representations in their 'pure' form; it also follows, and partly triggers, the informants' self-interpretative processes. In that way the anthropologist's and the informant's interpretations become intertwined in the final text; the practitioners' efforts to make sense of their own experience lie partly 'inside' the anthropologist's efforts to convey their practice into anthropological knowledge.

This leads into the second assumption, which has already been implied above: that experiential contrasts will tend to punctuate self-evident or doxic pre-understandings and trigger a need to search for explications. This typically happens when we (as anthropologists or as practitioners) meet unprecedented events. In this lies the possible fruitfulness of focusing on *new experience* as a point of crucial methodological importance: it is the point at which we become maximally able to compare researcher and informant.

MAKING SENSE

Turning our attention towards new or unprecedented experiences directs our attention towards the process of making sense, which I take to be crucial in the process of transforming social experience into anthropological knowledge. 'Making sense', as I intend it, carries the notion of appropriating new information and reconciling it with some pre-existing pattern of logic or sensibility. It overlaps closely with Vendler's definition of 'understanding' as requiring a constructive effort of the mind to supplement features that are not observable to the senses (Vendler 1984: 205), and further: 'To understand (such) a product of the human mind – from simple sentences to the loftiest creations of science and art – one has to reproduce the vital principle, which accounts for its visible appearance, in one's own mind' (ibid.: 206). Understanding defined in this way, as a creative process, operates on two different levels: the practical and the interpretative. On the practical level we demonstrate our understanding through action: we respond to particular situations more or less adequately. On the interpretative level, we are able to decipher the actions of other subjects in such a way that we seem able to tell why or how they take that particular shape. On both levels, we fill in gaps and supplement features that are not observable to the senses. And on both levels we can go astray (understanding may also be misunderstanding), hit the mark or add an entirely new twist to a problem.

We do not easily verbalize our own most self-evident practices. However, when we are met with practices that are alien to us but self-evident to others and hence not easily verbalized by them, we are normally puzzled,[1] and feel a need for explication. Anthropologists, as cultural novices, try to penetrate the self-evident understandings of the culturally seasoned. This search for explanations is often framed in the form of 'why' questions: the cultural novices hope for a verbal explanation as a shortcut to understanding. The anthropologist, anyway, has to transform his/her understanding into language proper. A written description is what the fieldwork is normally expected to result in, a description that is wrested from understandings which have come about in different ways and on many levels, The anthropologist has then partly observed and partly tried to learn bits of practice, interpreted signs and listened to speech.

The upsurge of reflexive approaches in anthropology can be

seen as a new twist to the discipline's long-established need for exploring the process of making sense. These approaches attack the problem by concentrating on the dialogue between researcher and practitioner – how they create knowledge together (e.g. Hastrup and Ramløv 1988), how the contrast between self and other steers the perception of the researcher and thereby sets the track for what anthropology comes to be about (e.g. Strathern 1988), and ultimately how the researcher invents the culture of the informant (e.g. Wagner 1981). There is more to Wagner's analysis than this, for he is also preoccupied with the way in which the practitioners invent their own culture by linking creativity to convention. This link is established across an experiential contrast. For the local practitioner, it is a contrast between past and present; for the anthropologist, it takes the form of a contrast between us and them. For both, the contrast entails a revision of previous understanding. It is precisely by exploring these contrasts – this inventive edge – that we can start building bridges between wordless experience and the linguistic description of it.

Let me revert for a moment to the distinction between practical and interpretative levels of understanding. The interpretation that the anthropologist has to make when concentrating on new experience is an interpretation both of culture and of the very process of making sense. This cannot be contained within the framework of what is usually labelled 'interpretative anthropology', in which one usually presupposes fixed meanings which are there to be unravelled. The point is, that along the inventive edge at least, meanings are still in the making. In a similar vein, Graham Watson has argued that 'culture, far from being a given framework that lies behind and is expressed in activities, is, rather, like the convict code, a flexible repertoire of interpretive resources drawn upon by participants in accounting for action' (Watson 1991: 89). We have neither a catalogue nor a text, and still, when information-processing takes place, there must be some markers, some kind of punctuation, that can be at least vaguely conceptualized. They lie on the borderline between analogic and digital communication, which will be further discussed towards the end of the chapter.

The transformation from experience to knowledge passes through stages of increasing articulateness, which, I suggest, can take the following course. Experience is initially stored in the form of images or *gestalts*, mental representations which can serve as models for future action without being articulated. But the acts themselves are observed by others as they are carried out, where-by they acquire a communicative aspect, they come to function as *representations* on an intersubjective level. At this point they enter a screen of symbolization and metaphorization in which polysemy, and hence potential creativity, is very wide. At an advanced stage of articulateness lies verbal discourse, which is intentionally steered towards intersubjective clarification and consensus; it will normally seek to control and reduce polysemy. At a still more advanced stage lies the scientific text, which by definition trans-cends normal discourse and tries to objectify it. But, as Watson observes, meaning is both indexical and reflexive. Indexicality refers to the context-dependency of meaning, reflexivity to the way in which accounts and the settings they describe elaborate and modify each other in a back-and-forth process (Watson 1991: 75). The difference between the scientific text and normal discourse is probably one of degree rather than of kind. No text can escape being simultaneously indexical and reflexive.

CAN EXPERIENCE BE SHARED?

A crucial question is whether experience can really be shared and, if so, what kind of sharing is feasible. As fieldworkers we try to come to grips with the informant's experience, of which we have no preconceived understanding but still aim at sharing. There are two important starting-points for this project. First, the infor-mant's daily experience can be compared to the researcher's in general terms of continuity or contrast. Second, we go through specific situations and events together with our informants, and can compare our comments with theirs.

On the surface, people who face the same events, or go through life careers which seem to be similarly structured in terms of the content and timing of major role assignments, can develop ways of communicating on a level of intersubjective understanding. But the communication, however meaningful it may appear, is likely to gloss over layers of different understanding, both between researcher and informants, and among informants.

I will revert to these problems later on. To specify and substan-tiate the discussion, I shall first give an example from my own field experience which exposes the intersections between continuity and contrast, on many levels, between a very limited number of parti-cipants. The participants are: a 'modern' woman, a 'traditional' woman, and myself as a fieldworker. The scene is a Malay village in 1987, where I did my first fieldwork in 1965.

The 'modern' woman – let us call her Noor – lived in a village which had retained many traditional features. Between the two of us a dialogue went on which revealed large areas of seemingly very similar experience, and some deep contrasts. Our individual local knowledge and experiential luggage seemed to converge on two points. I had known her as a young girl during my first fieldwork in 1965, when she, her parents and many of her other relatives had shared their lives and knowledge with me. In 1987 her life was structured in much the same way as I ran my own practical life at home. Unlike most of her neighbours, but like me when at home in Norway, Noor commuted to work in a nearby town every day and experienced the time pressure typical of suburban life. She felt insufficient as a mother and daughter when she compared herself to the ideal of being available full-time. She felt insufficient as a housewife when she compared herself to the ideals for smart middle-class cooking and home decoration which were advertised in the media. She was acutely anxious about her children's educational performance, and encouraged them to achieve and to strive for upwardly mobile careers. When she was tired, she often engaged in describing how she would spend her old age. She pictured herself vividly as sharing her present house with her daughter – she thought of having one of the downstairs rooms, for in her old age she would not want to climb the stairs.

When I focus on how she sticks tenaciously to her job and struggles to fit a number of activities into her daily schedule, I record strategies and worries which are typical of modern suburban life and strike me as acutely familiar. But when she reveals her image of growing old sharing her house with her daughter (and incidentally her husband, to whom she is happily married, is not visible in the image) I get a glimpse of an orientation and a value hierarchy which bring out difference rather than similarity.

She and I seemed to share an experience of never being up to the various demands in our lives, although the specific demands were culturally coloured in different hues. We shared the way life was structured in terms of time and space. It consisted in moving between compartments; the various demands spatially and temporally separated, and each one getting limited attention. We had meaningful conversations about this situation, and at least I felt that we reached a high level of intersubjective understanding. Following Unni Wikan, we can say that Noor and I 'shared space' (Wikan 1992: 463, quoting Tambiah), and that we obtained *resonance* because we each reached forward and tried to engage with the other's world (ibid.). In this sense, we shared experience.

In contrast to Noor and myself stood Limah, whom I describe as traditional. By the end of this description it will, however, become clear that the dichotomy between modern and traditional is not entirely satisfactory to describe the two cases, as both individuals use an experiential luggage which must be characterized as 'traditional' in their creative reaction to modern demands. The dichotomy traditional–modern is still useful in order to contrast the way in which they structured their lives temporally and spatially, and with regard to how they activate social relationships. As we saw, Noor is busy and compartmentalizes her day. Limah is equally busy, but she structures her life in a different manner, being available in all her role capacities in her neighbourhood on a full-time scale. She is in many ways an unusual woman, an efficient political leader and organizer of her neighbourhood. The base of her activities was a *kemas*[2] sewing studio where she instructed women who wanted to learn, and which was also open for those who needed to come and use a machine for their own purposes. But the sewing service was only part of her activities. She was also chairwoman of the local branch of the Women's Agricultural Association, and she was a mediator in various attempts at starting income-generating activities. Her network is firmly grounded in the village and stretches out to people in administrative positions. She does all her organizing in one place, and keeps a time schedule in which the opening hours of the sewing studio and the times for instructing children in Koran reading (another of her activities) are the only fixed points. She says that she 'never rests', but nevertheless does not complain about lack of time. By contrast to Noor she is exposed to the various demands simultaneously, and they get her attention in one big chunk. An illustration may help to elucidate the differences between the ways in which Noor's and Limah's days are distributed in time and space. In constructing the following diagrams I have used a division between three 'spaces' which I call 'family space', 'neigbourhood space' and 'other space'. This is, of course, a mechanistic and 'etic' division which may not make equal sense to the three of us. First and foremost, it is the division that I see as informative on the basis of how the bulk of my informants' activities are organized.

Figure 1 represents Noor's time–space organization. A striking feature is her relative absence from 'neighbourhood space'. Extra-domestic work and the bulk of her time with friends is located in 'other space', that is, outside household and neighbourhood. Noor's time–space organization resembles my own except on one point: the prayer-times punctuate her day, while my day is entirely secular. Her day resembles Limah's with respect to religious activities, but differs from it in other respects. While in Noor's case neighbourhood space is empty, it is full in Limah's case. There is a clear difference between Noor and myself when it comes to picturing the future. She has an image of old age which is very concrete; I shy away from picturing my old age as anything but a continuation, as long as possible, of an active state of being. My background is a Western discourse about the problems of old age, and an idea that it should be kept at bay.

So between the three of us there is a web of similarities and differences in the way our lives are structured, as well as in the way we represent the realities. Our representations can be seen in terms of different stages of distantiation and of punctuations which are governed by the contrasts that have occurred in our experiential histories and by the different goals with which we enter the communication.

Let us dwell for a moment on the difference between Noor and myself. Her image of her old age moved me in many ways: partly because I doubt that it will come true exactly as she describes it. If her daughters follow up her ambitions for them, they will be busy building their professional careers in a major town when she grows old, and even with a higher income than that of their parents they are likely to have more cramped housing conditions. It also moved me because I found it beautiful and extremely suggestive: it conjured up in one vivid image all that I had learned through two fieldworks about the closeness between female members of Malay extended families.

I recognized her description of her future as a symbol, or a metonym for an entire way of life, across the distance between our life worlds. I seized a piece of her imagery and stuffed it with meaning in a way which helped me to delimit a field of interaction and values which I took to be characteristic of her society. It was I who made it into a metonym – that was *my* mental operation, *my*

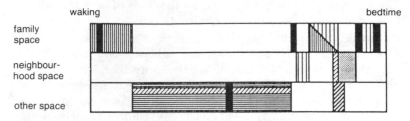

Figure 2.1 Noor's organization of time and space

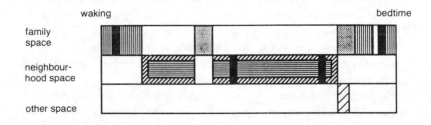

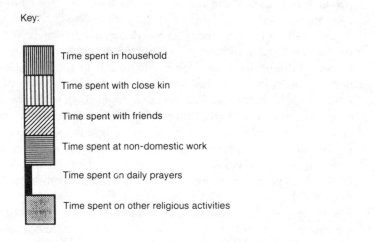

Figure 2.2 Limah's organization of time and space

reading of *her* practice and representation in my distantiation from observation and conversation to an analytic gaze at her society.

To Noor it is reality, the self-evident way of coping, which she has preserved as an image fostered in her early experience of normal family life. To her it is neither 'symbol' nor 'metonym'. But there is another point at which she has acquired a distance from features of her own background, and that has come about through the way in which she has dislodged her life from neighbourhood space. It is reflected in the way she describes the practice of more 'traditional' women, like Limah. The organizational substratum of Limah's activities is a strong tradition of ceremonial cooperation between neighbouring women. This is particularly displayed during life-crisis rituals, which take an outward shape of being very public, very formalized and based on an exchange of money and services which is calculated quite explicitly, and which also conveys a measure of prestige competition. Noor finds the pattern of village cooperation 'businesslike', and wants to conduct her own family events in a more private manner; she wants to erect a barrier between friendship and 'business'.

The way in which I see her dream about the future as a metonym of Malay family traditions is similar to the way in which she describes features of traditional ceremonial cooperation in a 'business' metaphor and sees it as metonymic of a whole way of ordering community relationships that no longer suits her. This is a contrast that has come to her along the temporal dimension of her own life-course, through formal education and new ways of forming friendships, as well as the new time–space organization that governs her days. The contrast that made me see her old-age dream as metonymic of a way of life arises in the interface between two spatially separated cultures.

THE INVENTIVE EDGE

The field example has illustrated some features of the 'inventive edge' inherent in cultural processes. The inventive edge follows contrasts that come mainly along two dimensions: time and space. The three of us have been faced with these contrasts in slightly different ways. We have all moved through time in our own life careers, facing new experiences that begged to be made sense of. Some of these are new only in the sense that the individual passes on to a new life-phase in growing up, having children, taking on age-appropriate responsibilities. All three of us have had these experiences. Other experiences are new in the sense that there are no or few culturally conventionalized ways of coping with them. Noor and I had such experiences when we were educated and took up jobs beyond the conventions in our mothers' generations. Limah responds to a new experience in a new political structure into which she tries to fit traditional skills. The anthropologist has made one major spatial move between two different cultures, a move which triggers reorientation, something culturally creative.

My metonymization of Noor's image is one such point, Noor's invention of a business metaphor is another. Less explicit examples are the ways in which both Limah and Noor work out their daily life in the interface between acquired knowledge and new challenges. I had as an ultimate purpose to create texts based on my insights from fieldwork, and sought to acquire an analytic gaze as a necessary step in that direction. Noor had a hunch of what kind of information it was that interested me, at the same time as she was genuinely fascinated by the chance our conversations gave her of reflecting on her own reality. Both of us were fascinated by the comparisons between our respective realities. The contrasts that made us create our various metonyms came to us across distances of time and space. They were, as mental operations, identical. Even if our specific experiences were different, there were enough similarities in the way our lives were structured to make us experience a 'shared space' and similar mechanisms of distantiation and metaphorization seemed to govern the ways in which we made sense of 'alien' practices.

In the above, I have used the terms punctuation and distantiation without discussing whether or not they could be used interchangeably. Punctuation is one of those uncommitted words that can capture a wide field of meaning, whereas distantiation has been given a precise meaning by Ricoeur, as the 'characteristics which effectively distance the text from the conditions of spoken discourse'. The act of creating a text and the life of the text have further been described as several instances and kinds of distantiation, but they are all locked within the confines of language: they move between speech acts, finite text, and the semantic conventions of originators and audiences (Thompson 1981: 13–14).

For some purposes it is important to stress the difference between the text and other forms of representation. This is because the text takes off from its context of origin and becomes subject to the different readings of the various audiences, a multitude of interpretations. But when we focus on the process of creating the text, it may be fruitful also to stress its continuity with other communicative and reflecting efforts, as it merely carries to an extra length a thrust which is generally present in human strivings toward externalization and representation.

As suggested earlier in this chapter, there is a process of reflection and representation which starts before language proper. What we could call a chain of emergent representations moves from wordless experience through doxic practice (Bourdieu 1977) to *gestalts* or images stored in mind for future practice (Rudie 1994), to symbols or metaphors fit for intersubjective communication, to direct language in speech and writing. The concept of distantiation as defined above is not sufficient to capture this process.

We must find a way to build up a more inclusive hermeneutic by means of including incorporating practices along with the inscribing practices, which have so far been the primary topic of hermeneutic analyses (cf. Connerton 1989). As suggested by Paul Connerton, body practice and commemorative ritual, with their inbuilt habit memory, are seen as promising fields to explore. Connerton is preoccupied with their stabilizing effect on societies, and claims that understanding stability is a greater challenge than understanding change. But it is also implicit (rather than explicit) in his analysis that such practices are malleable: 'When the memories of a culture begin to be transmitted mainly by the reproduction of their inscriptions rather than by "live" tellings, improvisation becomes increasingly difficult, and innovation is institutionalised' (Connerton 1989: 75).

This statement suggests two sides of the inventive edge, or two ways in which cultural re-creation and invention can come about: for beside the institutionalized innovation there is a constant flow of creative practice which can contain a high amount of *undetected change*. Noor's day-to-day experience seemed to infuse in her a feeling of continuity in her life which brought along images of long ago and blended them with new practices. I, who had been away for many years between my two field visits, saw a sharper contrast between past and present. For in my first fieldwork more than twenty years back I had *inscribed* what was then practice to her and frozen it in my text. Limah, who has been integrated in her neighbourhood for her whole lifetime, applies a traditional idiom of cooperation and sociality to new purposes. To me as an outside observer the inventive edge in her practice is very clear. She herself may not have an explicit concept corresponding to 'traditional idiom', but she certainly has a clear notion of trying to cope with a contemporary political reality as best she can by means of applying whatever skills she commands. Noor, who has recently diverted herself from her local background, sees the traditional idiom in local practices in contrast to her own practice, and probably fails to see their inventive edge.

The differences between these ways of making sense reflect our different experiential positions and interests. The similarity between them lies in the fact that they are all steps in the universally human effort of trying to bridge the gap between experience and representation. In that respect they are all mental punctuations within the limit of an inclusive hermeneutic project.

THE HERMENEUTICS OF CULTURAL INVENTION

So far I have applied the terms symbol, metaphor and metonym without distinguishing them carefully, my main concern being to stress how they constitute stages of information-processing, an embryonic discourse, or how they must find their place in an inclusive hermeneutic. As regards the paired concepts of metonym and metaphor, my usage is in tune with George Lakoff and Mark Johnson, as they state that

> like metaphoric concepts, metonymic concepts are grounded in our experience. In fact, the grounding of metonymic concepts is in general more obvious than is the case with the metaphoric concepts, since it usually involves direct physical or causal associations. The PART FOR WHOLE metonymy, for example, emerges from our experiences with the way parts in general are related to wholes.
>
> (Lakoff and Johnson 1980: 39–40; capitals original)

A recent concern with symbolization in anthropology sees it as an integrated part of social and cultural processes rather than just a way of speaking about something more 'real'. These analytical efforts take several forms – seeing symbols as 'the actualisation rather than the representation of people's shared understandings' (Strathern 1988: 174, quoting Clay 1977); as 'standing for themselves' and contributing to 'invention of culture' (Wagner 1981); as mental 'bricolage' (Sperber 1975). This approach to symbols often finds its themes in the body practices and representations of other cultures, and under this perspective the distinction between the symbolic and the practical melts down. This is not an unfamiliar thought in anthropology, although its full implications are only barely beginning to be spelled out. It is a leading theme in Marilyn Strathern's book *The Gender of the Gift*, and summed up in the remark: 'From our point of view, [these] are symbolic constructs; from the Melanesian point of view they are recipes for social action' (Strathern 1988: 271).

I touched on this perspective earlier in this chapter, when I suggested that practical acts acquire a communicative aspect as they are observed by others. This makes the distinction between instrumental and communicative acts into a matter of perspective in a reflexive process.

Anthropologists rarely get straight answers to their searching questions, with the result that alien practices remain enigmatic until they become commonplace. Such gaps between that which is fully internalized in self-evident practice and that which is still unfamiliar are the wellsprings of the 'symbolic mechanism'.[3] When a practice has become commonplace, it is internalized so that the practitioner is able to regenerate practice which is in tune with certain conventions, but this does not guarantee that one is able to explain it in verbal terms. The practices present themselves to the novice as images, and are stored analogically in that way, as mental representations. They represent the skills and the ideas of what a person is and can be, and lie so deeply ingrained in culture as to be perceived like nature. It was such an image, as recipe for action, that Noor brought out in her description of old age, and it was my distance from her reality that made me conceptualize it as a symbol or a metonym.

If the concept of distantiation is too specific to be applied to the embryonic stages of discourse, we still need to pay attention to the markers which punctuate the flow of information. The distinction between analogic and digital codes may be helpful in this respect. According to John Fiske, an analogic code works on a continuous scale, while a digital code is one whose units are clearly separated. He describes music as potentially analogic, though the notational system has given it characteristics of a digital code. Dance is analogic because it works through gestures, postures and distance, and is thus difficult to notate. Here we can remark that, when a dance is choreographed, an attempt is made to notate it according to digital principles. Punctuations are added for the purpose of description.

Nature, says Fiske, 'is generally composed of analogues: man, in trying to understand or categorize nature, imposes digital differences upon it: for instance the seven ages of man; or intimate, personal, semi-public and public distances between people' (Fiske 1982: 69–70).

In cultural processes analogic and digital principles intermix. The process of acquiring culture, whether we act as anthropologists or apprentice practitioners, can be characterized as an essentially analogic process which is punctuated by digital markers. Some such markers emerge as clearcut analytical or at least verbal categories; others are just stored in the form of images for further use, and then sometimes converted into metaphors or metonyms which can be used to reflect on more or less puzzling new experiences.

SOME TENTATIVE CONCLUSIONS

My concentration on the inventive edge of cultural processes is not, in this chapter, determined by a concern for the more familiar problem of continuity and change. Rather, my focus is chosen because I think it is a particularly promising field for capturing the experiential space, and sorting out the circumstances which can bring us from unreflected practice, to image, to symbol or metaphor, to explicit discourse.

The plasticity and creativity of the process of acquiring culture has been described by Tim Ingold in the following terms:

> For it is in and through relationships that persons come into being and endure in the course of social life. It might be helpful to think of social relations as forming a continuous topological surface or field, unfolding through time. Persons, then, are nodes in this unfolding, and sociality is the generative potential of the relational field in which they are situated and which is constituted and re-constituted through their activities.
>
> (Ingold 1991: 327)

In this perspective culture is seen as something that constantly happens, that is invented and re-invented, in the interface between individual and environment.

A topological field as introduced by Ingold is a field that can stretch and move into new shapes without being destroyed as a field, and the nodes may be highly instrumental in bringing this stretching about. Both Noor and Limah as described above have been such nodes, each in her own way. They have both integrated new experience into their practice, and brought it out in their relationships with others, in their environments.

The participant observer is another node, present in the field at two points in time, and bent on understanding social and cultural processes which have unfolded. Each time she shared some space with the informants, but they always shared more space between themselves. The 'stretching' performed by the individual partici-pants – the observer as well as the local practitioners – follows the same general rules when it comes to inventing culture and punc-tuating the flow of events by metaphors to conceptualize an under-standing. But the pattern of punctuations as well as the content of the metaphors varies among all the participants. The anthropo-logist, in her attempt to acquire the analytic gaze, tries to subsume the metaphors of the informants and make them into objects of analysis, at the same time as she creates metaphors at her own angles, and metonyms that eventually become decisive for the organization of the final text. The metaphoric and metonymic nature of the research process, however, becomes partly obscured in the text for two main reasons. First, we are not normally aware of the extent to which our conceptual system is metaphorical in nature (Lakoff and Johnson 1980: 3ff.). Second, a more thorough understanding of this point requires an analysis of *meaning in the making* along such lines as I have attempted in this chapter. And, as is obvious to everybody, my analysis has only touched the surface of a vast amount of information-processing that has taken place in a complex web of social interaction in the field.

NOTES

1 In a recent book Kirsten Hastrup focuses on the theme of puzzlement (*forbløffelse*). According to her argument, the hallmark of anthro-pology is the puzzlement that stems from experiencing cultural differ-ences, and 'although there are no more white patches on the ethnographic map, and no new peoples to discover, there are still untold depths to fathom in the way in which culture and society are shaped by people – and vice versa' (Hastrup 1992: 7; my translation).
2 Kemajuan masyarakat – Community Development Division of the Ministry of National and Rural Development.

3 Sperber sees 'the symbolic mechanism' as a definite cognitive faculty (Sperber 1975). I specifically wish to draw attention to it as a mechanism of information-processing.

REFERENCES

Bourdieu, Pierre (1977) *Towards a Theory of Practice*, Cambridge: Cambridge University Press.

Clay, Brenda J. (1977) *Pinikindu: Maternal Nurture, Paternal Substance*, Chicago: University of Chicago Press.

Connerton, Paul (1989) *How Societies Remember*, Cambridge: Cambridge University Press.

Fiske, Jon (1982) *Introduction to Communication Studies*, London and New York: Methuen.

Hastrup, Kirsten (1992) *Det antropologiske projekt – om forbløffelse*, Copenhagen: Nordisk Forlag AS.

Hastrup, Kirsten, and Ramløv, Kirsten, eds (1988) *Feltarbejde. Oplevelse og metode i etnografien*, Copenhagen: Akademisk Forlag.

Ingold, Tim (1991) 'Becoming persons: consciousness and sociality in human evolution', *Cultural Dynamics* 4: 355–78.

Lakoff, George, and Johnson, Mark (1980) *Metaphors We Live By*, Chicago and London: University of Chicago Press.

Malinowski, Bronislaw (1923) 'The problem of meaning in primitive languages', in C.K. Ogden and I.A. Richards, eds, *The Meaning of Meaning*, Oxford: Blackwell.

Ricoeur, Paul (1981) *Hermeneutics and the Human Sciences*, ed. and trans. John B. Thompson, Cambridge: Cambridge University Press.

Rosaldo, Renato (1989) *Culture and Truth*, Boston, Mass.: Beacon Press.

Rudie, Ingrid (1994) *Visible Women in East Coast Malay Society*, Oslo: Scandinavian University Press.

Sperber, Dan (1975) *Rethinking Symbolism*, Cambridge: Cambridge University Press.

Strathern, Marilyn (1988) *The Gender of the Gift: Problems with Women and Problems with Society in Melanesia*, Berkeley: University of California Press.

Thompson, John B. (1981) 'Editor's introduction', in Paul Ricoeur, *Hermeneutics and the Human Sciences*, ed. and trans. John B. Thompson, Cambridge: Cambridge University Press.

Vendler, Zeno (1984) 'Understanding people', in Richard A. Schweder and Robert A. LeVine, eds, *Culture Theory: Essays on Mind, Self, and Emotion*, Cambridge: Cambridge University Press.

Wagner, Roy (1981) *The Invention of Culture*, revised and expanded edn, Chicago: University of Chicago Press.

Watson, Graham (1991) 'Rewriting culture', in Richard G. Fox, ed., *Recapturing Anthropology: Working in the Present*, Santa Fe, N. Mex.: School of American Research Press.

Wikan, Unni (1992) 'Beyond the words: the power of resonance', *American Ethnologist* 19, 3: 460–82.

Chapter 3

Vicarious and sensory knowledge of chronology and change
Ageing in rural France

Judith Okely

This chapter is concerned less with the limitations of written, indigenous texts[1] than with those of the spoken word in conveying a people's changing and past experience. My material, based not only on one-to-one dialogue, but also on participant observation, contrasts vividly with the empirical research of oral historians and sociologists who, in addition to written sources, rely extensively on the interview, where speech is privileged.[2] In anthropological fieldwork, I drew on knowledge beyond language, less as extra-sensory perception than as that which comes from all the senses, both of the fieldworker and of the subjects. Knowledge was embodied through sight, taste, sound, touch and smell. Bodily movement, its vigour, stillness or unsteadiness, was absorbed. Spoken utterances, especially the brief and seemingly banal, made greater and profounder sense when placed in a broader, learned context.

My research involved the changing conditions and experience of the aged in rural France, so it was important to know something of their younger, working lives and the context from which they had emerged. They were now retired from wage labour or in other ways changed by a more explicit age categorization, although still clearly demarcated by class and gender. The majority were to be found in a market town. Many had moved with age and infirmity from their previous homes in the surrounding villages, where they had been involved with agriculture and related occupations. I participated in some of their day-to-day routines, whether in retirement homes, lodgings or their own homes. In addition, my residence in the villages and work on a small farm similar to those the aged had once known gave embodied knowledge of something of their past. My newly acquired knowledge and identifiable location among persons of the *pays* evoked points of recognition and continuity among many of the now urbanized elderly. The field-worker, *étrangère,* was made familiar to them and familiarized herself with their former landscape.

I wanted also to compare the conditions between different groups of the aged, especially in relation to wealth and class. The middle classes could avoid the municipal old people's home, or hospice as it was called, by purchasing or renting their own convenient homes near the centre of the town and paying for visiting carers. It became clear that the implications of biological ageing were less significant in retirement than privileged access through wealth to autonomous space (Okely 1986).[3] In this chapter, I shall concentrate mainly on those elderly who had moved to institutions.

Archaeologists have experimented in the reconstruction of a people's past by interrogating present-day inhabitants and the speechless landscape for clues which are consistent with past possibilities. My time-gap was far less problematic in that I could communicate with the former residents. Moreover, the changes stretched over only a few decades rather than centuries.

My specific example of attempting to grasp the earlier lives of the aged, now dislocated from their past in time and place, can be seen as an extreme case of what happens generally in anthropological fieldwork. Usually, the anthropologist in the field, while not faced with such a radical break between present dislocation from past continuity, is confronted by the disjunction between the subjects' experience of a culture and its decontextualized description by 'informants'. The very choice of the label informant betrays a positivistic dependence on the verbal, as well as a naive conflation of the actor's description or explanation with the actual experience or event. Knowledge and experience of another culture cannot be conveyed as uni-dimensional information. The subjects draw on the full range of unspoken knowledge, which in turn transforms the sense of linguistic utterances and any available written word.

The aged former labouring inhabitants of the Normandy locality were in many cases non-literate. In addition, they were not amenable to linear interviews. My sensitivity to non-verbalized knowledge had to be even greater than that normally recognized by anthropologists. Many of the aged had taken on the marginalized invisibility noted elsewhere by Barbara Myerhoff (1986). They were silenced in new ways if institutionalized and divorced from the utterances which come from external or domestic labour and family household routines. The gaze, however benign, of their professional carers changed their conversation. They were not practised in giving monologic accounts of either their past or their present. Besides, there were aspects of their current circumstances which were often best left unsaid. It is possible that they had to repress too strong a longing or consciousness of what they could no longer live and inhabit. Some, like those elderly studied elsewhere (Hazan 1980), chose to exist in a vacuum of present time.

SENSORY KNOWLEDGE

By privileging sensory knowledge in this chapter over speech and linguistic utterances alone, it should not be concluded that the argument is British empiricism re-emerging from Locke or Hume in twentieth-century clothing. The earlier belief that all knowledge could be traced back to immediate sense data, fails to recognize the way in which the senses are mediated, interpreted and conceptualized. We cannot prove that people's experience is identical merely because they have the same physiological senses. We cannot, for example, claim to know that we have experienced exactly the same physical pain or pleasure as anyone else. There is, even in the commonplace, room for doubt and the recognition of possible differences. On a grander scale, the anthropologist engaged in participant observation can never claim to have exactly the same experience as others, especially when from a different culture. The sense data are mediated, reinterpreted and reconceptualized. The experience cannot be exactly replicated.

Since sensory knowledge cannot be the direct reflection of reality, even members of the same culture cannot claim a complete correspondence in experience, instead they may creatively construct correspondences between themselves. This is what also occurs between anthropologist and subjects. In my examples, I show how there is a back and forth between what the subjects could convey and what I could respond to. The anthropologist cannot replicate others' experience, but she can use her own or what Nagel has referred to as 'the subjective character of experience' (1991: 166) for a vicarious understanding to surmise others' experience.

I contest therefore the view of anthropologists such as Clifford Geertz, who suggests that the endeavour of seeking shared experience should be abandoned. He was quick to denigrate any popular claim that anthropologists acquired a special empathy through long-term fieldwork (1974). More recently he affirmed:

> We cannot live other people's lives, and it is a piece of bad faith to try. We can but listen to what, in words, in images, in actions they say about their lives. As Victor Turner . . . argued, it is with expressions – representations, objectifications, discourses, performances, whatever – that we traffic. . . . Whatever sense we have of how things stand with someone's inner life, we gain it through their expressions, not through some magical intrusion into their consciousness.
>
> (1986: 373)

Notice that anything approximating to shared consciousness is safely dismissed as magical.

I would prefer to substitute for magic, sensory knowledge and one which is gained through experience of the everyday rather than confined to distilled external representations. I approach what has been called 'lived experience' (Bruner 1986: 7) in its widest sense, which embraces the commonplace and the everyday, rather than confining it to the representations and dramatized expressions selected by Turner, Geertz *et al.* in *The Anthropology of Experience* (Turner and Bruner 1986). There, experience is taken to mean something very specific: a highlighted event or production, separated from everyday practice. While Edward M. Bruner's introduction leans heavily on Dilthey's concept of experience (1976) as what has been 'lived through' (Bruner 1986: 3), Bruner, Turner *et al.* adopt Dilthey's answer to transcending 'the narrow sphere of experience' by 'interpreting expressions' (ibid.: 5). By contrast, I include the banality of daily practice and the often taken-for-granted ambience which is experienced through all the bodily senses. This embraces the non-verbal, although the odd verbal interjection may provide a clue to the former. Indeed, I argue that a single apparently throwaway remark may be the distilled clue to a total unspoken experience, if the anthropologist knows how to recognize it. Profound feelings may be disguised by linguistic banality.

The comprehension by the anthropologist of this experience has to be approached through the full range of sensory knowledge and a new intuition learned in fieldwork. The total experience of fieldwork is also used in unarticulated and unconscious ways to make sense of fieldnotes long after the events. Linguistic utterances cannot be the sole route to others' experience. Even in dialogue, the exchange and adjustments between persons are affected and enhanced by conscious and subconscious bodily knowledge. Participant observation enables the anthropologist to make interpretations through vicarious knowledge. This is of course always partial. The specificity of the anthropologist will also affect whether cross-cultural encounters are a contrast or a parallel with the anthropologist's previous experience (Okely 1992).

In some of the ethnographic examples below, I argue that the subjects also lived vicariously through my experience in the locality from which they had become separated. My cumulative experience in the field and a familiarity with aspects of the subjects' past or present through participant observation were conveyed back to them, not just through words but through their recognition that I had 'been there' and had experienced something similar through bodily presence, action and sight, sound, taste, touch or smell. I had engaged in agricultural labour of the kind they had once known. Here a distinction can be made between subjective experience which is individual, and creative understanding which is an approximation to empathy but never complete.

PARTICIPATION IN THE PAST

Textual critics and some anthropologists have examined the apparent devices used by anthropologists to confirm the authority of having 'been there' (Pratt 1986, Crapanzano 1986 and Rosaldo 1986). Although I do not see my interventions and exchanges with the aged as a calculated strategy, the reminder to the reader of the anthropologist's presence in final texts can be compared to my sometimes brief indications during fieldwork to the former villagers in retirement homes that I had been to their former domain. Once I had conveyed hints of my experience, a shared knowledge could be taken as given. My passing references did not so much give the anthropologist an unsought-for authority as afford the former villagers vicarious pleasure and recollections uncontrolled.

The extent to which participant observation in the surrounding hamlets made sense of the former residents' lives can be indicated in the contrast between my comprehension of the lives of those who were long-term inhabitants of the region and that of the lives of those who had moved from other places in France to one of the retirement homes in the fieldwork area. Mention of a village a few kilometres away drew blanks from the latter, while the locals smiled with delight. Even if they had not lived there, they could come up with an anecdote or the names of other residents. They could re-imagine themselves in that space, while now being relatively fixed. They were living vicariously through my current location. It needed only a few words to evoke their pasts through my present. By contrast, the incomers were themselves more dislocated than the indigenous elderly. Their dislocation matched that of my own at the start of fieldwork. They had no recognizable landmarks beyond the small walking-circuit which they might take on first arrival and which tended to diminish with frailty or indifference.

Just as the more distant incomers felt *dépaysés*, so also did I when attempting to construct their past in the light of their current circumstances. Their descriptions or accounts of their earlier lives remained disjointed: for instance, one man who had come from Dijon was identifiable only by that label. Neither I nor the other residents could supply his past local knowledge to recreate a sense of his past. There were some exceptions: for instance, the Parisian who could make use of shared knowledge of the metropolis. The fact that she had lived in Montmartre, a renowned landmark, encouraged questions from the locals about prostitutes. The place was also familiar to the anthropologist, so some knowledge, however different, could be used. In another case, the residents drew on regional stereotypes rather than shared concrete knowledge to recreate the woman's past. A Breton woman found herself the victim of ridicule similar to New York Polack jokes. Here her identity was fixed by visual details of demeanour. What she said was largely ignored. Somewhat absentminded and frail, she wore woollen knee socks which fell around her ankles. This confirmed her as a country bumpkin who knew no better.

A third woman came from Pas-de-Calais. I found a route to her past through images. After checking permission from the nursing staff, she was delighted to be 'allowed' to invite me to her room. She brought out a box of photographs. These worked as profound recreations of her past: I saw a robust woman with piled-up 1940s hairstyle and severe suit. She had fled the German invasion, driving a large commercial van. The pictures evoked comments and important descriptions. A mere tape-recording of her speaking in a formalized interview could not have conjured up the greater sense of her past which we mutually created with the aid of visual images. The more complete being conveyed in that encounter remained indelibly in the anthropologist's understanding of her and others of her kind. Every time I saw her again, I could also see something of the earlier chronology. Her presence at the Resistance and Liberation ceremonies, sparsely attended because of the town's political ambivalence, made greater sense.

It could be argued that my image of her is a haphazard construction based on idiosyncratic reactions to her salvaged souvenirs. I cannot fully articulate the powerful experience of the encounter. I was watching, listening and resonating with the emotions and energy of her living through photographs. It was vicarious living for the anthropologist who had not done fieldwork in her past but for whom the dulled and dog-eared photo images conveyed another time. The facts and dates of French history were made more meaningful, not simply in her verbal comments, but also in the knowledge that these photos had captured the physical stages from childhood to youth and middle age of this same woman embodied before me. Now stooping, suffering from severe varicose veins and with her once luxuriant hair just silver wisps, she radiated her previous *personnages* like an aura or photographic negatives.

My argument does not extend to the exclusion of words; the woman's comments were essential as captions and elaborations of the photos. However, the selective images of the past, which of course excluded so much, gave embodiment to a selective past which a purely verbal account would lack. Both of us pieced together the memories from whatever was picked up from the box, and created a synthesized whole. In reacting to the visual images, randomly stored, the woman was freed of linear chronology, any set piece for a life history and a purely verbalized description. The images did some of the work for both of us in ways which adjectives and other vocabulary could not supply.

In other contexts, photographs acted as more contrived cultural revelations. The selected icons of photos which the aged displayed at institutional bedside or on familiar sideboard in their own home were both cultural and individual presentations. Recollections by the elderly of a dead spouse were sometimes synchronized by their eye contact with the portrait on display. I was implicitly invited to imagine the individual as if always like this idealized and formal display. Blurred and spontaneous snapshots like those of the woman above were not the ones framed.

Other visual displays were not such clear routes to the individual's experience. The few pictures on display in the relatively stark hospice bedrooms turned out to be puzzling. One was of the promenade at Nice. For a while, I concluded that this had real past significance for the resident, who had no other personal objects in her room. When I commented on it she informed me that it had been given to her by a nephew on a rare visit. It was not possible to know what it meant for her to keep it on the wall. She appeared indifferent. Was it his gesture which counted? Had the image then seeped involuntarily into her spatial awareness? Words could not easily answer this. I was left with my own visual reaction to a place she had neither selected nor visited, but which she linked verbally only with her visiting nephew.

In my empathetic understanding of the aged, far more grounded was the interplay between participant observation in their former localities and their current more static existence in retirement. By living in the villages from which many had migrated when age and infirmity made it impossible to continue farming or other occupations, I was able to make acquaintances with their former neighbours and gain a perspective on aspects of their former working lives and surroundings. News that I was friends with certain individuals in a village brought unexpected entrée with poorer and non-bourgeois members of the town's club for the elderly: 'Once we heard that you were a friend of Madame G., we knew you were alright.' The village residents reminisced about their former neighbours. Just as important was the total picture which I acquired of village existence. By assisting in farm work, with the harvest, cider-making, cattle-feeding, hand milking (Okely 1991a), and joining in group gatherings such as the Armistice banquet, a summer dance and meetings of the clubs for the elderly (Okely 1990), I saw, felt, heard and tasted something of what the former inhabitants had known. My encounters back in town with them were enriched by this newly acquired knowledge. My vicarious experience was to be exploited to reconstruct and relive their own. It only needed a few key words or remarks to conjure up their memories and to imagine mutual knowledge.

The mere name of a locality was sufficient in some instances. A woman who once lived in a town about twenty miles away was transformed in posture and alertness when I indicated my acquaintance with the place. She beamed with pleasure when I pronounced the name of a china and household goods shop, where I had made a purchase. She was proud to identify with its high quality and reputation in her time. It was implicit, but never stated, that we were sharing images of the town, she did not have to give a verbal description of it. She could people my superficial acquaintance of it with her own memories. For a brief moment, perhaps, the scandal and grief of having been forcibly interned in the retirement home by relatives when she was in her fifties was dulled and she reminisced happily.

Inevitably, the ability to trigger off internal memories in others does not necessarily convey the same to the anthropologist. The examples above reveal that photographs awaken thoughts and speech, or that news of the anthropologist's field experience encourages rapport and identification, as well as nostalgia. In the example of the photographs, the anthropologist gains a privileged and visual perspective on a person's past. In the case of fieldwork in the person's former locality, the anthropologist is again able to add further dimensions to any purely verbal description of the past. She learns through bodily knowledge, whether via the senses in general or through the action of physical labour. To put it simply, the experience breathes life into words or silences, where the subject finds words a struggle or redundant.

Perspectives on the subjects' present and past experience can be acquired by other everyday gestures or activities which elicit apparently banal comments. In the following instance, the anthropologist was directly seen to be living aspects of the former lives of the residents. One day I entered the private, middle-class retirement home carrying a baguette of bread with my shopping-bag. The Parisian woman from Montmartre exclaimed with delight 'Mademoiselle, vous avez fait vos courses!' ('Mademoiselle, you've done your shopping!'). In everyday encounters in the town and villages, no one made such an excited comment. To buy one's daily bread was a commonplace. What was unsaid but conveyed in the woman's observation, was the surprised recognition that I had daily domestic tasks and poignantly ones which this woman no longer experienced. Few, if any, of the residents in this home had been involved in agricultural production, but the women had once taken responsibility for food preparation and domestic labour. In the residential home, all meals were provided in the *salle à manger*. The residents wanted for nothing, they were waited upon, others did the shopping for them, chose the menu, cooked, cleared and washed up. The majority of residents were of course too frail to take on any of these responsibilities, but they could still show that they missed these daily routines by taking vicarious pleasure in others continuing them. There is a special gender helplessness when women, by contrast to men, have to abdicate domestic labour to others (Evers 1981). For decades, this resident had bought her daily bread at a boulangerie round the corner from her Parisian apartment. Her few words had revealed more than the banal. In turn my participant observation at the home, seeing its routines and practices, gave added sense to her reaction and elaborated its unspoken, deeper meaning.

Many hours of fieldwork entailed minimum words in the company of the elderly, whether in the retirement homes or in the clubs. Among the most difficult aspects were the hours of playing dominoes in the town and village clubs. Then, communication was almost entirely non-verbal. It did not seem to require much intellectual concentration; or perhaps the need for single-minded application was extremely frustrating for the anthropologist who could not engage any of the participants in extended conversation. The players would sit sometimes for two hours at the table. Here it seemed that the impossibility of extensive verbal exchange was its very comfort. Conflicts were minimized. Individuals were recognized for exceptional skills at dominoes, others were pitied if they failed in its rudimentary requirements. Otherwise, a calm descended. Near-silent companionship could be savoured. The boredom or loneliness of widowhood and absence of former work routines could be filled in by a purposeful, short-term aim which obliterated past and future in the suspended present. Time and future death were temporarily defeated in the undramatic comfort of shared company. Some remarked bluntly that all they were now fit for was playing dominoes: 'Nos corps sont usés' ('Our bodies are worn out'). One man repeatedly drummed his fingers on the table as if frustrated by this bodily inactivity. In one village club, after several hours of dominoes, the members regrouped for the *collation* (snack), which entailed a generous supply of pâté, cheese and apple tart, washed down with cider or wine. Conversation then broke out. In another club, light feasting after dominoes was followed by individual singing with a microphone. The assembled company then danced in measured, snake-like and gentle procession around the hall to the sound of nostalgic gramophone records. In these examples, there was camaraderie and shared experience in near-silent games, singing of set pieces, music, dance and commensuality. Innovative verbal commentary was relatively unimportant.

THE FOOD AND DRINK OF ETHNOGRAPHY

The preparation and consumption of specific types of food and drink were a powerfully symbolic, rather than merely functional, feature of the people's lives, both in the past and in the present, if only in memory. The former *petits agriculteurs* (small farmers) had in addition been closely engaged in the production of food and drink, including that for their own consumption, during their working lives. The focus on food is more likely to be taken for granted by a French anthropologist nourished by a culture of *haute cuisine*, as confirmed in the following example. At a meeting of French and British social scientists in the late 1980s to exchange research ideas into rural change, many of the British were baffled at the apparent fixation of the French researchers on the need to study the impact of freezers on the rural household and economy (cf. Zonabend 1984: 43–4).[4] To the British, this seemed a trivial and mechanical object unworthy of further analysis. Notwithstanding, I recognized an echo from culinary priorities encountered in my own fieldwork. When relatives discovered that the director of the municipal retirement home ordered meat in bulk from a frozen-food company in Rouen, my village neighbours considered it a scandal sufficient to demand her resignation. This was seen to be an outrageous economy and an insult to the residents, who, as former *petits cultivateurs*, deserved local meat from animals brought to the town's abattoir. Many had once reared their own cattle and had developed discriminating palates which now they took for granted. Taste was an especially important part of their life experience, something which the palate of a British anthropologist had to try to acquire.

Although it has been argued that sight is the privileged, Western faculty replicated in fieldwork (Fabian 1983), this does not take into account differences between Western cultures. While Paul Stoller draws attention to the importance of taste in Songhay culture, in passing (1989: 15, 31) he nevertheless gives textual examples from French writers such as Montaigne and Lévi-Strauss who relish taste. The argument that insufficient attention is given

to the total world of the senses in representing cultures in monographs is nonetheless convincing.[5]

Although the sophistication of French bourgeois cuisine has
indeed been recognized outside anthropology, both within France
and beyond, less has been recorded about the culinary discernment of the rural working-class *petits agriculteurs* and *paysans*
(a term which now has derogatory overtones) and the rural petty
bourgeois. Bourdieu's *Distinction* (1984), while contrasting the
bourgeoisie and the working class, has not always adequately
distinguished the tastes of the urban and rural working classes,
especially the urban food consumers, as distinct from those persons in rural areas who may also produce what they consume. The
local significance of cider and other home produce is necessarily
lost in the macro-statistics of food purchases as percentage of
income. Indeed, cider consumption is presented only for skilled
manual workers and those of higher class echelons (ibid.: 181–2,
188–9).

Although there might be relative informality in presentation at
working-class meals, their content in my field area was not always
the grease and grossness, with function over form, that Bourdieu
has tended to suggest (ibid.: 177–200): 'As one rises in the social
hierarchy, the proportion [of income] spent on fatty, fattening
foods . . . declines . . . whereas an increasing proportion is spent
on leaner, lighter (more digestible) non fattening foods . . . and
especially fresh fruit and vegetables' (ibid.: 172). In this category
of 'more digestible', Bourdieu includes beef, which may unwit-
tingly reproduce the bourgeois and somewhat subjective assessment of culinary experience. In fact, the former and current *petits
cultivateurs* encountered in fieldwork had once or still relished
their own or local produce, which included farmyard chicken, 'free
range' eggs, veal, home-grown salad and freshly picked or home-
bottled vegetables and fruit, such as apples and pears. This type of
food does not fit with what Bourdieu has characterized as merely
'filling'. More importantly, the taste and consumption of home-
grown produce are strongly flavoured by symbolic associations
with person and place.

Bourdieu is convincing in the observation that the bourgeoisie
define their taste as that which is thought not to be working-class
(ibid.: 185). In my field area, the members of the local bourgeoisie
seemed unaware of the subtleties of the cuisine of those ranked
beneath them. The great divide came between those who regularly

drank local cider and those who denigrated it, expressing a preference for wine. The middle and upper classes complained that the cider gave them indigestion; that it was bad for the stomach (cf. Bourdieu 1984: 172). By contrast, the *petits cultivateurs* were proud to serve and drink locally produced cider, preferably from their own small orchards. They in turn denigrated commercially mass-produced cider, which was said to be spoilt by industrial chemicals.

An even greater joy for the soul and tastebuds was the *eau de vie* or cider brandy. There was rivalry and pride about one's own home-grown produce, made with the assistance of the distiller who visited each village in the autumn. One elderly couple who, in their seventies, had managed to remain in their own farmhouse while leasing out their few acres of land, were supremely proud of their cider brandy, produced for decades from the same orchard visible from their window. They had taken the trouble to have it inspected and tested at Rouen, where it was awarded an *appellation control-lée*. Like many others, they argued that they could recognize its taste blindfold, even alongside that of their immediate neighbour. At most club gatherings, and especially at the huge annual banquet, they took along a bottle to savour among their immediate companions. The key moment for the tasting was between the dishes, especially before the main meat course. Each diner was to swallow a small glass of the spirit in a swift gulp. This they excitedly explained to me was *le trou normand*, the Normandy drink which makes a space or a hole in the stomach for the next helping. The practice was especially elaborate at banquets. At home dinners, some women tended to see it as a requirement only for a man's digestive system (cf. Bourdieu 1984: 190–2).

At the annual banquet at the local authority home or hospice, attended by the mayor, *le trou normand* again made its appearance on the menu. But the spirit was diluted and modified by being poured on to a sorbet. Some of the elderly men residents were able to insist on being served theirs neat. One visiting woman councillor, a retired schoolteacher and guest at the mayor's table, explained that the sorbet mixture was better; the spirit was too strong and hard on the stomach. The comments resembled those made by others of her class about cider. Thus concessions were made to the visiting dignitaries sitting at the mayor's table. The minority tastes of the bourgeoisie prevailed over those of the less powerful inmates whose banquet it was supposed to be. By contrast, at the banquets of clubs where the non-institutionalized elderly still retained control over the preparation, if not the production of food, *le trou normand* was drunk according to working-class and peasant tradition.

Such culinary experiences were not just associated with banquets, but part of everyday consumption and commensuality. Participant observation among the often younger elderly or middle-aged in their own homes, at the clubs and in the surrounding villages revealed by way of contrast what the now institutionalized elderly once enjoyed, valued and experienced. The latter had lost relative autonomy, revelry and familiar, loved tastes in retirement exile.

The nuances of different tastes became apparent to me only morsel by morsel. On an early visit to the municipal home, in the company of a villager calling on her mother and aunt, I was introduced to the widow of the village butcher. When I asked her about the place, her main reservation and seemingly daily disappointment were conveyed in just two whispered words: 'La nourriture' ('The food'). At that stage of fieldwork, this seemed just a passing comment. Many banquets and farmhouse-dinner invitations later, I could comprehend her disappointed if not disgusted palate. I could not acquire her lifetime's subtle taste, but I had witnessed and shared the tastes of others in ways which could not be easily conveyed solely by language and at a distance from the meal table.

In seeing the very apple trees through the windows and eyes of their cultivators, I could empathize with the culinary sensibilities of those who could devour the fruits of their immediate landscape. However presentable the institutional meals, they could never be the same as the home grown. Even the rich cuisine served in the elegant *salle à manger* at the luxurious private retirement home where the Parisian found herself could not compensate for her loss of autonomy. Thus the losses and changes for palate and life-long routines became apparent not so much through their spoken or unknown absence as, more significantly, through the experience of their presence by the anthropologist in the company of other subjects elsewhere. I rarely tasted their institutional food; nor did I have to submit to the routines imposed by the staff. I did, by contrast, taste, hear, see, feel and move through aspects of their former existence. On my return visits to the homes, the residents responded not merely to my halting verbalized accounts, but also to the clues to some shared sensory knowledge. I had opened a way to their memories with which I in turn could find sensory correspondences. I had absorbed something of the conditions of their past existence through living in their former locality and experiencing its tastes, sights, sounds, smells and sights.

It was in the elaborate banquets arranged for clubs for the elderly and for mixed-age village events that I recognized the full drama of the production, preparation and consumption of food for the region's inhabitants. These banquets celebrated priorities of daily experience, although in concentrated form. The elderly set even greater store by the banquets than the young and middle-aged. The liveliest and most copious banquets were at clubs or village events attended by those elderly who had so far escaped institutionalization. The club for the elderly in the main town had fewer such elaborate feastings, and was under the firm control of a middle-class committee. Elsewhere (Okely 1990), I distinguished between Bourg, the main town, Pastorale, a village with an agricultural base, and Jonction, the home of many former railway workers as well as some small farmers. The annual club banquet at Jonction, the first to which I was unsuspectingly invited, began at midday and ended after midnight. There was a lull in eating and drinking between about 5 and 7 p.m., when the members, all of whom were over sixty, many over seventy, pushed back the tables, and sang and danced. (Even the local gendarme was puzzled as to why the hall lights were still on at midnight when the banquet had been scheduled for midday.) This was my first taste of *La Grande Bouffe*.[6] My body was so incapacitated that I spent the next twenty-four hours immobilised and fasting in bed. My dining companions had no such problems. I felt like the goose down whose throat grain is repeatedly stuffed in the process of *gavage* (force feeding). Its bloated liver destined for *pâté de foie gras* was one metaphor for the sensuous experience of fieldwork and research material to be digested.

A comparable event occurred at the Armistice midday lunch in Pastorale. I staggered home at about six o'clock in the evening, only to be visited at eight by several of the middle-aged farmers, who invited me to join, this time mainly their age group, for further four-course feasting until midnight. In addition to copious private lunch or dinner invitations, afternoon social calls to the elderly would entail a generous spread modestly called a *collation*, or snack. Many wonderful afternoons were passed in a haze of cider, wine, just *un goût* of brandy, or champagne at the château, with black coffee, pâté, cream gâteau, cheeses, apple tart or chocolate dessert. As my body ingested more and more, and as I observed the intensity of involvement and earthly joys of my companions at table, I digested the centrality of *la bonne nourriture* and *le boisson* to the local culture.

The capacity to enjoy the discriminating palate certainly did not diminish among the village residents with the immediate onset of old age. Eating and drinking filled the hours as well as the stomach. Those who complained of liver problems and received restraining medical advice, were seen as randomly unfortunate individuals. Others, especially women, interpreted medical advice about calcium to justify huge intakes of local cheeses. During their past days of heavy manual labour, it was clear that calories were quickly burned off. After retirement, however, the eating patterns were rarely changed. In the course of five years' acquaintance, I observed individuals who stopped heavy farm work then gain dramatically in weight. Eating good and familiar food while still living in their own homes affirmed their freedom from the constraints and deep-freeze economies of institutional menus. Few of such gluttonous joys were available for those in the municipal home, away from their villages and the clubs. But their parsimonious words did not adequately convey these lost sensory and convivial experiences. Just a few comments from the hospice residents gave me the clues, without recreating their pasts.

A people's spatial sense is greater than just the sense of sight; it extends to bodily memory and total ambience. This is again something which cannot be reduced to words alone. An individual feels 'at home' within a long familiar space even though s/he may not be able to describe how or why. Removal from that familiar space and daily routines can highlight for the anthropologist and the subject what had once been taken for granted (Okely 1986, 1991b). In the retirement homes, I was given a few verbal clues, which were poignantly selective or condensed. I was better able to comprehend those clues when I compared the residents' spatial ambience with that of the village homes, farms and landscape. My comparison was built on a fieldwork familiarity with both their past and their present locations. As I sat with the aunt of one of the village visitors at the hospice in her shared room, I asked her about the differences between her current and previous residence. Her reply was as stark as her personality: 'Eh bien, j'avais ma maison, mon jardin et mon chien, j'étais heureuse' ('Well, I had my house, my garden and my dog, I was happy').

After some months of inhabiting and hence experiencing her past locality, I was able to visualize the sort of house which she once inhabited. Her niece lived in an extended wattled and beamed house overlooking her farmyard and orchard. Even if the aunt had lived in the more austere architectural alternative of red-brick village house, it would have had a certain cosiness and would be externally softened by the ubiquitous geraniums at the doors and window sills in summer. (The hospice residents had no plants either inside or on sills.) The village interiors had a unique look, called a Normandy interior. It took time for me to get used to the terracotta floor tiles, the multicoloured wallpapers and the seemingly random array of ornaments. There were patterned net curtains halfway up the window. Always central to the home was the kitchen table covered by patterned oilcloth; a very altar cloth. Around this, all social life was conducted. Whenever I visited someone in her own home, I was soon asked 'Qu'est-ce-que je peux vous offrir?' ('What can I offer you?'). The very phrasing implied that the hostess was ready to supply anything requested. Hospitality was at the heart of the home. In the residential homes, there was no kitchen table to be seen. The means to share food and drink in simultaneous sensory experience was absent. The main social exchange seemed of necessity limited to the verbal.

CONCLUSION

I have presented an extreme case of what is in effect standard to anthropological fieldwork: the project of constructing the world of others in ways which go beyond or indeed belie the subjects' statements about their world. Anthropological fieldwork is a total bodily experience, not one merely dependent on verbal accounts. Contrary to those, like Geertz, who fear the mystery of empathy, I suggest that the anthropologist has no choice but to use body and soul, in addition to intellect, as a means of approaching others' experience. Linguistic utterances may be a clue, but they cannot be depended upon. There is also the full range of bodily senses.

In this ethnographic case, I have explored how the institutionalized elderly, away from their original homes and villages, are exiled from aspects of their life experience. Past images, such as personal photographs, act as powerful recreations of their lives, portrayed beyond a linear, pre-ordained format. In living in the village localities from which the elderly came, I was able to reconstruct something of what they once lived. Especially significant were the sense of place, the personal home and its associations, the taste and sight of home grown produce, local cuisine and drink, the revelry of banquets and neighbourhood commensuality. Silent games in known company gave wordless comfort, and daily domestic or work routines, not ritually framed, were valued when lost or changed. By introducing the institutionalized elderly to my recent experience in their past locations, I awakened identification and correspondences. The anthropologist and the subjects lived vicariously through one another.

I do not, in emphasizing the vast area of non-linguistic knowledge, mean to imply that language is a subordinate or even a redundant means of knowing. I wish to draw attention to the context in which language takes meaning, to the places where language is inappropriate, and finally to the instances where spoken utterances may belie what is said. Psychoanalysis reveals how speakers are adept at disguising truths from themselves and their listeners. The anthropologist has to have the perception of a psychoanalyst to spot the hidden, often contradictory, meanings in both utterance and silence. But in the discipline of psychoanalysis, knowledge is primarily dependent on the verbalized. There is not the comparable sensuousness and embodied knowledge involved in participant observation fieldwork.

The anthropologist's long-term participation encourages a grounded knowledge which is then used vicariously as a means of comprehending others' experience. Whatever its hazards and limitations, this is the most appropriate medium available. In many instances, anthropologists have not been fully aware of the extent to which they have relied on this unarticulated embodied knowledge to make sense of and to interpret their fieldwork. Instead, they have mystified themselves and their readers by an instrumental and retrospective language of disembodied objectivity.

At the end of fieldwork, the anthropologist is faced with the challenge of transforming the total experience and its messiness into words. No words may adequately redescribe that knowledge, but there are still choices between words. Neither I nor the subjects in the field were poets. It is not surprising that the totality of sensory experience cannot be conveyed. Perhaps nineteenth-century novelists came closest to detailed descriptions of the material world and its individual characters. Since then, however, the nineteenth-century realist project has collapsed. The rest of us have to recreate others' experiences through refracted means.

NOTES

1 Some of the ideas for this chapter were crystallized by my reading of Hastrup 1991.
2 Zonabend's work (1984) on indigenous history in Minot appears to depend largely on oral and written accounts, although her co-residence in the village is likely to have alerted her to the people's priorities and influenced the format of the questions asked.
3 Fieldwork for this research was financed by the Economic and Social Research Council 1985–6, with additional assistance for follow-up visits from the Fuller Fund, Department of Sociology, Essex University.
4 Personal communication Sue Wright.
5 Stoller was converted from the worst excesses of instrumental 'data collection' in the name of linguistic anthropology (1989: 4–5) to what should be regarded as essential experiential fieldwork.
6 In this case Bourdieu's words are apt: 'The art of eating and drinking remains one of the few areas in which the working classes explicitly challenge the legitimate art of living. In the face of the new ethic of sobriety for the sake of slimness, which is most recognised at the highest levels of the social hierarchy, peasants and especially industrial workers maintain an ethic of convivial indulgence' (1984: 179). Nonetheless, the food served at such banquets by carefully vetted caterers was remarkable for its quality, not simply its quantity.

REFERENCES

Bourdieu, P. (1984) *Distinction: A Social Critique of the Judgement of Taste*, trans. R. Nice, London: Routledge & Kegan Paul.
Bruner, E. (1986) 'Experience and its expressions', introduction to V. Turner and E. Bruner, eds, *The Anthropology of Experience*, Chicago: University of Illinois Press.
Crapanzano, V. (1986) 'Hermes' dilemma: the masking of subversion in ethnographic description', in J. Clifford and G. Marcus, eds, *Writing Culture: The Poetics and Politics of Ethnography*, Berkeley: University of California Press.
Dilthey, W. (1976) *Dilthey: Selected Works*, ed. by H. Rickman, Cambridge: Cambridge University Press.
Evers, H. (1981) 'Care or custody? The experiences of women patients in long-stay geriatric wards', in B. Hutter and G. Williams, eds, *Controlling Women: The Normal and the Deviant*, London: Croom Helm.
Fabian, J. (1983) *Time and the Other: How Anthropology Makes its Object*, New York: Columbia University Press.

Geertz, C. (1977) '"From the native's point of view": on the nature of anthropological understanding', in J. Dolgin, D. Kemnitzer and D. Schneider, eds, *Symbolic Anthropology: A Reader in the Study of Symbols and Meanings*, New York: Columbia University Press.

—— (1986) 'Making experience, authoring selves', in V. Turner and E. Bruner, eds, *The Anthropology of Experience*, Chicago: University of Illinois Press.

Hastrup, K. (1991) 'Beyond words: on the limits of writing in social anthropology', paper for 'The Multiplicity of Writing and Social Anthropology', Seminar at the Department and Museum of Social Anthropology, University of Oslo.

Hazan, H. (1980) *The Limbo People*, London: Routledge & Kegan Paul.

Myerhoff, B. (1986) '"Life not death in Venice": its second life', in V. Turner and E. Bruner, eds, *The Anthropology of Experience*, Chicago: University of Illinois Press.

Nagel, T. (1991) *Mortal Questions*, Canto edn, Cambridge: Cambridge University Press.

Okely, J. (1986) 'The conditions and experience of ageing compared in rural France and England', Final report to the ESRC, Swindon, England.

—— (1990) 'Clubs for Le Troisième Age: communitas or conflict', in P. Spencer, ed., *Anthropology and the Riddle of the Sphinx*, London: Routledge.

—— (1991a) 'Defiant moments: gender, resistance and individuals', *Man* 26, 1: 3–22.

—— (1991b) 'Age and place in rural Normandy', unpublished paper presented to the Department of Social Policy, University of Edinburgh.

—— (1992) 'Anthropology and autobiography: participatory experience and embodied knowledge', in J. Okely and H. Callaway, eds, *Anthropology and Autobiography*, London: Routledge.

Pratt, M.L. (1986) 'Fieldwork in common places', in J. Clifford and G. Marcus, eds, *Writing Culture: The Poetics and Politics of Ethnography*, Berkeley: University of California Press.

Rosaldo, R. (1986) 'From the door of his tent: the fieldworker and the inquisitor', in J. Clifford and G. Marcus, eds, *Writing Culture: The Poetics and Politics of Ethnography*, Berkeley: University of California Press.

Stoller, P. (1989) *The Taste of Ethnographic Things*, Philadelphia: University of Pennsylvania Press.

Turner, V. and Bruner, E., eds (1986) *The Anthropology of Experience*, Chicago: University of Illinois Press.

Zonabend, F. (1984) *The Enduring Memory: Time and History in a French Village*, trans. A. Forster, Manchester: Manchester University Press.

Chapter 4

Veiled experiences
Exploring female practices of seclusion

Karin Ask

Malinowski's maxim for anthropology, to convey a sense of what it is like to participate in other societies and cultures, continues to inspire anthropologists in various ways. A Bangladeshi colleague once told me about her plans to shoot a moving picture with a veil thrown over the lens, to evoke a subjective experience of purdah to people who had never worn the veil. Similar experiments have been suggested by among others Paul Stoller (1989), who recommends a return to our senses through the media of film and narrative ethnography. Both suggest ways to capture 'that which goes without saying' by adding to or circumventing the use of words.

My attempts to convey a sense of purdah are pedestrian by comparison. Though there are ample descriptions and theories on the phenomenon, I find the topic still warrants our attention on several scores; while the 'muteness' of women in anthropological texts is broken, the authority and authenticity of their voices are often muffled in the interpretations of cultural constructions. Female seclusion in the form of purdah will serve as my case in point. I will focus mainly on the non-linguistic aspects of purdah as signs made corporeal by the female body. I ask how these signs are given meaning in a zone of experience where tacit knowledge is transmitted through non-verbal means. The extent to which the meaning of these symbols and practices is shared, is empirically examined by analysing everyday recurrent experiences of women.[1]

First, the meaning of purdah is mostly inferred from discourse of honour, social rank and religious morals, that is, from a male's point of view. The woman and her body are twice hidden, and we fail to analyse the emotional and corporeal grounding of purdah as a meaningful practice for the individual actor.

Second, the case of purdah is an apt starting-point to examine

how the shifts in our positions and perspectives implied by participant observation influence our construction of anthropological
knowledge. The methodology aims at situating us on the same
plane as the subjects we study and observe, while to understand
and explain we go beyond.

Third, contemporary Islamization processes often give control
of women and the female body (literally as well as metaphorically)
a prominent place in their political rhetoric. The ensuing confrontation between lived experiences of purdah and its representation
in public discourse is another impetus to rethink anthropological
theories about purdah.

KNOWLEDGE AND EXPERIENCE

'It is because subjects do not, strictly speaking, know what they are
doing that what they do has more meaning than they know'
(Bourdieu 1977: 79). Starting from a description of women's and
girls' location in and use of space, I describe everyday experiences
in relation to sensual interactive processes. Through a contextualization of conventional practices of female seclusion, I focus on
corporeal aspects of purdah such as control of gaze, voice, mobil-
ity, use of space and cloths. The analysis draws on concepts from
practice theory (Bourdieu 1977) and semiosis (Singer 1982). I use
the concept 'embodiment' in a restricted sense to refer to processes of learning involving corporeal practical mastery. I find this
usage fruitful to distinguish operations mastered in a practical state
from their transformation to represent, in the sense of 'embody',
values and ideas. When referring to this last meaning, I use the
term representation. Part of this knowledge is submerged in the
body, embodied through training as skills and habits, normally not
reflected upon. This knowledge is retrieved through memories that
evoke emotions and frame judgments and understandings. Other
parts attain the level of discourse, in which case it is made explicit
and externalized through language and symbols. In this process
the relation of power is evident in confrontations over *correct*
practice and interpretation. Experience is analysed as a process
where an actor's place in social reality makes her perceive and
comprehend as subjective '(referring to, even originating in, oneself) those relations – material, economic and interpersonal –
which are in fact social and, in a larger perspective, historical'
(Lauretis 1984: 159).

STRUCTURING THE FEMALE BODY

Female seclusion in the form of purdah is only one entry on the long list of practices that in various ways, more or less drastic, modify a woman's perception and control of her body. As a female participant observer in 'purdah society' my first reaction was a feeling of utter discomfort at being ogled in the streets of Rawalpindi. While I considered myself well prepared in terms of anthropological theory on the subject, I was utterly unprepared for my feelings of, and reactions to, being uncovered and exposed. In the vignettes that follow, I describe encounters and observations that alerted me to various dimensions of the bodily feeling of purdah. The presentation is organized to illustrate the experiential feelings of central elements of purdah like separation and conceal-ment, identity and boundaries.

DISCIPLINING THE GAZE

At the time of fieldwork (1978–80) a vigorous debate ran in various Pakistani (state-controlled) media on the need to Islamize all sectors of society. The political rhetoric for an Islamic society used the slogan 'Chader aur char diwari', which literally translated means 'The shawl and the four walls'. The objects referred to evoke an image of the purdah-keeping woman locked up in her home, only leaving the protection of the four walls when duly covered and chaperoned. In the village of my fieldwork, the women commented that this was only more example of hollow words from the military regime. All their big words about Islam concentrated on eye-catching cosmetics without any radical re-structuring of practices. The visible accoutrement of *burqa* (an enveloping cloak) and *dupatta* (transparent veil that covers head and breasts) in no way guarantees that the woman inside is pro-tected and morally pure. The women said that the heart of the matter was 'Ankhoon ki Purdah' (literally translated, 'The purdah of the eyes'). The saying about the eye cropped up in several contexts. To explain to me, they would point at the Kohistani girls working as servants in their houses, the nomadic Gujer or Pathani women peddling cloths and say, 'They have no shawl and do not stay within their own four walls, but do you think that means they are not keeping purdah? They are strict people, and good Muslims!' Their explanations to me about variations in the manifestations of purdah point to an understanding of female modesty as dependent on the women's morals and knowledge. This conceptualization makes it in a certain way nonsense to speak about more or less purdah observance; either you do or you do not keep purdah. This does not imply that women did not distinguish between more or less strict rules for seclusion, but they did insist that the system was dependent on their free will.[2]

There are several contrasts indicated by the image used in the official slogan and the local saying. Bodily self-control is evoked by the saying of the eye, the sign indicates a personal and free will exercised. The official slogan's reference to shawl and walls indicates concealment and control of the female figuratively as well as concretely. The reference to the eye should not be understood simply as a linguistic symbol. It does point to deliberate techniques to control the gaze, as I was to learn during painstaking instructions on how to control facial expressions, how never to meet the eyes of a man in public without losing important details of a street scene, how to avoid smiling and laughing in public, and how to conceal your lips behind your hand and *dupatta*.

This training aptly points to the self-disciplining exercised by purdah-keeping women; however, the intimidation and discipline wrought by violence inflicted on women should not be minimized. Women partake in vicarious experiences that remind them of their vulnerability, even behind the shielding of veils and walls. Stories circulate that constantly alert them to the horrors of abductions, rapes and murder. It is a very real threat to some, and a hazard to more, in the domestic as well as in the public sphere. The Pukhto proverb 'Women have no noses. They will eat shit!' has a gruesome presence in the women walking the countryside and towns, a patch of cloth over the place where their noses have been cut off in retaliation for breaches of the rules of modesty and shame.

To me, this saying about the eye indicated a vantage-point from where to make sense of the intriguing *pas-de-deux* of purdah which I witnessed on various occasions. It also made sense of my own feelings of embarrassment and of being trapped by the others' gaze. Below I give an example of this socially guided perception of seeing and being seen. It brings about an awareness that makes a woman highly attuned to her interlocutor's perceptions and reactions.

A PLUNGE INTO THE WATER

A group of women and girls and I went to take a bath after a long day's work. The place chosen was situated under a steep bank overhanging the riverside. On top of the embankment ran a road going into the town centre, the bazaar area. Thinking that I by now (two months after starting proper fieldwork) was well attuned to the rules of seclusion, I was utterly unprepared for the episode that followed. The women and girls took off all their clothes and ran stark naked into the river, leaving me standing behind, embarrassed in a bathing suit. Coming out of the water the most they did to hide their 'shameful' parts was to hide their breasts behind their unloosened plaits and place a hand over the pudendum, rather like the painting by Botticelli. To my prudish questions if they did not feel ashamed thinking of the men who might see them from the top of the embankment, they replied laughingly, 'Why should we? How would they recognize us naked? We keep purdah, don't we?' My further attempts to put questions to them about feelings of shyness and shame caused a lot of merriment and giggles behind the veils of the *burqa* on our way home through 'the women's street'.

This bathing scene was not unique; another time we went bringing clothes for washing. A tenant from the village came by, bringing cattle for drinking farther down the river. He had to pass close by, carefully groping his way along the steep riverside. The self-evident dimension of concealment and hiding seemed to be flagrantly ignored in both cases, which bewildered and, yes, shocked me. On the analytical level, reflecting on the experiences, I did of course see the logic of the women's answer. Also, bearing in mind the identity of the bathing nudes, they enjoyed the protection of their position as wives and daughters of local landowners. However, with all the evidence of their talk and attempts to avoid shameful action, I could not make sense of their behaviour in terms of their personal feelings. In other words, I wondered how their self-conscious limits for behaviour related to the arbitrary boundaries set by the cultural institution of purdah as a shared set of ideas on honour and shame. Certainly the men in these cases contributed to the maintenance of a separate 'room' for the women. Should the definition of the situation break down, however, the women would be the ones to take the burden of blame.

TELLING SILENCES

The sexual bond and relation of intimacy between husband and wife are publicly silenced by the non-use of the terms for husband *mian/khawand* or wife *biwi/trimti* in reciprocal address or in reference to the couple. The spouses refer to each other by the euphemism *gharwahla* (of the house). This is the case until you have a child and can indicate your spouse by addressing and referring to him/her as so and so's (child's name) mother or father. A telling consequence of this linguistic usage is that the wife's place and position are not vocalized as such if she stays childless, if her body does not bring forth the continuation of her husband's line.

The daily usage of kinship terms objectifies relations of authority; this is exemplified by juniors showing respect for their senior by not using personal names. Children are explicitly told not to 'take the name' (*nam lethe*) of their elders, nor display unwarranted intimacy by the use of personal names. The use of correct language by which to address and refer to kin is explicitly stressed through instructions and corrections of the children.

Given the dominant practice in marriage and subsequent residence for the new couple (frequent endogamy within the patrilineage and patrilocal residence), the use of correct teknonyms for affine is an experience and a vocabulary where the women are more drilled th ᦙ are the men. The dominant discourse, however, concentrates on the importance of patriliny and the tracing of kinship links through men.

In joking, women often take delight in teasing each other to produce a slip of the tongue on the subject of the forbidden and unspoken, for example the sexual relation to a husband. A young wife pregnant with her third child spoke constantly about Ahmed *ki Abu*, Ahmed's father (her husband), who had gone on pilgrimage, *Haj*. Every night she wondered aloud if he got enough food, if he was safe on his journey and so on. The other women in the household had finally heard enough talk about this wonderful man, so they started a game of questioning and teasing to get her to 'take her husband's name' (*nam lethe*): 'Who is he who has placed the seed inside your womb? Is your bed too cold to sleep in now that your what's-his-name is away?' They did not manage to get her to pronounce his name; instead she gave skilful repartee with innuendoes about the sexual appetites of her sisters-in-law:

'Were they making *bistre* (quilts) every night?' The remaking of quilts involves the opening of old stitches so that the cotton inside can be properly aired through beating with wooden sticks, thus making a better stuffing of the quilt. *Bistre karna* is often used as a metaphor for sexual intercourse.

THE GIRL AND HER CHANGING BODY

The restrictions of purdah are at their height for young unmarried girls and married women. The proof of boundary-crossing from childhood to young woman is a girl's first menstruation. From this day she is *jawan*, that is, 'young'. No public rituals mark this transition; she will continue to wear the same type of clothes as before, but her mother, her elder sisters and brothers and her sisters-in-law will become more vigilant that she remembers to cover her head and hair with the *dupatta*, uses a *chader* when leaving the compound, and so on. She will be instructed as to which objects not to touch on her 'unclean' days, and what religious duties are suspended on these days. The processes changing her body are only named in private between sisters and mother, and are not linked explicitly to sexuality, fertility and birth of children. The young girls do hear about and are involved in events linked to the pregnancies and deliveries of their sisters-in-law. I was struck by the lack of hiding of these facts in the families, even if one was reminded that it is *sharmwali bat* ('shameless talk') to bring them up outside all-female fora.

Growing up, the young girl will many times have participated in the welcoming of a new bride (a *duhlen*), and kept a girl of the village company during the nights before her departure to her conjugal home. These are both occasions when the body and sexuality are in focus; through singing, dancing and joking the references are many and not always subtle.

The girl is instructed to move within different boundaries and in a narrower terrain than her brother. She must internalize a feeling for a mental map to know when it is appropriate to draw the veil (*dupatta*) over the head, when to don the shawl (*chader*). This constant manipulation of clothes is something learned by observation, imitation and correction, as is the control of body movements, eyes, voice and how to choose the correct words in conversation. This meticulous and concrete moulding of the female body is further analysed below.

WHAT DRESSES REVEAL AND CONCEAL

The clothes a woman wears, and when and where she wears them, are in many societies used as a gauge of her morals or sexual availability. So also is the case in Pakistan. In the propaganda for an ideal Islamic society the topic of proper Islamic dress was prominent. The use of *dupatta* became obligatory for the female staff on the national television. Another new directive was the use of *chader* with the school uniform for all female students. Also in the local discourses on femininity, religion and morality, women's dressing prompted discussions.

One incident concerns proper female attire for a festive occasion, the wedding party of a man in the village. On this occasion his two sisters showed up in saris of an Indian cut: i.e. the blouses were short, leaving the abdomen visible as well as their arms naked. The two girls became the topic for gossip among the women in the village for weeks after. Their 'foreign' and shocking ways were endlessly rehashed as an example of disregard for proper behaviour. The use of saris is rare in this area, though the trousseau often includes one or two pairs. These two sisters were unmarried, and the festive attire for unmarried girls at a wedding would rather be a *gharara* (*shalwar* with generous width of pleats from the thigh down) with a close-fitting tunic and a *dupatta*. Wearing saris that showed their midriffs, as well as discarding the cover of the *dupatta*, certainly indicated a frivolous disposition. In this context there was also reference to and praise of the one woman of the village who was a Hindu by birth, but had discontinued the wearing of a sari after her marriage to a man of the village and her conversion to Islam. A context for this discussion is of course the traditional one where elder women always use the chance of a wedding to scrutinize the 'available' young unmarried women present. But, in addition, the constant contrasting with the former Hindu woman served to link the question of dress to religious and national identity, signifying proper religious loyalty.

A popular new Japanese fabric with the catching name of *Sharmili* ('modesty') was launched on the Pakistani market. The silky fabric became a success, what every woman had to buy to follow the fashion for the celebration following the fast. The mocking comments from men who were pestered with demands for money to buy yards of this cloth for the coming celebrations, were, 'What's next, now women are buying *sharm* (modesty) in the bazaar!' In other words, a contradiction in terms, modesty available for money in the marketplace.

TALK ABOUT SHAME AND MODESTY

Conventional symbols appropriate bodily experience, bringing them into relation with public symbols making a culturally constructed world appear as a 'natural' fact. These practices are embodied from early childhood; they are constructed by daily practices, becoming habitual as evocative devices for rousing and domesticating emotions of modesty (*sharm*), long before they are articulated as abstract concepts. On the one hand the institution involves the most intimate organization of bodily experience; at the same time it refers to and symbolizes abstract political and religious principles. The girls are constantly admonished to epitomize *sharm* in the sense of modesty, while shunning it in the sense of shameful behaviour. In most analyses of purdah practices and norms, the concept of shame is contrasted with and evokes honour as its opposite. Unni Wikan argues that the pervasive employment of these concepts reflects a male bias in ethnographic analysis, which ascribes honour principally to males, 'leaving women with, if anything, only shame' (Wikan 1984: 635). Her argument certainly captures an important aspect of the discourse on purdah as I experienced it in daily interaction with children and their parents. While the concepts for shame are used automatically in normal everyday talk, the words for honour (*izzat, gheirat*) were seldom heard in daily casual conversation. One could discuss a person's conduct and characterize him as *sherif* (noble), or *izza-twahla* (honourable), but then the discourse often involved a generalization that lifted the person and events referred to out of an immediate, everyday, mundane context and made of them an occasion to illustrate an edifying example of moral principles.

Everyday interaction offers many occasions when a girl might be reprimanded for *sharmwali bat* (shameless talk), or when she will explain her manners, why she refrained from doing or saying certain things, by the words '*Muje sharm ati hai*' (literally: 'Shame came to me'). The value and sentiment of modesty and shame are recurrently objectified through the language.

If we compare the experiential quality of the concepts, a salient difference is that girls must exhibit control of self to avoid being reprimanded for shamelessness. Boys on the other hand must give priority to behaviour that reveals acts of control of others in public arenas, to win honour. The limiting case for men is then the control of 'their' women, the weak point where their cherished self-image can be utterly sullied.

I suggest that the central value of *sharm* (in the sense of modesty) as imprinted upon and represented by the female body, is made corporeal and linked to emotional experience and put into language for girls in ways that *izzat* is not for boys. In Charles S. Peirce's words it produces 'a habit-change, a modification of a person's tendencies toward action resulting from previous exertions' (quoted in Lauretis 1984: 174).

An internal view on socialization to exemplary behaviour must differentiate the imposed link between emotion and cognition according to gender. In the present context, the presumed necessity of purdah is implied by the concepts of *nafs* (sensuousness, appetite or passion) and *aql* (capacities of knowledge, intellectual reasoning, moral action) in a way that seems to suppose that women have more passion than their knowledge can control. As Fatima Merinissi (1985) has noted, the texts and practices referred to make the question of protection ambiguous: is it men who must be protected against women's sexual appetites and passion, or the other way around? Metaphors linked to emotion are subordinated and devalued by comparison to the qualities of thinking and rationality, which are presumably the prime domain of men. However, intriguingly, boys are expected to attain the quality of adulthood and the congruent capacity of *aql* later than do girls, though the women are not supposed to excel men.

Both sexes are encouraged to strike the correct balance between *nafs* and *aql* as a prerequisite for honourable dealings. But the point of equilibrium is different for the two. This is revealed in subtle ways by the kinds of praise or negative sanctions that the two genders meet through interaction.

CHANGES IN THE BAZAAR

Several of the actions taken to Islamize society, such as campaigns against prostitution and black marketeers, focused on the bazaar area. An example of this is the 'cleaning' of red-light areas, that is, bazaars where brothels are traditionally found. Another initiative taken was to paint over film posters (that is, those prominently displayed on buildings centrally located) showing the 'nakedness' of women. The confusion produced by the changing borders in the urban landscape was thus expressed in a letter to an English newspaper: 'One can no longer discern decent women from prostitutes by sight. The latter have assumed hypocritical fashions and donned the veil, and now you risk meeting them everywhere, even in decent neighbourhoods' (*The Muslim*, 27 October 1979). The term *bazaari* meaning 'from the bazaar' is also used to scold somebody for showing improper, vulgar behaviour. The public signification of boundaries for the secluded woman, paradoxically, infuses the public arena with indexical signs of femininity and sexuality through the very concealment of the female body. The inversion of the 'hidden woman' is exemplified by the many representations of the female body in film, on posters, inscribed and sung in poems and stories, where the sexual connotations are strong.

USE OF PLACE, ASPECTS OF MOBILITY

The Swati women of the village seldom went to the bazaar, and when they did they had to get permission from their guardians, husband or father. I have tried to describe how the cultivation of the senses evident in women's uses of language, space and eyes incarnates a strong sensitivity to place and awareness of identity. Their crossing of boundaries is clearly signalled by the clothes they wear and how they don them. Leaving her own village, a woman will wear a shawl (*chader*) or cloak (*burqa*). As spontaneously remarked by one woman who drew the veil over her face at exactly the same spot when crossing the fields surrounding the village, 'We don't have to cover our faces as long as we are on our own land.' This notwithstanding the fact that there was no difference between persons who might see you on the footpath ten metres *before* or ten metres *after* the invisible line dividing own from others' land. Going to the bazaar women choose their own streets, known as 'the women's streets', even if they are fully veiled and already rendered 'invisible' by the conventional donning of a *burqa* or a *chader*. The avoidance of public recognition extends to not greeting persons of the opposite gender, even if they are close male relatives whom you cannot marry. The two parties immediately withdraw in opposite directions should they by accident meet each other.

BODY, EXPERIENCE AND LANGUAGE: CONCLUDING DISCUSSION

We presume that a lot of interpretation of experience goes without saying, that it is literally dependent on our five common senses of seeing, smelling, hearing, touching, tasting. Returning to my point of departure, I have tried to describe how I made sense of information gathered through participating in and observing elements of purdah practices.

Most interpretations of the purdah omit analyses of relationships between the signs as information-bearing vehicles in public, and their emotional and habitual grounding as meaningful practices for the individual actor. My investigation of the habit formation of purdah tries to focus on social contexts, practical action and experience. Analysing current political mobilization using metaphors of gender relations calls for an investigation of how embodiment forms a link between cognition and experience: how cultural understandings are stored via real experiences in concrete social contexts in real human bodies. This presents us with the task of relating cognition and emotion to the analysis of experience, so that experience acquires inter-subjective significance, and memory and habits extend beyond the individual to a social repository of experiences and to traditions.

I think that the probing of practices that go without saying is especially pertinent in the context of changes, of destabilization of the authoritative discourse. At such junctures, people often start to question or reinterpret traditions and discard practices. Telling information on the difficulties in disembodying purdah practices came from a university teacher who tried to discard the use of the veil when she went to market. She told me how brave she felt entering a shop without the flimsy, transparent *dupatta* around her neck.

A large part of the embedded cultural understandings comes first through experiences of the body. Embodiment forms the non-arbitrary link between cognition and experience, and hence memory and meaning are understood and stored via real experiences in concrete social contexts in real human bodies, male and female.

This is where the anthropologist has to start, if she wants to comprehend the habit formation of purdah. It is not a matter of empathy; I certainly did not enter into the women's streams of consciousness by joining them in a bath, or donning a veil. It is, rather, a matter of systematically probing the practices that go without saying in those unfamiliar zones of experience that we choose to study with all our senses.

NOTES

1 The analysis presented is based on fieldwork in Hazara, Northeast Pakistan from 1978–80. The fieldwork was conducted mainly among Swati landowners, which of course colours my subjective experiences of purdah.
2 I do not intend to imply that women as a category internalize and practise *ankhoon ki purdah* in the same way nor without resistance. Undoubtedly there are big differences in how individual women's lives and daily routines are affected according to class, age and livelihood. However, there are collective experiences that take hold of and structure public arenas in ways that affect all women disregarding individual practises and motivations.

REFERENCES

Ask, Karin (1984) 'Family life and socialization: growing up as a girl in Hazara Northeast Pakistan' (in Norwegian), unpublished MA thesis, Department of Social Anthropology, Bergen University.
Bourdieu, Pierre (1977) *Outline of a Theory of Practice*, Cambridge: Cambridge University Press.
Lauretis, Teresa de (1984) *Alice Doesn't*, Bloomington: Indiana University Press.
Merinissi, Fatima (1985) *Beyond the Veil: Male–Female Dynamics in Muslim Society*, London: Al Saqi Books.
Mumtaz, Khawar, and Shaheed, Farida (1987) *Women of Pakistan: Two Steps Forward, One Step Back?*, London: Zed Books Ltd.
Singer, Milton (1982) *Man's Glassy Essence: Explorations in Semiotic Anthropology*, Bloomington: Indiana University Press.
Stoller, Paul (1989) *The Taste of Ethnographic Things: The Senses in Anthropology*, Philadelphia: University of Pennsylvania Press.
Wikan, Unni (1984) ' "Shame and Honour" a contestable pair', *Man*, 19: 635–52.

Chapter 5

Shared reasoning in the field
Reflexivity beyond the author

Peter Hervik

'Do you keep a shotgun in the house?', Paulina asked confiden-
tially. She had already told friends, neighbours and others that I
had a large shotgun, without knowing if this was true. Paulina
lived with us during our fieldwork in Mexico and helped with
household chores.[1] To protect herself and us against trouble-
makers she had declared to anyone interested that I kept a
shotgun.

Paulina quite obviously feared being robbed or assaulted by
criminals and drunken men. She knew of many incidents in
Oxkutzcab and enjoyed telling stories of how drunkards got into
fights, how intruders had violently ripped off golden chains worn
by women, and how men had entered houses stealing anything
from machetes and kitchen utensils to chickens and pigs. When
answered in the negative, her question about the shotgun was
turned into a direct request that I bought one for our common
protection. In the face of her stories there was a definite need for
this precaution.

We (Paulina, Manuela, the ethnographer and his family) were
part of the same setting in a relationship that was based in mutual
trust and to a certain extent shared responsibility. Paulina was well
aware of our vulnerable situation, and her personal engagement
went far beyond the social responsibility of an ordinary senior
housemaid (*muchacha*). Phrased differently, Paulina reflected and
acted consciously upon her own situation, and her reflexivity
embraced my family. Her awareness of our situation led her to
publicize my capacity to protect not only herself but the entire
unsuspecting household. Rather than language, it took shared
social experience of living with Paulina to gain the tacit knowledge
and social intimacy necessary to understand her question, and to

explain why she had used language to build a shield of protection without having evidence to support her claim.

Paulina mobilized her own family in the second evening to turn blankets into sleeping-bags for the hammocks. The first night sleeping in a thatched-roof house in airy hammocks had proved a chilly affair. Getting acquainted with and later becoming friends of Paulina's family gave further glimpses of her reflexivity. Paulina had quit her job at a tortilla factory in order to work for us. Her promise to help was a strong and dedicated one, which she took great pride in fulfilling. She was the elder sister (*kiik* in Maya) who in the absence of responsible brothers (*suku'un'ob*), felt obliged to provide residential security for her parents.[2] From the very beginning she was meticulously engaged in helping us in all sorts of ways.

My general ambition in this article is to present a reflexive perspective, which could reconstruct and perhaps innovate the debate on how we perceive and understand social practice. The assumption I will seek to substantiate is that reflexivity can be seen as a prominent means of transforming social experience in the field to anthropological knowledge. In other words, the concept of reflexivity may provide the connection between shared social experience and a more general understanding of culture. Shared social experience does not imply identical experience: this is impossible. It simply implies that we attend to similar categorical conventions and practical tasks. The awareness of living in a common world encourages sameness and fosters an image of shared social experience (Wikan 1991).

One possible outcome of shared social experience is shared reasoning, which borders on the concept of reflexivity I wish to elucidate in the present article. Without preempting the issue, I shall stress from the outset that I do not see reflexivity exclusively as a matter of investigating the position of the author and the production of texts. Rather, it is part of the intersubjective context of the fieldwork.

Reflexivity that bends back on the individual cannot be separated clearly from reflexivity of the group. Paulina's questioning and reasoning are an illustration of native reflexivity, but it is also a kind reflexivity that reflects back on her own as well as my family at least as long as she lived with us.

In the following, I will present small instances from my fieldwork to illustrate further how reflexivities operate and evolve in the course of fieldwork and how subjects change positions in the process. This, in turn, will enable me to discuss the general features of reflexivity as I understand them and to compare them to other approaches.

FIRST-HAND EXPERIENCE

'Reflexive' anthropologists have disclaimed the use of arrival scenes in ethnographic writing (Clifford and Marcus 1986; Marcus and Cushman 1982; Tyler 1987). In their view, the narration of first encounters serves the sole function of establishing the ethnographer's credibility and authority. Visualized direct experience tends to make readers believe in the author's statements, and belief has an almost axiomatic status as knowledge (Sweetser 1987). The target group for this criticism is the 'modernist' writers who appear in the introductory remarks only to vanish as the monograph gets serious.

The critics treat arrival scenes almost exclusively from a literary perspective. They tend to forget that they actually may reflect important first-hand experiences. Regardless of how the first-hand experiences are used in the text, we can assume that the 'arrival' itself was an important experience. Any ethnographer would probably agree that first encounters generate personal alienation and a sense of extreme relativism that forever marks off the 'field'. First experiences belong to an experiential space that cannot be done away with by literary criticism.

In the first few weeks of fieldwork the cultural knowledge of the fieldworker differs maximally from that of the local people, and inevitably predicaments arise, as the following scene will illustrate. During a pilot project, I had once met a local schoolteacher and activist, Carlos, who promised to facilitate my impending fieldwork. He did so out of his dedication to improve the socio-economic conditions of the Mayas, and to enhance Mayan cultural self-esteem (Hervik 1992a). Carlos took us to a local family of very limited means to seek assistance. Carlos's brokerage promised well, as he was an intimate friend of the family head, with whom he had often cooperated in various community affairs. Carlos was the patrón of this relationship. As an added advantage, he could present the arrangement in their native language, Maya. A daughter was to live with us, to help with the children and household chores. We had agreed with Carlos that the entire family could be crucial to our practical 'Mayan' enculturation. However, the family head declined our offer.

Despite our different cultural backgrounds and disparate lived experiences, Carlos and I had compatible interests and agreed on this mutually beneficial arrangement. However, my arrival in the field revealed an unexpected incompatibility not only between me and the family head, but also between Carlos and the family head. My cultural knowledge was maximally different, so to speak, from theirs, but still congruous to Carlos and incongruous to the family head. Reflections with Carlos on this experience were the first step towards learning local cultural knowledge.

Regardless of the disparity of our cultural knowledge, Carlos, his family and I could cooperate, and slowly I was able to close in on the differences. Carlos gave me lessons in the Yucatec Mayan language. He introduced words akin to each other and insisted that I pronounced them correctly and learned what they represented in the Mayan language. Thus, the Mayan words, *k'aan, k'áan, k'a'n, kaan, kan, ka'an* mean respectively mecate (a measure of 20 by 20 metres), hammock, strong, snake, four and sky. Everyday situations easily revealed what I meant, despite my incorrect pronunciation. After all, one does not confuse the meanings of words in concrete situations, for instance sleeping on a snake (rather than in a hammock).

The cultural broker Carlos is a native of Oxkutzcab. He was educated in Mexican revolutionary ideology and influenced by the ideas of President Lazaros Cardenas (1934–40). During his training he gained knowledge of how the bureaucracy operated, and at the same time he became increasingly aware of his Mayan identity and the conditions of the Mayan people in the villages. Later, upon settling in Oxkutzcab, Carlos turned this self-reflexivity into cultural activities. He took the initiative of establishing a local Mayan theatre group for instance. Today, he is the writer, instructor and manager of the troupe, who has as one of their plays *The Auto-da-fé – or Shock of Two Cultures*. He based the play on the historical *auto-da-fé* in Mani (1592), but wrote it from a contemporary perspective with a call for attention to the socioeconomic conditions of his compatriots, and to raise their awareness of colonial exploitations (Hervik 1992a).

Carlos organizes and stages 'culture' reflexively. For that reason, I believe, he began teaching me to distinguish between like words, plants, fruits and vegetables, rather than leaving me to 'learn by doing'. Participating in community life would eventually provide a context for the correct usage of each word. His insistence that I learned the phonetics of Mayan words correctly turned out also to be his way of maintaining that the Mayan language could fulfil all and even more functions than Spanish. Thus, he took great pride in taking me to the exotic corners of the Mayan language. He explained that different forms of talk were distinguished, such as *x-ye'-ye'-táan* (imitation), *p'as t'aan* (exaggerated imitation), *ketlán t'aan* (competent speech), *bobo' chi'* (speech without content), *p' u'* (used for the sound of spitting but without spitting) and *a-k'ankubul*, which is a rare phenomenon used when milpa farmers see a small yellow powderish cloud rise from the cornfields. If it occurs the corn will not be any good. For Carlos, my interest in 'culture' implied that I intended to learn the rules. As long as this was the case, I was no threat to his position as cultural broker and local expert.

His broker position differed radically from the local perspective of a Mayan woman. On a first visit to her family compound I told her that I had come to Oxkutzcab to learn the Mayan language. Upon discovering my objective she turned to me and said '*Diga, sama yan inkinsik unpeel*' ('Say, tomorrow I will kill a chicken'). This practical remark referred to her activities the following day; her doings took preeminence over the words.

Knowing history and culture does not mean knowing rules and structures, but knowing how to make oneself understood, i.e. to articulate taken-for-granted schemata (Tyler 1978: 119–20). Likewise from a linguistic point of view:

> Expert native speakers produce and understand speech unreflectively, without evaluation of alternatives and without following rules as such. Instead, relying on extensive familiarity with situations and their outcomes, the expert simply does what is to be done in recognizable situations.
>
> (Hanks 1990: 71)

Our continuous involvement with local people and their practices increased our skills and made us capable of enacting Mayan ways, which we could not have learned by way of Carlos's verbal instruction.

MAKING SENSE

Recent advances in cognitive science have given us important general insight into what goes on in social experience in terms of background knowledge. In this field, it is widely accepted that, in understanding, we combine two forms of knowledge, which Cicourel has called schematic and local knowledge. Schematic knowledge, roughly equivalent to cultural models (Holland and Quinn 1987), is embodied in prefabricated representations of objects and their relations, and depicts regularities of practice.[3] Cultural knowledge, which is organized in cultural models (ibid.), is embedded *in* and sensitive *to* the contexts (Cicourel 1986: 92). Cultural knowledge is available to us through 'unreflected common sense and habit', by others called 'habitus', and it orientates and naturalizes action (Hanks 1990: 6). Such cultural knowledge is often transparent to its bearers: 'Once learned, it becomes what one *sees with*, but seldom what one *sees*' (Hutchins 1980: 12). It is neither conscious nor unconscious; it is implicit meaning, indicating that it exists in a practical state in the agents' practice (Bourdieu 1977: 27). The application of a cultural model is called local knowledge. It is produced as 'an emergent element of the particular setting and the participants project and revise their immediate comprehension over the course of an exchange' (Hanks 1990: 70). Cultural models provide a resource for understanding, for the negotiation of understanding, in short, for making sense of experience (Cicourel 1985, 1986).

A cultural model without application is like having 'a script and an empty stage but no action, because the actors remain anonymous and disembodied' (Hanks 1990: 11). Therefore, it must be studied in practice. Cultural models cannot be taught exclusively by linguistic means but must be acquired through embodiment. The notion of a cultural model is a way of describing knowledge that cannot in and of itself account for how this knowledge is used, even though it is produced from repeated experiences. Reflexivity and resonance come into play and reveal how cultural models are resources for thinking and understanding experience, rather than fixed rules for action.

The notion of resonance indicates that there is more to thinking than 'thinking'. The Balinese ask: 'Can anyone think without the heart?' (Wikan 1992: 463). Without resonance there will be no understanding. Resonance demands:

> a willingness to engage with another world, life, or idea; an ability to use one's experience . . . to try to grasp, or convey, meanings that reside neither in words, 'facts', nor text but are evoked in the meeting of one experiencing subject with another or with a text.
>
> (ibid.)

To transcend the words and to judge correctly what people are doing, we need to attend to the speaker's intention and the social position speakers emanate from. Resonance is a non-verbal means to this end.

Paulina was doing more than spreading tactical untruth for self-protection. Her emotional involvement grew as she was adopted in the household and became ever more engaged in the family's welfare. She obviously liked to be with us and loved the children. Trying to make me buy a gun turned out to be an effort that went beyond protecting her own interest; it was a means of building a social shield around the household and making life more pleasant and secure.

Since cultural models are generated from repeated experiences, it follows that cultural models change more slowly than local knowledge and according to different principles (Hanks 1990: 11). However, in the early experiences of fieldwork when cultural knowledge differs maximally, cultural models are likely to change rapidly.

The sharp and visible contrast between academic and local categorization and their embedded cultural models becomes less and less important as the fieldworker spends hours reflecting on these contrastive encounters. In the process, we think of these people less as different, and more as variants of 'us' (Rorty 1989: 461). Repeated experiences of real people cannot be flattened out by unit categories. Thus, experience makes its way into the category system (Ardener 1989: 169). Categories coexist with their perceived attributes in the form of prototypes and cultural models. Therefore, categories and language cannot exhaust reality, but it must be re-created in separate terms (Ardener 1989, Hastrup 1989).

Elsewhere, I have used the notion of cultural model to explain the relationship between the social categories Maya and *mestizos* (local term for Maya people) (Hervik 1992b). Local brokers in Oxkutzcab, including Carlos, share the local cultural model of *mestizo*, which forms part of a more inclusive model of Mayan culture encompassing achievements of the Mayan civilization. Lay people in Oxkutzcab do not perceive the hieroglyphic writing, ruins, stelae, paintings in the caves, etc., as part of their cultural identity or heritage. The brokers *do* consider the contemporary Mayas an integral part of the Mayan culture and civilization, and it is their ambition to heighten the local awareness of this heritage. Carlos's attempt to bridge the two cultural models had consequences for the way he taught me about language and culture. He 'declares' culture in an effort to preserve it. Accordingly, he insisted on explaining the potentiality of the Mayan language and the details and richness of contemporary knowledge in daily practices. He taught me language and cultural practices by speaking about them.

In some sense cultural models contain more knowledge than can be instantiated in practice. What is brought into action is selected or distilled, but not arbitrary since it is based on – and revised by – past experiences. A single element of an encounter can instantiate the entire cultural model, later giving way to unexpected knowledge. In many situations knowledge can be omitted because of previous shared experiences of a similar kind (cf. Holland 1985: 390–1).

Knowledge may also be attached or projected as a substitute for inaccurate memory or simply lack of knowledge. Dorothy Holland has researched the reasoning applied to brief first encounters in the social worlds and their subsequent familiarization. Her research shows that sometimes when women's first impressions of brief encounters with men were highly negative (e.g. the baseball player with an aura of a jock), they turned out to be really friendly and considerate. The baseball image instantiated the entire cultural model of the jock type of male, only later to be revised upon requiring additional knowledge of this man (ibid.: 395–6).

In another example Cicourel has shown that in diagnosing doctors need to rely on disembodied schemata. Everyday language and technical language would only partially reveal schematized knowledge and local conditions. In order to translate the language of interaction with patients into formal diagnostic categories and the lexical elements associated with them, and subsequently into intuitive clinical procedures and knowledge, schematized knowledge of a different level was brought in. Obviously, it also led to incidents where the wrong cultural model of an illness was chosen

(Cicourel 1985); thus it was incongruent with the real-world illness.

What comes out of this is a new attention to the reflexive nature of people's realities. People do not follow the economic dictates, the politically obvious, the psychologically plausible or the socially expected. They reflect and play theoreticians in the field weighing pros and contras and shuffling chunks of knowledge around, regardless of whether it can be located within a traditional Mayan or modern Mexican universe for example.

Today, I am no longer able to distinguish clearly between my general knowledge of Maya culture at the time of arrival and what I learned subsequently. My experiences of the first phase of field-work have to a certain extent been transcended by cultural models gained from shared social experiences. I can recollect feelings and understandings of the first-hand experiences, but I make sense of them in new ways, because the local knowledge that I bring into them has evolved.

SHARED REASONING

An immense stock of knowledge is omitted or taken for granted, hidden in unreflected habits. If we recognize that a substantial part of cultural knowledge (including language) is learned out-of-awareness, then people will not be able to explain how culture and language as such operate. Through enculturation during fieldwork we as ethnographers learn to distinguish between what is import-ant and what is unimportant in culture – that is the difference between happening (blink) and the event (wink) – and our knowl-edge of the difference is tested. In order to distinguish events from happenings we must acquire the cultural knowledge that exists prior to events, events being the relation between a happening and the cultural field (Sahlins 1985: 153).

From our very first days in the field, we were involved in the thoughts and sufferings of our maid's family. Paulina's father, Don Iz, was a Mayan milpa farmer who had acquired three small parcels of land to grow corn, fruit and vegetables. One day he complained that he had not slept at all the previous night. He had great pain in his stomach and could not work. He was uncertain of whether he should go to a traditional shaman (*j-men*) near Peto or to the clinic in Oxkutzcab for treatment. On the one hand he did not trust the doctors at the clinic. They had once prescribed medicine with a high content of sugar to his wife. She had diabetes and the medicine almost killed her. For six days she was in coma at the clinic, and she needed to spend an additional two months recuperating.[4] One of Don Iz's daughters refused to let doctors examine her for a severe chest pain. She was embarrassed to reveal her naked breasts to a male doctor. Don Iz was sceptical about the clinic, and the one daughter living in the household gave new strength to his scepticism. On the other hand, he told that he had gone to a shaman in Oxkutzcab several times. The shaman had composed a medicine of different plants, but it did not remove the pain. Instead, he considered consulting a well-known shaman in Cantamayec near Peto.[5]

I was convinced that Don Iz had a severe stomach ulcer and revealed possible sources of stress. This was soon confirmed. When I asked about his son who lived in the house – he has one other son and eight daughters – he became upset. Don Iz could never be sure if his son would take part in the hard work in the fields; his wife and daughter were unable to work owing to the diabetes and the chest pain, and he himself was too sick to work. How was he to manage?

I was in no position to tell whether the shaman or the clinic would be able to help him. I kept thinking of a piece of advice given to me by a Danish doctor in a similar situation. He claimed that plain yogurt is the best means for treating excessive production of stomach acid. But under the circumstances, it seemed absurd simply to suggest that Don Iz should eat yogurt. Instead, I explained to him that his condition seemed similar to what my wife, Lisbet, had suffered from a long time ago. As I finished my explanation his eyes lit up, and quietly he suggested that Lisbet and I should accompany him to the shaman for another diagnosis. We could tell the shaman about Lisbet's stomach ulcer. Such information would be important for an accurate diagnosis, and the shaman could compose a more adequate medicine.[6]

This is an instance of what I call shared reasoning; in this case it was triggered by the emotional involvement in each other's families. We tried to find a proper course of action to get Don Iz back on his feet again, and it involved different but congruent cultural models. Our shared reasoning illustrates a kind of reflexivity which is embodied in culture. Although our cultural models certainly differed, we could share a kind of reasoning in which they worked together. Disparate though they were, they became resources for a shared reflexivity. The case shows that reflexivity cannot be reduced to a mental process of the individual, or be separated from the reflexivity in interaction. The Mayas say that each person is a different world, meaning that there are sharp limits to the degree to which one can share feelings and know another person (Hanks 1990: 92). The notion of resonance does not deny difference; difference is embedded in the notion. Resonance bridges differences and implies that we embody cultural models in practice and allow ourselves to be involved personally.

Another example illustrates participation on the border of native shared reasoning. In this case the shared reasoning concerned the illness of one of my children and took place within the household, though it only later involved the entire household.

One evening Paulina took our twins, Thomas and Simon, to buy sweets. When she came back to the house, she laughingly told us that a drunken man had come by and complimented Simon (then 18 months old) by saying 'Que bonito el niño' ('What a beautiful boy'). At night Simon became ill with high fever, vomit and green diarrhoea. The next day Paulina was worried.[7] When the other girl, Manuela, who helped us during the day, arrived the two of them discussed earnestly and semi-secretly what to do. For a while they would not say anything. Finally, Paulina revealed that she was convinced that Simon had been hit by *el ojo* (the evil eye), cast by a drunken man who admired him. We had to prepare a bath with different medicinal plants for him and his twin brother for protection. Manuela pulled me aside and told that she knew about the evil eye but personally did not believe in this tradition. She was trained as a nurse, and the treatment for the eye went against what she was taught at the nursing school. Nevertheless, she did encourage us to bathe the twins as prescribed. It was too risky to refuse. If it did not work we could take him to a doctor for treatment.[8] The bath did prove effective.[9] The following days either one or the other twin had the wrong side turned out of one sock or the T-shirt to prevent being struck again by the evil eye.

Paulina's reflections on what happened to Simon and on her own role as caretaker of the children were effectively wordless. Her reflexivity can be seen as an attempt to attune two different cultural models: one informing her of what to do with a child struck by the evil eye, the other concerning her relationship to us as employers and patróns. For Manuela the choice of treatment was a pragmatic one. Her reflexivity involved herself as a modern

Maya and how to maintain this image in front of Paulina and in front of us, while she ascertained Simon received proper treatment.

For us, the entire happening came to constitute an event, that is, a culturally marked happening of significance. The verbal communication was only a small part of this identification of the event. Once the ethnographer has learned to distinguish events from happenings, encounters will contain more shared reasoning, emotional involvement and perhaps conflicts of interest, as the next example will show.

Nowadays, as ethnic populations are becoming increasingly global, Carlos, the cultural broker, considers himself the 'local ethnographer' of Oxkutzcab, and better at it than any professional anthropologist. My growing knowledge of Mayan culture seemed to threaten his position, yet he discovered that the kind of insight I sporadically presented to him did not fit into his cultural model of ethnography. To him, an ethnographer's task is to learn as intimately and implicitly as possible the cultural knowledge of the local population. He did in fact have an enormous stock of knowledge – even publishing small books and writing for a major newspaper.

Most anthropologists would agree that they can never master cultural knowledge as fully as local experts, but then this is not the purpose of anthropology as a social science. Anthropological knowledge is different from cultural knowledge. One way of identifying this difference is through a separation of knowing and understanding. 'Knowing' points to a social space of intimate and implicit native knowledge. Knowing differs from the external, detached and explicit 'expert' 'understanding'. 'We "know" the social space as participants and we "understand" it as detached analysts' (Hastrup 1992a: 6). Our anthropological knowledge can of course be questioned on various grounds, but 'whatever we might "know", a genuinely anthropological understanding is different from mere knowing. The kind of truth anthropology aims at is a general one, which lies beyond any particular narrative' (ibid.).

Regardless of whether shared reasoning produces consent or conflict, it expresses a reflexivity in a world into which the ethnographer is becoming increasingly integrated. In the process, the congruent relationship in the beginning of my fieldwork with Carlos became more and more incongruent. I gained more local knowledge from shared social experience, for instance in the form of shared reasoning. But as my resonance with Don Iz's family grew my local skills and cultural knowledge expanded, and the relationship to Carlos was transformed. Speaking with him about encounters, practices and language transcended direct participation.

Shared reasoning and the embodiment of tacit cultural knowledge are the first steps towards understanding and ultimately towards written anthropological knowledge. Yet, reasoning itself still does not take the full step from 'knowing' the social space as participants to 'understanding' as detached analysts (Hastrup 1992a: 6).

THE GENERATION OF ANTHROPOLOGICAL KNOWLEDGE

Some general concepts can now be established which relate to the epistemological and the reflexive processes involved in the cross-cultural space of ethnographic fieldwork.

Individuals bring various degrees of prestige, knowledge and power into interaction. Participants have different access to the intended meanings of words and actions. In practice theory, the idea of *congruence* refers to the assumption 'that the differences in perspective separating actors are, until further notice, irrelevant to their activities' (Hanks 1990: 44). Shared conventions or shared practices are possible without language skills or shared cultural models:

> What *is* relevant is that participants assume they identify and comment on the same objects in the same world. . . . The level of referential uniqueness sustained by speakers is set relative to their motives; some referential contexts require finer individuation and more precise agreement than others.
>
> (ibid.)

Some internalized background knowledge – based on shared social experience – is necessary to separate *intended* and *interpreted* meanings of actions. That is the difference between the speaker's intended meanings and the semantic reference, the relationship between language and what it represents on a given occasion (ibid.: 30). Incongruence is incompatibility of differences; experience is social but not shared.

The dichotomy of intended and interpreted is found, for instance, in the official census of the population of Oxkutzcab, taken every tenth year. According to the census, there are always almost five times as many people who are 60 years of age as there are people aged 59 or 61. Precise age is not reckoned among the older generation. However, the census form presupposes precise information, and people therefore produce answers that they believe are correct or sound reasonable. The demographic information of the census clashes with cultural knowledge of age in a shared practice which *seems* perfectly compatible but *is* incongruent. The subjective experience of age differs from objective measurements of age: numbers are unreliable. The incongruity can only be sustained owing to the presentation of demographic information as detached from local practice and according to its own rules. 'Most of reality is indifferent to our descriptions of it' (Rorty 1989: 7).

In the above example of shared reasoning between Don Iz and myself concerning his stomach pain, I contend that reflexivity exceeded the individual. We were both aware of Don Iz's suffering and we tried to formulate proper care and relief in a creative process that involved different and partly shared cultural models and idiosyncratic experience. Reflexivity belonged to the interaction. This does not deny the coexistence of individual reflexivity, even during the interaction, but the reflexivity inherent in the shared reasoning cannot be reduced to the sum of two reflexive individuals. Moreover, 'the anthropologist is not involved as an anthropologist, but as an individual and a representative of a cultural category' (Okely 1992: 24).

The shared reasoning between Paulina and Manuela led at first to muteness and an unsuccessful attempt to hide valuable but sensitive knowledge of an old-fashioned tradition in a modern scenario; then to an open dialogue concerning proper diagnosis between them, me and my wife. In this case, the gradually established joint reflexiveness made us not only aware of the interpretation of illness, but also alert as to how knowledge of the disease was negotiated by drawing on a number of different available resources. In this example, shared reasoning could not have taken place, I believe, without a close relationship. Moreover, it would make little sense to reduce reflexivity to an individual practice.

As a preliminary conclusion we can say that anthropological knowledge is generated by a process that takes off in a shared experience followed by shared reasoning. This, finally, leads to a discussion of reflexivity as such.

REFLEXIVITY

Reflexivity is a condition embodied in anthropological practice. It is beneficial as 'a continuous mode of self-analysis and political awareness' (Callaway 1992: 33). In this wide sense, reflexivity refers to the conscious use of the self as a resource for making sense of others. During participant observation or, more generally, shared social experience, the ethnographer moves back and forth between giving in to the alien reality, i.e. 'becoming' part of the local community without completing the process, and reflecting at a distance. On the one hand, the ethnographer embodies cultural ideas and practices and undergoes vicarious experiences, and, on the other, he detaches or dissociates himself from this embodiment in order not only to grasp the personal alienation and extreme relativism (Hastrup 1990: 45) but also to relate participation to the intellectual practice of the discipline. Such a practice has the individual ethnographer as a starting-point, but he is not the issue.

Distance (or detachment) can be emotional, personal, cognitive and physical; it is not fixed, but fluctuates and ranges from moments of complete identification to hostility: 'Distance is constitutive of the fieldwork experience and the writing of the ethnographic text' (Kondo 1986: 84). One dimension of distance is that between experience and fieldnotes. Fieldwork and fieldnotes are intimately connected, even though most ethnographers see them as incompatible (Jackson 1990). Fieldnotes are liminal; they are written in the field and usually in private, while the ethnographer is detached from participation. Regardless of the ethnographers' discomfort in spelling out their experience, fieldnotes make up a first written indication of the individual self-reflexivity which is the first step on the road towards anthropological discursive reflexivity.

If we are to use the notion of reflexivity to link experience and writing, we need to be aware of the limits of the ethnographer's individual reflexivity. People are part of a social space, simultaneously defined by it and its active, conscious and reflexive definers (Ardener 1989: 211–23). People are reflexive in practice without necessarily being 'reflexive' as authors; they are self-aware and aware of others including the ethnographer. This reflexivity, which is part of the human condition, takes place regardless of whether the anthropologist is present or absent. As ethnographers we only experience the reflexivity of others when we are present. In turn, this presence makes us a source to be reflected and acted upon by local people who – like ourselves – change positions within their experiential space.

Reflexivity does not belong to an individual or cultural vacuum but to a cross-cultural encounter: it is not the unmediated world of the 'others', but the world between ourselves and the others (Tedlock 1983: 323). The experiential space of the fieldworker is the source of anthropological reflection (Hastrup 1992b: 117). Reflexivity is an aftermath of experience. Accordingly, it is not produced by 'external ideas, values, or material causes, but by one's subjective, personal engagement in the practices, discourses, and institution that lend significance to the events of the world' (Callaway 1992: 37). In the ongoing cross-cultural encounter the anthropologist and participants are constantly changing their positions as subjects and objects. Since any person is a positioned subject:

> reflexivity inevitably forces us to think through the conse-
> quences of our relations with others, whether it be conditions of
> reciprocity, asymmetry or potential exploitation. There are
> choices to be made in the field, within relationships and in the
> final text.
>
> (Okely 1992: 24)

Reflexivity in this discursive sense does not directly involve the reflexivity of others. My reflexivity is not included in that of Paulina, and vice versa. Analytically, they form two separate reflexivities. Empirically they can hardly be disconnected. They belong to the same social space and at times they merge into shared reasoning. Shared reasoning emanates despite the different sources brought into the exchange but evolves from those very differences.

Ethnomethodologists insist that reflexivity is an essential condition of social life. If not, ethhnomethodology would have nothing to reflect upon and be reflexive about (Platt 1989: 640). Some anthropologists replicated this view. Thereby, they blurred the potential of reflexivity as a constructive tool that opens the way for new insight in the process of generating knowledge and saw it as a means of deconstructing anthropological authority. Ethnomethodologists assert that all utterances possess the inescapable, latent properties of being indexical and reflexive. Indexicality means that a word or an utterance not only has a trans-situational but also a distinctive context-dependent meaning. Reflexivity consists of those practices that simultaneously describe and constitute a social setting (Rogers 1983: 93). For example, 'all talk is essentially reflexive or self-descriptive in that the resources being mobilized in establishing the sense of the conversation are also being invoked or consulted as part of the assembling of sense' (ibid.).

Anthropologists use the notion of indexicality and reflexivity expounded by the ethnomethodologists with a similar emphasis on language. Reflexivity here

refers to the way in which accounts and the setting they describe mutually elaborate and modify each other in a back-and-forth process. Accounts, which describe a setting, are made up of expressions that derive their specific sense from that setting. It is important to note that accounts are not interpretations superimposed on a preexisting reality; rather, they are constitutive of that reality; they make it what it is.

(Watson 1991: 79)

With this notion of reflexivity we have come a long way from 'benign introspection' (or perhaps 'reflection') and the implied narcissism (Woolgar 1988: 22). It refers to the process of 'thinking over' an experience or 'what we are doing': 'Narcissus is reflective, but not reflexive – he is conscious of himself as an other, but he is not conscious of being self-conscious of himself as an other, thus not able to detach himself from the initial experience of alienation' (Babcock 1980: 2).

While this helps us getting beyond allegations of narcissism, the distinction is not particularly advantageous, since it inflates the use of the mirror as a metaphor. Thinking is no longer a reflex arising from seeing oneself in the mirror, but becomes reflection on the act of standing in front of the mirror reflecting on oneself. Such a strict linear reflexivity will lead scholars to focus on the author and the author's reference to himself in the activity of writing, which is the product of science. The term reflexive denotes 'any text that takes into account its own production' (Latour 1988: 166). In other words 'reflexive knowledge contains not only messages, but also information as to how it came into being, the process by which it was obtained' (Myerhoff and Ruby 1982: 2). These authors continue:

> To be reflexive is to be self-conscious and also aware of the aspects of self necessary to reveal to an audience so that it can understand both the process employed and the resultant product [the text] and know that the revelation itself is purposive, intentional, and not merely narcissistic or accidentally revealing.

(ibid.: 6)

Attention to the interdependence between writer and the 'world' led to a sense of crisis of representation which, for instance, can be seen in a postmodern anthropology style of writing where the writer is not only legitimized but also celebrated for his narrative creativity.[10] However, to turn reflexivity into an issue of the author's presence in the text, of being conscious of the production of the text, and subsequently to turn the ethnographic genre into a question of literary artistry is to reduce anthropology to that 'text' which we have tried to escape for a decade.

Stephen Tyler's version of postmodern anthropology is a study of man talking:

> Discourse is its [postmodern anthropology's] object and its means. Discourse is both a theoretical object and a practice, and it is this reflexivity between object and means that enables discourse and that discourse creates. Discourse is the maker of the worlds, not its mirror, for it represents the world only inasmuch as it is the world. The world is what we say it is, and what we speak of is the world.

(1987: 171)

Although reflexivity and discourse (natural discourse as well as scientific texts) are regarded as essential features of anthropology, according to Stephen Tyler, we must resist the temptation to let the burgeoning discourse industry plant the idea that discourse in itself *constitutes* the world, while it actually just *contributes* to our understanding of it. This is not to say that I discredit discourse analysis in the sociolinguistic sense of the term, that is, as flows of conversation or text beyond one sentence (Goodwin and Duranti 1992); but I doubt the usefulness of turning everything social into discourse. My point is that reflexivity belongs in the world and not in spoken words and discourse.

CONCLUSION

Reflexivity has most often been defined as an essential feature of discourse and as awareness of the process whereby knowledge is produced. My proposition is that this reflexivity in written text and in discourse differs from the reflexivity in the 'world'. No discourse about 'us' and the 'other' can create a common ground for human solidarity and understanding (Barth 1993).

A reflexivity in the 'world' can be acquired through shared social experience based on involvement with others in everyday contexts of practical action (Wikan 1992: 471) and involves vicarious experience in both directions, from ethnographer to local persons, and vice versa.

Reflexivity is not exclusively a process of language and it is at best insufficient to treat reflexivity as an individual conscious activity. Reflexivity does not rise from painstaking generalizations from one's own first-hand experiences, but from the combination of one's own experiences and images presented in stories, myths, accounts and vicarious experience.

Since reflexivity starts from shared social experience, it is crucial to relate the total fieldwork experience to the shifting positions of individuals in the cross-cultural encounter. The relationship to Carlos changed from one of congruence to one of incongruence, from indispensable to dispensable. My focus shifted back and forth between experience and reflections of experience in a spiralling process attempting to reach generalizations, and I changed from working with Carlos as a cultural broker and my only informant to working with many underprivileged people who were illiterate and extremely poor. This shifted the emphasis from verbal to silent knowledge. The cultural broker is trained in delivering monologues of rituals, plants, events, whereas Don Iz, Paulina, Manuela and others did not possess this capability, although some of them were gradually gaining this skill.

Through shared social experience of people's lives, thoughts and sufferings, we gain insight into the collective beliefs stored in cultural models. Sharing life and thoughts with people in common experience is a question not of native substitution, but of mismatching categories, 'the experience of relativism not as a form of anti-objectivity but as our only mode to objectivization' (Ardener 1989: 212–21). In this process a space is created where shared reflexivity becomes an essential tool for gaining cultural knowledge.

Reflexivity and categorization go hand in hand: not as a result of reflexivity and language in themselves, but as a consequence of the embodied prototypes and cultural models. Categorization is an ordering device for both inner understanding and social inter-action. Categories might be applied for real-world experience, or in presupposed, simplified worlds, but once established their sig-nificance and adequacy are reflected upon. To take this reflexivity as the constituting feature of reality would in my opinion be off the track, however.

I have argued that anthropological knowledge takes as its point of departure shared social experience, shared reasoning, the re-flexivity of others and the ethnographer. It belongs to a different register with distinct goals that transcend local knowledge. Anthropological knowledge is not about representing native voices or about evoking lived experience by narrative construc-tions, but about generalizing the particular in a separate discourse.

NOTES

1 The fieldwork was supported by the Institute of Anthropology, University of Copenhagen and a grant from the Danish Research Council for Development Research (DANIDA). The fieldwork ma-terial is presented in my Ph.D. dissertation (1991) and in shorter pieces in (1992a, b). This article has benefited tremendously from sagacious criticism from Kirsten Hastrup and Fredrik Barth, to whom I wish to extend my gratitude.

2 Shortly after Paulina had begun working for us, she asked to be paid eight months ahead. She needed this sum to buy a plot of land where her parents could live. Salary and the price of this plot of land defined each other. At the time, her parents lived in a rented traditional thatched-roof Mayan house.

3 I shall use the notion of cultural model in order to stress the relative nature of knowledge and only use schema/schematic when the cited author explicitly and exclusively uses this term.

4 The expenses involved for patients can be excessive. Don Iz had to pay for bloodtests at the price of 85.000 pesos each, equivalent to payment for one month of work.

5 In Peto and surrounding areas, people claim that the more skilled shamans live in Oxkutzcab and Mani.

6 Once again, the medicine had no effect, nor would any medicine prescribed by the clinic, had he gone there instead. His stomach ulcer had developed because of his social conditions and family situation,

none of which could be alleviated by any kind of medicine, traditional or modern.

7 Incidentally, the word for 'worry' in Maya *sèentuklik* translates approximately into 'think intensely' (Hanks 1990: 93).

8 The 'eye' is related to the hot–cold opposition known throughout Mesoamerica. Adult men sweating from physical labour, menstruating women, couples after having sexual intercourse (Hanks 1990: 89) and drunks possessing an excessive amount of heat can convey the heat to a child (up to 5 years old), resulting in the eye. Handsome children and twins are more prone to receive the eye.

9 A shaman is able to direct you to the person who gave the eye. If this person holds and touches the child the proper heat will be restored (Hanks 1990: 89). However, few people wish to confront a man who gave the eye when drunk even if they know who it was. Since the diagnosis for the 'eye' is straightforward – the distinct symptom being green diarrhoea – composing a bath with the proper plants is the normal procedure of tackling the eye. If the eye is given by a pregnant woman, medicine must be obtained from a shaman.

10 The label 'postmodern' was invented to describe a certain condition that reigns after the days of 'modernism', which in fact is claimed never to have existed. The confusion, I believe, is caused by the criticism of authors who sought to establish ethnographic authority by literary conventions (modernism). But literary conventions are precisely only conventions, ethnography authority is not real, hence 'modernism' does not really exist.

REFERENCES

Ardener, E. (1989) *The Voice of Prophecy, and Other Essays*, ed. M. Chapman, Oxford: Blackwell.

Babcock, B.A. (1980) 'Reflexivity: definitions and discriminations', *Semiotica* 30: 1–14.

Barth, F. (1993) 'Assessing anthropology', in R. Borofsky, ed., *Assessing Developments in Anthropology*, New York: McGraw-Hill.

Bourdieu, P. (1977) *Outline of a Theory of Practice*, Cambridge: Cambridge University Press.

Callaway, H. (1992) 'Ethnography and experience: gender implications in fieldwork and texts', in J. Okely and H. Callaway, eds, *Anthropology and Autobiography* (ASA Monographs 29), London and New York: Routledge.

Cicourel, A.V. (1985) 'Text and discourse', *Annual Review of Anthropology* 14: 159–85.

—— (1986) 'The reproduction of objective knowledge: common sense reasoning in medical decision making', in G. Böhme and N. Stehr, eds, *The Knowledge Society*, Dordrecht: D. Reidel Publishing Company.

Clifford, J., and Marcus, G., eds (1986) *Writing Culture: The Poetics and Politics of Ethnography*, Berkeley: University of California Press.

Goodwin, C., and Duranti, A. (1992) 'Rethinking context: an introduction', in A. Duranti and C. Goodwin, eds, *Rethinking Context: Language as an Interactive Phenomenon*, Cambridge: Cambridge University Press.

Hanks, W.F. (1990) *Referential Practice: Language and Lived Space among the Maya*, Chicago and London: University of Chicago Press.

Hastrup, K. (1989) 'The prophetic condition', in M. Chapman, ed., *Edwin Ardener: The Voice of Prophecy*, Oxford: Basil Blackwell.

—— (1990) 'The ethnographic present: a reinvention', *Cultural Anthropology* 5, 1: 45–61.

—— (1992a) 'The native voice and the anthropological vision', *Social Anthropology/Anthropologie sociale* 1, 3: 173–86.

—— (1992b) 'Writing ethnography: state of the art', in J. Okely and H. Callaway, eds, *Anthropology and Autobiography* (ASA Monographs 29), London and New York: Routledge.

Hervik, P. (1991) 'The position of language and cultures in the Yucatecan landscape', unpublished Ph. D. Dissertation, Copenhagen: Institute of Anthropology.

—— (1992a) 'Mayan culture – beyond boundaries', *Ethnos* 57: 3–4.

—— (1992b) ' "Learning" to be Indian: aspects of new ethnic and cultural identity of the Maya of Yucatán', *Folk* 34: 63–80.

Holland, D. (1985) 'From situation to impression: how Americans get to know themselves and one another', in J.W.D. Dougherty, ed., *Directions in Cognitive Anthropology*, Urbana and Chicago: University of Illinois Press.

Holland, D., and Quinn, N., eds (1987) *Cultural Models in Language and Thought*, Cambridge: Cambridge University Press.

Hutchins, Edwin (1980) *Culture and Inference: A Trobriand Case Study*, Cambridge, Mass.: Harvard University Press.

Jackson, J. (1990) ' "Déjà entendu": the liminal qualities of anthropological fieldnotes', *Journal of Contemporary Ethnography* 19, 1: 8–43.

Kondo, D.K. (1986) 'Dissolution and reconstitution of self: implications for anthropological epistemology', *Cultural Anthropology* 1, 1: 74–88.

Latour, B. (1988) 'The politics of explanation: an alternative', in S. Woolgar, ed., *Knowledge and Reflexivity: New Frontiers in the Sociology of Knowledge*, London: Sage.

Marcus, G., and Cushman, D. (1982) 'Ethnographies as text', *Annual Review of Anthropology* 11: 25–69.

Myerhoff, B., and Ruby, J. (1982) 'Introduction', in J. Ruby, ed., *A Crack in the Mirror: Reflexive Perspectives in Anthropology*, Philadelphia: University of Pennsylvania Press.

Okely, J. (1992) 'Anthropology and autobiography: participatory experience and embodied knowledge', in J. Okely and H. Callaway, eds, *Anthropology and Autobiography* (ASA Monographs 29), London and New York: Routledge.

Platt, R. (1989) 'Reflexivity, recursion and social life: elements for a postmodern sociology', *The Sociological Review* 37, 4: 636–67.

Rogers, M.F. (1983) *Sociology, Ethnomethodology, and Experience: A Phenomenological Critique*, Cambridge: Cambridge University Press.

Rorty, R. (1989) *Contingency, Irony, and Solidarity*, Cambridge:

Cambridge University Press.
Sahlins, M. (1985) *Islands of History*, Chicago and London: University of Chicago Press.
Sweetser, E.E. (1987) 'The definition of lie: an examination of the folk models underlying a semantic prototype', in D. Holland and N. Quinn, eds, *Cultural Models in Language and Thought*, Cambridge: Cambridge University Press.
—— (1990) *From Etymology to Pragmatics: Metaphorical and Cultural Aspects of Semantic Structure*, Cambridge: Cambridge University Press.
Tedlock, D. (1983) *The Spoken Word and the Work of Interpretation*, Philadelphia: University of Pennsylvania Press.
Tyler, S.A. (1978) *The Said and the Unsaid: Mind, Meaning and Culture*, London and New York: Academic Press.
—— (1987) *The Unspeakable: Discourse, Dialogue, and Rhetoric in the Postmodern World*, Madison: University of Wisconsin Press.
Watson, G. (1991) 'Rewriting culture', in R. Fox, ed., *Recapturing Anthropology*, Santa Fe, N. Mex.: School of American Research Press.
Wikan, U. (1991) 'Towards an experience – near anthropology', *Cultural Anthropology*, 6: 285–305.
—— (1992) 'Beyond the words: the power of resonance', *American Ethnologist* 19, 3: 460–82.
Woolgar, S. (1988) 'Reflexivity is the ethnographer of the text', in S. Woolgar, ed., *Knowledge and Reflexivity: New Frontiers in the Sociology of Knowledge*, London: Sage.

Chapter 6

The mysteries of incarnation
Some problems to do with the analytic language of practice

Angel Díaz de Rada and Francisco Cruces

This paper is an exploration of the space between words and practice.[1] We will deal with the relation between the analytic language used by the anthropologists and the social practice and experience of the people they study. An ethnography is both a process and a product. As a process, it involves everyday interactions, comprehensive experiences and local knowledge. As a product, its result is a written text intended to encourage a scientific and universalistic understanding. We will focus on the contrast between these two diverging logics, which are inherent in the anthropological task. In particular, we will explore the conceptual vacuum that appears as the researcher translates embodied practices into analytic categories.

TWO ETHNOGRAPHIC SKETCHES

Two years ago, Francisco attended a rock concert in Madrid for the first time in his life. His companions explained to him that, although hundreds of youngsters were jammed together, this concert was not a prime example of a good concert. There was no *marcha* (action; literally, 'to get going'). The singers were not really *enrollados* (letting go), and the *ambiente* (atmosphere), although not ideal, could not compare with that of other occasions they had experienced. They recalled situations when people had rushed to the front to be close to the lead singer; touching moments when the singer really gave it his all; the audience swaying and jumping around in unison to such an extent that one left 'dripping with sweat'. That was real *marcha*.

Francisco shares with many other young madrilenians a basic vocabulary to speak about ludic situations, like concerts, in general, public celebrations and parties of all kinds. *Marcha*, *ambiente* and *enrollarse* are part of such colloquial and common-sense categories. During his fieldwork, Francisco was confronted with the use his informants gave to these words in the very context of the festivals. By means of them they seemed to shape and express their experiences of joy and togetherness.

Francisco was never led to ask directly about the meaning of these words: he knew it on an intuitive basis. But, as an ethnographer, his task was to rationalize and clear up their semantic domain. What did people really imply with *marcha* or *ambiente*? To what extent could categories of this type be analytically separated from the sensations, feelings and actions of the individuals involved?

Let us begin with the second of these terms, *ambiente*. In Madrid the following joke is told. A grain of sand is making his way through the big city. After a long haul he arrives at the city edge. He finds a good vantage-point and sees the desert beyond the last suburbs. '¡Qué ambientazo!' ('So that's where it's all happening!'), he cries.

The punch line of this joke lies in its crude objectivization of what we refer to as the *ambiente* of a public situation. It rejects the common-sense notion that a party is something more than a load of people thrust together, like grains of sand in the desert. But at the same time it reflects that *ambiente* denotes a loss of personal space. For example, a concert without a good crowd, without a rush to get to the centre of the floor and close to the singers, would hardly be considered to have 'a lot of' *ambiente*.

The term *ambiente* defies clear definition. It is above all a form of metaphorical reference to what is taking place in the party. By means of such metaphor social interaction and experience are understood in terms of the air we breathe, the 'atmosphere' inside which we live. *Ambiente* describes the copresence of a quantity of people, but also the quality of the setting generated for participation. As natives of a culture in which the party situation is important, we learn to use this thermometer of its good or bad functioning. We are able to say when there are indicators of good or bad *ambiente*. We also speak about 'a lot of' *ambiente* or 'a little' *ambiente*. The concept brings into close relation the external conditions of the ritual (numbers of people, intensity and order of stimuli and actions) and its meaning. It makes us perceive the people present as an ensemble, an integrated whole. It converts 'a lot' into 'good'.

The notion of *marcha* is an even more illustrative example of this conversion of quantity into quality. In the context of the rock concert, it is held that the *marcha* is the indicator *par excellence* of its success or failure. There are concerts with 'a lot' and others with only 'a little' *marcha*. However, people are not sure how to define it. It refers simultaneously to a form of collective behaviour and to an individual experience. For example, a singer might ask his audience, 'Have you got a lot of *marcha*?' In the same way, someone may opt not to find a place at the front because he does not feel that he has 'enough *marcha*'. Sometimes, it is said that the *marcha* 'is in the body'. Nevertheless, *marcha* does not simply evoke a subjective, individual state. It is also something which, objectively visible for the participants, is noticeable from the outside as an attribute of situations. 'There's a lot of *marcha* here' means that there are a good number of people who are exteriorizing their experience in their behaviour, synchronizing their movement to the rhythm of the music. The *marcha* is simultaneously experienced as an external stimulus and as a disposition to be active.

These, like many other similarly ineffable concepts, describe the social setting from the starting-point of synaesthetic representations and metaphorics of bodily experience.[2] But, in carrying out this semantic rodeo, they become normalized and gain social meaning. *Marcha* describes something more than dance or movement, in the same way as *ambiente* describes something other than pressure, crowd and pushing. This something else is what we could call the 'social plus'[3] which every situation geared to enjoyment produces. By means of it the quantity and the quality, the behaviour and the experience turn out to be very difficult to discern by the participant. It is in this sense that we have coined the expression 'mysteries of incarnation', in order to underline the fusion in these situations of conventional meanings and bodily movements, collective patterns and subjective conceptions and feelings.

Unlike Tamara Kohn, Peter Hervik and other authors in this volume, Francisco knew fairly well how to 'behave appropriately' in the new ethnographic context. But, was his experience the same as that of the rest of the participants in the rock concert? It could be. The point is that, to a certain extent, his analytic tools as anthropologist had little to do with his social experience as native.

Without resort to local categories, any description of the ritual process would have missed what seemed to be most relevant for the participants.

In this case, the problem for the observer was to illuminate the ambiguities of the process by means of which a set of collective, stereotyped and recurrent actions become experience for those who participate in it. Labels such as *ambiente* and *marcha* point to such practical and ambiguous incarnation, which only reveals itself to the observer in its external manifestations.

Anthropology does not have exact translations for experiential terms like *marcha* or *ambiente*, terms that are both representational and pragmatic. Native languages are capable of integrating such ambiguities synaesthetically and metaphorically, pointing to the bodily and subjective dimensions of experience and to the socially objectified in a single move. The questions that arise then are: does the analytic jargon of anthropologists grasp what the practice holds of an experience as much as these native symbolic mediations do? How can we reconstruct what the subjects do with what the exterior does to them?

A second ethnographic sketch may give a clearer insight into the problem. Angel counselled as an educational psychologist at a public high school in Madrid. The students' parents were mainly qualified manual workers and white-collar workers. The formal counselling programmes informed about university studies by means of texts, talks, classroom discussions and booklets. But the school experience around these matters was a continuous frustration, because the hopes so fostered met with the resistance of conceptions originated in another field of social practices, that of family relationships, which, without having been formalized in procedures of cultural transmission, displayed greater efficiency than the explicit, programmed efforts of the counsellors. From his double role of psychologist and ethnographer, Angel was able to sense the perplexity which was produced by the breakdown between the optimism of the textual descriptions which codified this information ('a world of paper', as one pupil would say in a discussion group), and the wider reality of the universe of their sociocultural practices. The students at the school had explicit intuition of the rupture between the representations of the world projected by the school and immediate learning from their direct experience.

Psychologist (ethnographer):   And what about you? Have you decided which degree you're going to study yet?

First Pupil: I still haven't made up my mind. Because . . . I don't know. I'd like to do journalism or law. I'd like to be a journalist, I'd like to be a lawyer. But you don't know what the courses are going to be like. You don't know what you're going to study. You haven't got a clear idea of what you want to do.

Second Pupil: You just haven't got a clue about the different careers.

First Pupil: That's right. You *see* journalists, you *see* lawyers, and obviously you like it. You say 'great', 'wonderful'. It's really attractive because they've already got work and everything. But then you say 'I'm going to read journalism.' What are you going to *do* in the course? You don't know. We don't really know anything about the *content* of the course. You just *know* the future – things about what journalists and lawyers do once they've got work.

Psychologist: Would you have a better idea of things if you were aware of the course content?

First Pupil: The thing is, it's not just the content of the courses. Because you get there and it turns out to be a different *world* than the one you imagined. I know a lot of people who . . . I don't know . . . who started a career eager to study only to find out they didn't like the *rhythm* at the university. Or . . . I don't know . . . the lecturers, their attitude. Well, I don't know . . . It's easy to lose faith.

In the context of the classroom, pupils tried to make sense of their personal situation using categories drawn from their lived reality. While the counselling programmes focused on things like 'contents', 'visions' and 'knowledge', pupils stressed 'actions', 'rhythms' and 'worlds'. By such oppositions the agents in the classroom intended to illuminate the realm of the university, which from the high school they could only contemplate at a distance. But the pupils' problem (and also that of the ethnographer) was the sharp hiatus between the two sets of categories.

Both ethnographic cases illustrate the ambiguities of social experience and the incarnation of objectified processes in it. Seeing how rituals like rock concerts invoke non-explicit meanings and efficient experiences, as well as how the pupils in the school acquire preferences and notions about formal academic contexts, we learn that in social practice there are meanings which are not definable other than *in* and *by* action itself. Often, the protagonists do not know how to answer the question about what something means, but they are able to point out significant issues in a deictic or presentational way.[4] From this perspective, the native discourse remains a necessary road of access to the meaning of practice, even if it is hardly ever translatable or transparent. The native conceptual mediations of practices are, irretrievably, instruments of action and understanding, so that categories like 'world', 'rhythm', *marcha* or *ambiente* serve to do the very thing they are attempting to reflect.

Besides, the sketches suggest shortages in the ethnographer's vocabulary in order to speak, by means of a propositional mode of discourse, about the ambiguous, vague and locally embedded conditions of the actors' experience. In the sections below we will discuss these and other problems which social scientists, particularly anthropologists, seem to face as they seek to represent social practice in the sphere offered by their observational language.

PRACTICE, ACTION, LANGUAGE: SETTING THE PROBLEM

Any attempt to situate the concept of social practice should begin by considering the Weberian project of elaborating a comprehensive sociology, that is to say, of penetrating the internal conditions of social action. Under the label 'comprehension', Weber recognized an interpretative limit wherever the researcher was incapable of attributing rationality to the actions. Beyond this limit, the interpretation had to give way to comprehension, as 'the essentially negative form of satisfying our demand for a causal explanation with respect to the "interpretation"' (Weber 1985: 81). Social action theory, from its beginnings, restricted practice to the scope of the rational action by which an agent finds himself involved in a universalizable calculation of motives, means, ends and values (Habermas 1982, 1989a).

This way of understanding practice left out anything that did not fit into the rational characterization of the action. Seen as rational action, practice became above all reason (practical reason, as it has been designated by Marshall Sahlins (1976)). This inspired a somewhat ethnocentric vision: a social world perceived in terms of the way the formal institutions we live by (and in) recognize themselves. Outside such an epistemological enclosure remained all those facets of action which did not match with narrowly instrumental or utilitarian guidelines (cf. Godelier 1990: 209–39). Practice in general had been instituted as the residues, as the remainder.

For anthropology as an empirical discipline, the penetration of this left-over is, however, crucial, and not simply due to the *horror vacui* which the old holistic aspiration provokes in it. It is also the case because for the ethnographer everyday practices are not merely the object of research, but the primordial means of constructing the object itself (cf. Stocking 1985, López Coira and Díaz de Rada 1990). To put it in Gumperz's words:

No matter what seemingly reasonable, utilitarian justification members might give for their practices, the anthropologist tends to see behavior as having both rational, or goal-oriented, as well as conventionalized, arbitrary, and culture-bound components. It is the clarification of the role of ritualized, routinized, unconscious, and often glossed-over aspects of behavior, of the way they enter into everyday instructional tasks, that best characterizes the anthropologist's contribution to our understanding of human society and the role of language in it.

(1975: xii)

Notwithstanding these salutary purposes, the main obstacle of any ethnographer in actually performing such a programme is to cope with the sharp differences that contrast the real practices which agents carry out in their daily life with the language used by theorists to order, classify, interpret and explain these practices. The 'glossed-over' aspects of behaviour seem to possess a rationale of their own, different from the rationality of action as reflected in the systematic reconstructions of the observer. This gap or *décalage* between two diverging logics has for a long time been a focus of interdisciplinary confluence. Authors as diverse as Pierre Bourdieu, Jean Lave, Michel de Certeau, Mark Johnson, James W. Fernandez or Stanley J. Tambiah have coincided in pointing out the deficiencies and traps of a logistic or intellectualist reduction of social action and experience.[5] All of them suggest the existence of what could be called a conceptual vacuum inevitably dividing the analytical categories (clad in words) from the practices analysed (embodied in action, routines, schemata, bodily movements, etc.).

The predominance of textual and representational metaphors of culture and behaviour in sociocultural studies might be seen as an attempt to prevent such a gap. Since Austin it has been common to consider language as action, paying attention to its pragmatic dimensions and to how speakers 'do things with words' (Austin 1971). On the other hand, the interpretative tradition of anthropology is distinguishable for its special sensibility with regard to the meaning which human groups give to their practices. It pays attention to the expressive qualities of action beyond the purposive ends which may guide it.

Nevertheless, this convergence which brings language and action closer together, in conceptual terms does not cease being somewhat asymmetrical. When we examine the background of metaphors and models upon which our understanding of what people say and do rests, we perceive a large imbalance in favour of terminology based on language, text or discourse, as opposed to a relative scarcity of vocabulary to speak directly about practice in its own terms. We have more words to describe other words than to explain what is done with them.

Obviously, what we call metaphors of language, discourse and text are no more than a heterogeneous collection of categorial instruments with very different implications. The emphasis of linguistic relativism in the grammatical structure of languages is far removed from the universalizing interest of French structuralism in the phonological mechanism of binary operations. This in turn differs considerably from the attention given recently to matters such as the pragmatics of language-use, sociolinguistic change, f :·rative language, the construction of discursive coherence, or the dialogic nature of speech. Too often, the structure of language has been taken as a model for all practice. Since language was understood as a body of objectified social conventions, cultural interpretation took the form of a sort of cryptological activity of decoding or deciphering. The prevalence of the external interpreter banished the actual agents. In the face of that, the metaphors of 'dialogue' and of 'translation' drastically reopen the relationships of the theory with its object, cultural diversity. In a concert in which many voices are heard and in which many logics interact, the scientific institution renounces the pretence of being the only form of mediation (Cruces and Díaz de Rada 1991).

Among these different metaphors of practice (and, more fully, of culture) there is a continuity which interests us. They are rough proposals seeking to close the gap between descriptive languages and the actions described, and implying an attempt to conserve their particularity, their wholeness in a local context: that which Fernandez has termed the 'embeddedness' of meaning (Fernandez 1978: 221). In order to recuperate the logics, the voices and the senses which sociological objectivization annuls, textual metaphors suggest an 'as if': read the ritual as if it were a text; analyse the rules of descent as if they obeyed a code or logical schemata; contemplate ways of eating, walking or working as if we were dealing with a grammar.

The use, often implicit, of this type of textual metaphors may represent an important conceptual aid. But its feebleness can be seen in the mysterious, if not paradoxical, appearance which the processes of transmission, incorporation and execution of practices tend to take on when the language of theory is superimposed on them (as happened in the 'mysteries' of our sketches). In Certeau's expression, practical knowledge appears then as a *docte ignorance*: an unconscious wisdom, a knowledge without awareness (1979: 136–41). If there are 'logics', 'voices' or 'forms of knowing' in the practices themselves, the inevitable inertia of the analytic language and the routines of writing which we employ as observers tend to blur their *locus*. We are no longer sure of where to situate them, or to whom we should attribute them. At the start, there are silent practices on the data side, and clear and abstract concepts on the theory side. As the investigation advances (especially as it is being written), there appears an elucidation of meanings which is located somewhere within the space that separates the constructions of the anthropologists and the actions of the agents. It is not simply that theory takes on local contents (e.g. lexical loans of difficult translation, like *mana, taboo, potlach* or *soul*). In a correlative way, it becomes difficult to discern the degree of psychological reality of these 'forms of knowing' and 'meanings', caught halfway between the tools of the anthropologist and the empirical context.

The distinction competence versus performance will illustrate our point. The Habermasian separation between the reconstructive sciences of competence and the empirical sciences of performance is well known (Habermas 1989b: 313). Such a distinction vanishes from the moment when the model reconstructed by the researcher from his own knowledge of rule (whether grammatical, pragmatic or logical) has to be postulated as a factor present in the mind of the subjects. Henceforth, the 'reconstructive' discourse becomes 'empirical', a fact evident in the *rapprochement* that Habermas himself has been forced to make with the more empiricist and analytic traditions of social research.

Textual metaphors, together with other heuristic devices, tend to represent human practice in a roundabout way. We wonder if this tendency might not be due to the nature of the ethnographic work in itself. In so far as we, anthropologists, are to interpret practices which others carry out, we are placed at the following crossroads: (1) impose every significance on native practices from the outside (from the system of relationships set up by the language of observation); (2) make the practices speak more than they actually do, in a show of ethnographic ventriloquism. In the former case, native practices, subordinated to a network of causal relationships and statistical distributions, tend to go dumb: justifications, agents and *manières de faire* become blurred (Certeau 1979: 20). In the latter case, their assimilation to language, discourse or text tends to textualize them in excess, superimposing the particular coherence of a written and propositional mode of discourse on the conditions of practice, which are, as we will try to argue, extremely different. It is as if the significance of practices, real and relevant, but barely transparent, had to be reconstructed at the level of theory, whether by means of the dominant categories of the analysis of meaning, or by means of local concepts, lexical borrowings which exercise a similar mediation between behaviour and its sense.

An instance of the first temptation could be to understand the pupil's troubles in our second sketch in terms of 'school failure'. An instance of the second one are the statements by journalists in Madrid newspapers, reading the rock concerts as 'acts of love', 'explosions of energy' or 'forgetfulness of everyday sorrows'.

These common dilemmas of any fieldworker reveal the existence of terminological problems when it comes to speaking of schemata for action and patterns of experience. Sheltering in, or returning to, antimentalist or objectivistic prejudices is not a satisfactory solution. Adopting an objectivistic position prevents the very problem from emerging, because such a perspective disdains from the outset the explanatory relevance of the incarnated senses of native experience. On the contrary, we take their relevance for granted. The closer our look at such issues, the deeper our understanding of the social process.

This does not mean the encumbering of any mystical subjectivism. It does mean the reassessing of our analytic tools in order to grasp the nuances of human behaviour. What is needed is to specify in which ways the construction of the analytic concepts of the observer differ from the practical knowledge of the agents. In other words, it is necessary to reflect on the nature of our own language of analysis when contrasted with the specific conditions of social practice and experience. This is the purpose of the following section.

FROM THE COHERENCE OF ANTHROPOLOGICAL DISCOURSE TO THE CONDITIONS OF SOCIAL PRACTICE AND EXPERIENCE

If the different conceptual languages of anthropology have any common trait, it is that of discursive coherence: an order of meaning which it is supposed contains, at the very least, the capacity to re-present and evoke a given sociocultural world. Such a representation is supposed to be orientated towards a scientific community, in which a rationalistic scrutiny and discussion demands a certain degree of validity (adequacy and relevance of the representations) and liability (stability of the representational code). The coherence of anthropological discourse establishes itself thanks to the predominant use of an expressive medium (verbal language in writing), in which certain basic properties, for our purposes, stand out (Table 1).

This language allows a propositional expression of knowledge, a shaping of ideas which operates by means of reference to a world represented with claims of truth. The propositional construction of discourse tends to prevail over the non-propositional aspects of language (for example, the intentional and pragmatic components of communication) and over the properties of reality which cannot easily be contained in language itself (Goody 1990). In this way this expressive mode is able to reduce reality to language, and language to a network of propositions.

Given that these properties of the propositional mode are quite unavoidable within the context of the scientific communication, it would be inaccurate to take this reduction as a form of reductionism. We know that sociocultural reality and experience cannot be

Table 1 Anthropological discourse versus social practice and experience

The coherence of anthropological discourse	The conditions of social practice and experience
Propositionality	Total fact Integration Presentational mode Ambivalence Opacity
Discreteness	Temporal and social continuity Rupture of symbolic distinctions
Articulation	Polithetia
Seriality	Substitutability Multimedia Simultaneity
Panopsis	Partiality Opportunism Local character
Reversibility	Privileges temporal relations Enunciative present Irreversibility

identified with propositional language, but we have to express our ideas by means of this mode if we are to construct a rational space of dialogue. Propositional language provides the resources for it, but it sets the limits at the same time. For example, it is able to include rhetorical tropes which can partially reflect the displacements and continuities we operate in our social practice. As anthropologists we are used to making quotations such as *ambiente, marcha*, 'world', verbal expressions which our informants mention as a part of their experience. The point is that, in the context of anthropological discourse, these tropes and native terms have to be subordinated to a sense of coherence universally understandable. The propositional language can include these experiential windows only by reducing their divergent 'logic' to the convergent logic of scientific representations. As a consequence, native vocabulary may be elevated to the realm of irreducible or ineffable. As we have shown explicitly, anthropology is forced to appropriate the native terms as encapsulated experience even in the case of the study of our own societies, when anthropologists are real agents of the sociocultural process they try to depict.

As a written text, anthropological discourse presents itself in a discrete, articulate and sequential medium. Analytic description has to be fragmented and discontinuous, but if it aspires to reach the composition of an order it has to submit itself to a criterion of articulation which confides a necessary meaning to the elements (and also to their possible substitutes) in a logical series.

Finally, the expressive medium makes possible a panoptic vision of represented reality (Certeau 1979: 82–9; Bourdieu 1990: 83). The permanence of the inscriptions gives control over the totality of the expressed knowledge. Written texts provide a simultaneous vision of the before and after. In addition, diagrams and synoptic drawings redirect the attention in all conceptual directions. Consequently, anthropological discourse can give way to an experience of reversibility in the utopic and u-chronic field of textual references: it can retract or justify itself a posteriori, it can bring together that which reality obstinately separates, and it can separate for analysis that which in the world of life is given in compact experiences.

On the other hand, what can we say about the experiences that are brought to life by practice or incarnated in practical and common-sense labels such as *marcha* or 'rhythm'? Essentially, social practice, in Mauss's definition, presents itself to agents as a total fact (1979: 258–63). We are speaking of an immediate, integrated experience in which the exercise of communication is not primarily engaged with an attempt at analytical clarification. Rather, this exercise is penetrated by actions and interpretations of actions which constantly intertwine elements coming from different perspectives, levels and fields of reality. Properties such as ambivalence, ambiguity, contradiction and conflict mark important domains of sociocultural life. Let us look, for example, to the dynamics of domination. It is common to separate the dominants from the dominated by well-defined frontiers. But in these kinds of relationship we have to assume an important degree of ambivalence, since some part of the comprehension of reality sustained by the dominants is integrated in the perspectives of the dominated. And what the dominated take from the dominants cannot be reduced to a mere addition of elements but comprises a relational and transformational sphere of operations (Grignon and Passeron 1982: 49–96). The cognitive, symbolic and ritual realms share similar properties as well. Their realities have to be grasped by playing with the ambiguities of the displacement and condensation of meaning, processes of inchoation and lightening (Fernandez 1986). In their very constitution, social life and experience owe their structure to a structuration that is continuous, and crossed by contradiction and conflict (Willis 1978; Giddens 1984).

Being made to a certain extent by representations, experience is above all a presentational fact. By contrast to a representational mode, a presentational one operates analogically, in the presence of face-to-face interaction and by means of complex wholes of unbounded information. In a presentational mode, communicated contents and media of communication are intricately linked. Words and other representational tools do things, or are even processed as if they were things. In summary, the agents' knowledge is quite far from the intellectualized imagery of our academic milieu: the body is in the mind (Johnson 1987). As Certeau indicates, everyday practices are opaque, since in their very performance they conceal the meanings which the analyst believes he can see in them. This is not to say that the practical experience is contrary to all kinds of self-reference. Social agents in their everyday life monitor their behaviour at a practical stage. Their knowledge is practical knowledge.

Social practice constitutes the space for all types of social, cultural and temporal continuities. On the one hand, the agents construct and interpret the present contexts in the terms of other ones. In each particular experience, they are loaded with the burden of wider and more comprehensive experience. On the other hand, they bring into play, according to each case, both the long *durées* which penetrate the sense of collective history, and the short time-spans which allow the agents to play with the short distances of face-to-face relationships.

Analytical requirements of modern science seem to fragment social reality into domains: economy, art, kinship, religion. This approach, being necessary for rational understanding, does not fit with the ways in which the agents perceive and create the world, however. A single action can usually be found saturated with meanings which refer to a wide range of fields. For instance, a move in the domain of religion can yield effects in the domain of economy or kinship; and it can even yield unintended effects precisely because the agent is not completely conscious of the whole set of relations and mediations. This constant exercise of rupture and reconstruction of symbolic distinctions seems to be one of the main traits of everyday practices.

As a consequence, the criteria of practice are not clearly defined guidelines. They are ones which operate according to polythetic and fuzzy classifications,[6] where the appearance of a given element usually corresponds not to a logical series, but rather to an indeterminate sequence of substitutions. The meaning of the actions and practical representations cannot be reduced, from an information-alist perspective, to plain information (in the narrow technical sense of a reduction of uncertainty), or even to a componential set of attributes semantically elaborated. To a certain extent, the meaning of the 'meaning' has to be assessed in the field, contrasting the common-sense definitions with that of the social sciences.

Social practice brings into play a range of communicative and expressive channels. It is, by definition, a multimedia complex (Tambiah 1985: 145) whose global meaning does not lend itself to a reduction to what happens in each of the media separated from the rest. As the agents never cease to act, these media operate simultaneously. The regulation of the interactions should be thought of as if it were a dance (Gearing 1979).

Practice is partial and opportunist. Everyday interests play not in absent arenas, but in concrete and proximate relations of force. Agents may try to satisfy their most immediate interests, against the satisfaction of other ones attributed to them from a panoptic, rational and scientific perspective. Besides, practice is local in space and in time. Its temporality (like that of enunciation) is projected from the present and in the present. Although there might be evocation, there can be no turning back; although there might be anticipation, there is no prediction. Each moment of the action establishes itself in a specific *locus* from which it is not possible to sight the full group of relationships. For this reason, reversibility is unlikely in practical experience. By contrast to the panopsis which is brought about by written conceptual language, practice seems blind and fateful.

SOME NOTES ON REFLEXIVITY

It could be said that our ethnographic argument and that of Tamara Kohn (in this volume) follow opposite roads, although not necessarily opposed ones. Instead of the external view of a stranger entering a radically alien culture without a full mastery of its language, our ethnographic sketches are based on a previous linguistic understanding of the contexts studied. While Kohn's paper tends to find mutualities between the ethnographer's and the native's direct experience of the culture, we have, conversely, underlined the ruptures and breakdowns among a diversity of levels of comprehension inside a single culture.

What we have attempted here is to call for a notion of reflexivity removed from the intellectualistic and logocentric assumptions of Western thought. By 'reflexivity' we mean a basic and general human capacity for self-reference that takes both representational and operational forms. We do lack a positive, crystal-clear definition of what a 'practical reflexivity' is all about. But, as a matter of fact, the chief challenge for understanding practice is to account for those reflexive conditions of human action that are not properly contained in the models of language, text and discourse.

The problem of reflexivity so understood cross-cuts common oppositions like linguistic experience/prelinguistic experience, on the one hand, and others' ethnography/home ethnography, on the other. It implies that (1) practical experience cannot easily be labelled as 'extra' or 'prelinguistic' (or, consequently as 'merely linguistic' either). In other words, practical realities are 'linguistic' and 'extralinguistic' at the same time: words are just one of the sources by which cultural agents reflect upon themselves. Self-reference and self-mention are obviously significant skills, although not necessarily restricted to explicit verbal behaviour. (2) The coherence of anthropological discourse is just one mode of reflexivity. Anthropology does not have the sole right of it; as a matter of fact, the ethnographies show, although in a partial way, the many faces of native reflexivity. Human beings are able to take themselves as objects of reflection in ritual performance, in everyday routines, in marked speech, in political action, in the process of institutionalization, and wherever they create and recreate culture by means of practising it.

In our view, the existence of the aforementioned gap or *décalage* which divides the analytical categories from the ones embedded in social practice and experience is quite indifferent to oppositions such as prelinguistic–linguistic, others–us. On the basis of the first, Kohn compares her experience with that of young brides coming from outside the communities she studied. On the basis of the second, Peter Hervik elaborates on the concept of reflexivity in fieldwork as cross-cultural space. Our hypothesis is that, in any case, the vacuum we have been trying to describe will always appear in the ethnographic process, even once the ethnographer has acquired the cultural and linguistic competence which can be considered as adequate in methodological terms, and whether he/she is a member of that culture or not.

Of course, our characteristic position as observers may affect this vision. As has been stated above, for us there was no prelinguistic shock at all; at least, not in the extreme way it could happen to a naive alien ethnographer. Before entering the field, we had experiences at parties, concerts and schools. As native ethnographers, we both had to cope with the paradoxical task of translating the experiential categories of our social world into anthropological ones (rather than doing it the other way round). But this common trait should not conceal the fact that, in a complex, urban, plural society, the range of virtual positions for an observer is wide and manifold. Working as a technical consultant in a formal institution differs greatly from entering the arena of a rock concert as an anonymous voyeur. Only the fiction of being 'natives' of such contexts could lead one to neglect these differences.

Our topic of discussion can then be restated as the existence of a diversity of modes of reflexivity that are not correctly settled when the problem is reduced to a contrast in terms of 'they' (the natives) versus 'we' (the members of the ethnographer's culture of origin). For, whether 'native' or 'foreigner', 'local' or 'alien', the anthropologist is always an intruder. It is for this reason that we have focused on the analytic tools of anthropological discourse, and not on the ethnographer's particular cultural background. The fiction can no longer be maintained that the anthropologist belongs to a single, unique culture. As a matter of fact, nobody does; everyone is, to a certain degree, native of a diversity of levels of inclusion within sociocultural borders. Very often, when anthropologists speak in terms of the they–we opposition it is no more than a rhetorical device, useful for expositional purposes, but misleading to the extent that it reproduces an insular conception of cultures. Identities are not only multilevelled, but mobile: what the ethnographer gathers always depends on his/her own relational definition with respect to others. It is, say, like a snapshot of a crowd in movement. Our urban fieldwork 'at home' leads us to a sensitive recognition of these facts. Often our informants were as permeable to a universalist and rationalist motto as we were, and we had to negotiate our views with them on an equal basis.

In order to account for the complexity of this issue, it should not be enough, therefore, to trace a crude line between the coherence of anthropological discourse and the conditions of social practice and experience. The anthropological discourse is also due to a process of practical experience. Conversely, non-anthropologists seek for coherent interpretations of the world they live in. This is specially true when they are demanded to elaborate rational reconstructions about their own culture, as is the case in the ethnographic interview. It would have been necessary to carry out, so to speak, a fourfold comparison, contrasting the observer's theoretical discourse (a) with research as a specific form of practice and experience, (b) with the conditions of the observed practices, and (c) with the construction of discursive coherence created by the informants.

In highlighting the problem of a conceptual vacuum in the analytic language of practice, it has not been our intention to criticize the worth of the irreplaceable heuristics based as much on a social action theory as on textual metaphors. Rather, we have explored some of the conditions of any analytic effort in relation to the social world. The research activity generates effects over the object of study. Often, ethnography as a product overshadows ethnography as a process; a process which is rooted in the quicksands of non-transparent experiences and loose, fuzzy and sketchy domains of social practice. Every research has its mysteries of incarnation. In this respect, we anthropologists are not any different from those around us.

NOTES

1 Written with the support of the DGICYT (Spain), as part of the programme 'Changes in Values and Political Behaviour in Different Contexts of Social Transformation'. Our acknowledgments to Paul Cunliffe, Rochelle Robertson and Katy Elder for their help in editing the manuscript.
2 Synaesthesis is a rhetorical trope which expresses properties that belong to a sensorial modality as if they belonged to another, i.e. 'a sweet melody', 'a hot rhythm'.
3 The evolutionist theories of religion defined 'ritual' as a medium of communication with the supernatural world. Further developments of the concept have enlarged their field of application, taking it as a category of action in its own right rather than as the result of a body of religious beliefs (Velasco 1986: 65–75). 'Social plus' refers to the expressive quality of ritual acts that lies beyond any means-to-ends explicit calculation. For an elaboration of this concept, see García, Velasco *et al*. 1991: 264–5.

4 The distinction 'presentational' versus 'representational' will be discussed below. On presentational, participatory and iconic coding, see Tambiah 1990: 84–110.
5 A diversity of critical labels reminds us just how lacking our attempts usually are and what the dangers of confusing both levels of reality could be: 'philologism' (Bajtin, quoted in Bourdieu 1988: 116), 'objectivism', 'theoricism', 'logicism' (Bourdieu 1988: 119; 1990: 25–41), 'intellectualism' (Evans-Pritchard 1989: 41; Fernandez 1978: 220–5); 'psychologism', 'formalism' (Polanyi 1976: 155–78), 'utilitarism' (Sahlins 1988: 162–5), 'rationalism' (Lave 1989: 172–6; Tambiah 1990). All of these concepts, although often linked to an explicit critique of Enlightenment and modern suppositions of social action theory, generally point to a breakdown of greater importance which affects sociocultural research as a whole.
6 While in monothetic classification the criteria are always hierarchical and independent, polythetic classification melts heterogeneous levels of hierarchy within non-independent sets of categories.

REFERENCES

Austin, J.L. (1971) *Palabras y acciones. Cómo hacer cosas con palabras*, Buenos Aires: Paidós.
Bourdieu, P. (1988) *Cosas dichas*, Buenos Aires: Gedisa.
—— (1990) *The Logic of Practice*, Stanford, Calif.: Stanford University Press.
Certeau, M. de (1974) 'Des espaces et des pratiques', in *La Culture au pluriel*, Paris: Union Générale d'éditions.
—— (1979) *L'invention du quotidien, I: Arts de faire*, Paris: Union Générale d'éditions.
Cruces, F., and Díaz de Rada, A. (1991) 'Traducción y derivación. Una reflexión sobre el lenguaje conceptual de la antropología', *Antropología* 1: 85–106.
Evans-Pritchard, E.E. (1989) *Las teorías de la religión primitiva*, Madrid: Siglo XXI.
Fernandez, J. (1978) 'African religious movements', *Annual Review of Anthropology* 7: 195–234.
—— (1986) 'The mission of metaphor in expressive culture', in *Persuasions and Performances*, Bloomington: University of Indiana Press.
García, J.L. (1987) 'El discurso del nativo sobre su propia cultura. Análisis de un concejo asturiano', *Fueyes dixebraes de lletres asturianes*, 23: 113–24.
García, J.L., Velasco, H., *et al.* (1991) *Rituales y proceso social. Estudio comparativo en cinco zonas españolas*, Madrid: ICRBC, Ministerio de Cultura.
Gearing, F. (1979) 'A reference model for a cultural theory of education and schooling', in F. Gearing and L. Sangree, eds, *Toward a Cultural Theory of Education and Schooling*, New York: Mouton.
Giddens, A. (1984) *The Constitution of Society*, Cambridge: Polity Press.

Godelier, M. (1990) *Lo ideal y lo material*, Madrid: Taurus.

Goody, J. (1990) *La lógica de la escritura y la organización de la sociedad*, Madrid: Alianza.

Grignon, C., and Passeron, J.C. (1982) *Sociologie de la culture et sociologie des cultures populaires*, Paris: Gides.

Gumperz, J.J. (1975) 'Foreword', in M. Sanches and B.G. Blount, eds, *Sociocultural Dimensions of Language Use*, New York: Academic Press.

Habermas, J. (1982) *Conocimiento e interés*, Madrid: Taurus.

—— (1984) *Ciencia y técnica como 'ideología'*, Madrid: Tecnos.

—— (1989a) 'Aspectos de la racionalidad de la acción', in *Teoría de la acción comunicativa: complementos y estudios previos*, Madrid: Cátedra.

—— (1989b) '¿Qué significa pragmática universal?', in *Teoría de la acción comunicativa: complementos y estudios previos*, Madrid: Cátedra.

Johnson, M. (1987) *The Body in the Mind: The Bodily Bases of Meaning, Imagination and Reason*, Chicago: University of Chicago Press.

Lave, J. (1989) *Cognition in Practice*, New York: Cambridge University Press.

López Coira, M., and Díaz de Rada, A. (1990). 'Los antropólogos vistos por sí mismos. Un planteamiento para el análisis de la reversibilidad', in J. Bestard and J. Frigolé, coord., *Trabajo de campo*, Granada: Universidad de Granada, Actas del V Congreso Nacional de Antropología.

Mauss, M. (1979) 'Ensayo sobre los dones. Razón y forma del cambio en las sociedades primitivas', in *Sociología y antropología*, Madrid: Tecnos.

Polanyi, K. (1976) 'El sistema económico como proceso institucionalizado', in M. Godelier, ed., *Antropología y economía*, Barcelona: Anagrama.

Sahlins, Marshall D. (1976) *Culture and Practical Reason*, Chicago: University of Chicago Press.

—— (1988) *Cultura y razón práctica*, Barcelona: Gedisa.

Stocking, G.W., Jr (1985) 'The ethnographer's magic: fieldwork in British anthropology from Tylor to Malinowski', in G.W. Stocking Jr, ed., *Observers Observed: Essays on Ethnographic Fieldwork*, London: University of Wisconsin Press.

Tambiah, S.J. (1985) 'A performative approach to ritual', in *Culture, Thought and Social Action: An Anthropological Perspective*, Cambridge, Mass., and London: Harvard University Press.

—— (1990) *Magic, Science, Religion, and the Scope of Rationality*, Cambridge: Cambridge University Press.

Velasco, H.M. (1986) 'Rituales e identidad: dos teorías y algunas paradojas', *Revista de occidente*, January: 65–75.

Weber, M. (1985) 'Roscher y Knies y los problemas lógicos de la escuela histórica de economía', in *El problema de la irracionalidad en las ciencias sociales*, Madrid: Tecnos.

Willis, P. (1978) *Aprendiendo a trabajar. Cómo los chicos de la clase obrera consiguen trabajos de clase obrera*, Madrid: Akal.

Chapter 7

On the relevance of common sense for anthropological knowledge

Marian Kempny and Wojciech J. Burszta

The aim of science is to provide a representation of reality, but the social sciences deal not only with mere objects, but first and foremost with social (cultural) realities as products and subjects of human experience – of sensation, feeling, thought and action. That cultural reality cannot be represented simply, and that it can only be grasped through the experience of dwelling in the world, is one contribution of anthropology as social science. In the light of the above, what anthropology is really all about is to render mutually intelligible the different ways of experiencing the one human world. Consequently, anthropological knowledge seems to serve as a means to reconcile the alleged unity of mankind with an enormous variety of cultural forms.

From the very outset anthropology has faced a bundle of problems in its endeavour to deal with social experience in other cultures. These problems can be seen as a direct result of this interpretative exercise; as Kirsten Hastrup (1987) puts it, the crucial problem is – how anthropology comes to terms with life.

Until recently, the concept of common sense had only appeared sporadically in anthropological works as a subject-matter or theoretical category. Its relevance to the problem mentioned above will frame the following discussion. That is, by clearing up the notion of common sense as it is used by Clifford Geertz, we want to contribute to the understanding of anthropological cognition.

We suggest that the specific character of the reality facing an anthropologist in another culture is an unavoidable result of his/her own reality or 'common sense'. To put it another way, our starting-point is that a certain category is needed as a bridgehead between the subjective experience and anthropological knowledge, 'objectivizing' the former. As we will try to argue, it is 'common sense' that fulfils this task, being a common core or cultural knowledge universally shared.

We will show the importance and properties of common sense understood as the experiential mood upon which other cultural forms are parasitic, while tracing it back through the models used for conceptualizing the relationship between anthropologist and cognized culture.

ANTHROPOLOGICAL KNOWLEDGE AND CULTURAL REALITY: THE EXTERNAL STANDPOINT

To get a better understanding of the background to this problem it should be noted that early attempts at interpretation employed what we might call 'natural objectivity'. That is, the cultural reality which the anthropologist encountered in the field was treated as external, as one which 'objectively' existed 'out there'. As a result, anthropologist/researcher attempts at subjective construction of other cultures stressed the importance of functions as the 'naturally objectivized' phenomena are investigated, rather than investigating their socio-subjective cultural meanings. In the process of objectifying in this way the researcher stripped them of their humanistic coefficients because it was believed they distorted reality. Let's take a simple example: Bronislaw Malinowski, the founder of the functionalist school, described culture as a system whole which was particular and context-conditioned. However, his approach to culture so defined was a particular one. Functionalism treated 'the native's point of view' as important for the anthropologist at initial stages of research. The real goal of 'scientific' anthropology was after all to discover the laws which governed culture and social life, whereas natives had no idea about them because '[they] obey the forces and commands of the tribal code, but they do not comprehend them; exactly as they obey their instincts and their impulses, but could not lay down a single law of psychology' (Malinowski 1922: 11).

The metatheoretical premises that gave rise to this approach are clear. That is, and following the rules of objectivist epistemology, anthropological studies aimed at reaching an autonomously existing object which is independent of any subject, be it a representative of the culture investigated or the anthropologist himself.

This statement holds true for both Malinowski's functionalism and Lévi-Strauss's structuralism.

At the same time, all these 'modernistic' theories present culture (society) in a rather pictorial way. The objects of these theories are certain wholes, whose parts 'function', 'become separate', undergo 'structuralization' or merely exist (to a greater or lesser extent timelessly). R.J. Thornton (1988: 292) has observed that these images refer to certain metaphorical images:

> These images of social wholes are usually framed in terms of metaphorical images of organic bodies (function, functionalism), texts (signs and symbols, hermeneutics), trees (branches, evolution), rivers (flow, history), geological and architectural formations (strata, structuralism and Marxism) or machines (process, economics).

When we refer to the most common models which are used to help explain the nature of cultural phenomena, i.e. to the metaphorical images of the organism and language, we can see clearly that such theories must be formulated, so to say, 'from outside' because in each case the observer is outside the object he is investigating, or even looks at the investigated reality through a kind of transparent medium – the ethnographic text. What comes to mind here is Bentham's metaphor of 'a scientific prison', of which Michel Foucault has made us aware anew.

It becomes clear in this context that the 1980s failed to produce any new theoretical '-isms' which would enjoy such unrivalled dominance (cf. Ardener 1985). It was also a period in which anthropologists ceased to treat their interpretations as the 'objective' reflection of the external reality. The division between the observers and the observed has disappeared. Moreover, according to Geertz's claim, even the line between mode of representation and substantive content is hardly drawable in current anthropological approaches to culture. Consequently, the status of anthropological knowledge seems to be under threat, as these comments imply it has nothing to do with social reality as experience, but rather its source is scholarly artifice (cf. Geertz 1973: 16). Hence the need to answer the following question: what relationship can be established between the 'truth' and the 'fiction' of the knowledge which is being acquired by anthropology?

ANTHROPOLOGICAL KNOWLEDGE AS A SYMBOLIC FORM

What can be said about the above will again be a simplification. The collapse of the neopositivist model of practising science has led to a fundamental change in the way we understand the nature of anthropological knowledge. We can say that for modern anthropology the metaphor of 'a mirror in which Man sees his reflection' has taken on a new relevance. Just like present-day postmodern philosophy, which has been forced to admit that there is no mirror which faithfully reflects reality (cf. Rorty 1979, 1989), anthropology too has ceased to be treated as a mirror reflection of other cultures existing 'out there'.

Nowadays everyone is expected to understand the necessity of studying the cognitive relationship which binds the anthropologist to the object under scrutiny: that is, to look at anthropological 'others' while, at the same time, watching (as in a 'mirror') him/herself looking at the reality of other cultures. This is why anthropology has to be assisted by meta-anthropology, which is a reflection on the cultural condition of anthropology itself. In other words, many researchers have come to realize the necessity of something which is called an 'anthropology of anthropology'.

An 'anthropology of anthropology' should help explain the nature of anthropological study as culturally specific, historically placed, socially constituted and reflecting philosophically defined paradigms which define the intellectual boundaries of the specific forms of European thinking (cf. Scholte 1983). In other words, anthropological knowledge should be treated as a symbolic form which, to a certain extent, will always be a product of the anthropologist's culture. Consequently, it means that the clear and sharp division between the researcher and the researched, between the researcher's culture and other cultures, will be forgotten.

The reflexive quality of anthropology which makes the anthropologist acutely aware that his own cultural reality, i.e. the system of imaginings generated by his/her culture, cannot be anything but a subjective product of its participants also forces him/her to perceive the cognitive situation as a kind of cultural participation. Thus emphasis must be laid on getting anthropologists involved in the social situation which they are studying. It would seem that one of the results of such processes is the departure from the concept of studying 'social wholes'. The departure, in turn, directs the anthropologist's attention to researches into the sphere of cultural phenomena which is referred to as 'discourse' or 'practice' (see Ortner 1984).

The consequences for the perception of the nature of culture and for the ways of studying it are clear. By its very nature this kind of approach opposes the idea of 'objective' culture as something shared by a community of individuals who have similar cultural equipment. It also opposes the model on which structuralism especially is based, i.e. one which regards culture as a global structure – one that is similar to *langue*, as Saussure understood it, which allows to bring out the meaning of an element of culture by relating it to other elements of the system and to internal relations that exist within this very structure.

THE ANTHROPOLOGIST'S JOB IS NEVER DONE: INTERPRETATION

Reference to 'discourse' or 'practice' directs the anthropologists to another structure which is much more heterogeneous, individual and accidental, although no less complex. An important question now arises: how, through discourse episodes, is this structure created, and what are its features to be? We will attempt to answer this question by referring to Clifford Geertz's (1983) concept of culture – the evolution of his ideas corresponds to the changes in anthropology which are mentioned above.

Geertz's approach in *Local Knowledge* is usually described as antifundamentalist, i.e. as rejecting the doctrine of 'untainted' observation. The very nature of the knowledge of intentional phenomena, the kind of phenomena the anthropologist deals with, makes this knowledge fragmentary and bases it on the 'shifting sands' of interpretations. Every attempt at an analysis of culture begins with our own interpretations of our informants: who they are, or who they think they are. In other words, we at once make indistinct the difference between, let's say, the culture of Bali as a 'natural' fact and culture as a theoretical unit. Just like Sperber (1985), Geertz (1983) treats ethnographic writings as interpretations of second or third order, if we accept that only the proverbial 'native' who lives amidst his own culture is able to interpret it in a totally original way, 'at first hand'. If we take the original meaning of the Latin word *fictiō* – the creation, the shaping of something which does not necessarily have to be invented – as untrue, we will see that Geertz identifies anthropological interpretations as fiction in this sense, i.e. with a kind of literary fiction. The world presented by the anthropologist in his/her work cannot be verified simply by comparing it to the external reality. Anthropologists are not always aware of the fact that culture exists, develops, undergoes certain transformations, whereas anthropology exists in books, scientific papers, lectures, museum exhibitions, video cassettes or films. What we deal with is culture which is interpreted in some way or other (see Geertz 1973: 16).

As a result, the problem of valid anthropological interpretation comes down to establishing shared meanings between the participants in the discourse, i.e. between the subjects of a culture and the researcher. The ethnographer gets involved in the social discourse and records it, thus passing from temporary events to their description which exists in the recording: it is only these descriptions as records that can be verified again. We record the meaning of a cultural act, not the act itself. Moreover, Geertz reminds us, anthropologists are unable to be true subjects of the culture they are studying, and thus anthropologists do not record 'raw' discourse but only the part of it which their informants make understandable for them. According to Geertz the fact that he/she is not fully participating in the discourse should not discourage the anthropologist – 'it is not necessary to know everything in order to understand something' (ibid.: 20). Anthropology is not about discovering the 'continent of meaning', but a gradual drawing of conclusions from the guessing of meanings which are increasingly well understood.

The main characteristic of the interpretative approach is integration: how the interpretations are constructed and how they are textually represented in a discourse about the subjects which have been studied. The point is to maintain a balance between a reflection on self and other in the discourse, and the meaning itself in the same text. The most important task in implementing interpretative theory is not to produce a codification of abstract regularities, but to make thick, multi-dimensional contextual interpretative descriptions possible.

In order to emphasize the anti-reductionism of his own attitude towards research, Geertz (1983) does not hesitate to call interpretative anthropology 'a strange science' which the deeper it penetrates the more incomplete it becomes – completeness of cultural analysis is an illusion of science, a throwback to the days when positivist concepts dominated it. As a result, symbolic culture is considered to be an autonomous sphere that cannot be explained by historical determinants, biological urges, unconsciousness or economic laws. Geertz's concept of ideology as an expression of cultural identity (ibid.: 193–233) is a classic example of cultural system becoming autonomous.

Following Wittgenstein, Geertz knows very well that the anthropologist cannot become 'a native' and that he is unable 'to see the culture he is studying through the eyes of its subjects'; therefore he cannot follow exactly conceptual patterns which are totally alien to him. One of the things anthropology can do, however, is broaden human discourse; a thick description reveals the interrelated sets of symbols anchored to the context of local culture. As a result, understanding human culture stresses its typical quality without reducing its particularity.

According to Geertz's concept, it is local knowledge that sets the framework of a cultural system by defining the public world of individuals. This perception of a cultural system, however, aggravates the difficulties arising from the proposition to 'thicken' the network of meanings in order to copy better and better the complex whole of characterizations and imaginings. The whole, however, remains

> vernacular characterizations of what happens to be connected to vernacular imaginings of what can happen . . . This is doubtless more than a little vague, but as Wittgenstein, the patron saint of what is going on here, remarked, a veridical picture of an indistinct object is not after all a clear one but an indistinct one. Better to paint the sea like Turner than attempt to make of it a Constable cow.
>
> (Geertz 1983: 215)

COMMON SENSE AS A HARD CORE OF ANTHROPOLOGICAL KNOWLEDGE

The example above of the way Geertz is attempting to describe the picture of an indistinct object results from his analysis of common sense as a special kind of cultural system. His treatment of common sense as an object of anthropological studies on a par with traditional subject-matters of research – magic, religion, art and myth – also reflects the theoretical/methodological challenges with which this discipline is confronted nowadays.

Geertz's use of common sense is also an attempt to rephrase and deal with some of the previous paradigmatic controversies in which anthropology has been engaged. For example, he believes the question of primitive rationality to be wrongly put. In essence his dispute is not whether the so-called traditional societies have some elementary education, law or ideological doctrines, but rather – which in the categories of 'cultural holism' is entirely senseless – to what extent, if at all, cognition in primitive communities is integrated into a system (see Geertz 1983: 75).

Common sense is regarded by him as a category which enables a particular explication of the problem. 'It is, in short, a cultural system, though not usually a very tightly integrated one, and it rests on the same basis that any other such system rests; the conviction by those whose profession it is of its value and validity' (ibid.: 76). In short, it refers to 'a desire to make the world fully understandable'. Therefore, argues Geertz, it is a conceptual framework which is as totalizing as any other such form: 'it pretends to reach past illusion to truth to, as we say, things as they are' (ibid.: 84).

Geertz makes it clear, however, that the question of common sense is far more problematic and requires more detailed studies than might appear from the perspective of the modern Western European culture. It is absolutely necessary, for instance, to distinguish between the immediacies of experience and the reflective treatment of them. In other words 'common sense' understood as an individual experiencing of the daily-world reality (which is characterized by a feeling that this world is ready-made, unquestionable and independent of us, something that we experience immediately and truly) is to be contrasted with common sense as a relatively integrated system of reflections over reality (i.e. colloquial wisdom):

> If common sense is as much an interpretation of the immediacies of experience, a gloss on them, as are myth, painting, epistemology, or whatever, then it is, like them, historically constructed and, like them, subjected to historically defined standards of judgement. It can be questioned, disputed,

affirmed, developed, formalized, contemplated, even taught, and it can vary dramatically from one people to the next.

(ibid.: 76)

Hence the importance of this category of phenomena for the development of each human culture. In his *Philosophical Investigations* Wittgenstein uses a metaphor of language as a town in which common sense as one of 'the oldest suburbs of human culture' is characterized by a desire to master the world cognitively, 'moving beyond the maze of little streets and squares toward some less casual shape' (quoted ibid.: 77). Therefore it is also a universal cultural form, omnipresent despite the changing quality of its content and of the sphere to which it is to relate.

Though, on its way to universality, common sense runs into the problem of subjectivism, Geertz avoids this by defining common sense as 'wisdom of the anthill', which refers to certain fundamental assumptions which integrate individual cultures rather than to some thought reality of an individual: 'Common sense is not what the mind cleared of cant spontaneously apprehends, it is what the mind filled with presuppositions . . . concludes' (ibid.: 84).

As a result, common sense offers a rough description of reality which allows its members to identify and classify their environment in a common form. Thanks to this they may operate on it in a number of ways: in other words, it is common sense that primarily gives access for both the insider and the outsider to a social reality which may be then experienced and represented by means of different cultural frames of reference (e.g. magical, aesthetic, scientific, etc.).

This role common sense plays can be proved even if the cultures being studied are remote. This can be exemplified with a particular case, e.g. traditional peasant culture in Poland (especially that of the nineteenth century). Such a study was based on the assumption that members of the so-called traditional peasant culture had developed a specific system of normative and directive propositions, which were reflected in particular types of cultural forms and practices. For instance, religious behaviour was regulated in a subjective way by means of suitable judgments (norms and directives) which operated globally by settling in the social consciousness a set of symbols that is called religion and is individually respected by its members. Furthermore, all actions and products were shown to be under the control of members of a particular culture who build up, more or less consciously, an appropriate 'stock' of judgments. It can be argued in the case of the above-mentioned Polish peasant culture that a large framework of such judgments mainly refers to 'common-sensical' ways of experiencing reality.

First of all, the background to the common-sense realm of this folk culture revealed the following basic features: (a) isolation; (b) Catholicism; (c) the verbal transmission of tradition. The consequences of the horizontal (geographical) isolation and the vertical one (i.e. the social distance) are easily traced or observed in the attitudes of peasants towards the reality they lived in, which could be described as conservatism, ritualism, sensualism and moral relativism (cf. Stomma 1986). Though common sense serves as a practical instrument of making the world familiar and understandable, at the same time interpretations peasants used to carry out of the immediacies of 'empirical' experience have always been 'ideologically' biased (e.g. distorted by magical–religious beliefs). This is also visible in their language expressions and usages. Bourdon and Lazarsfeld (1965) have called some of these idioms 'mother formulas', which express for instance that 'things are to be as they are', and 'things are as they are to be'.

However a problem arises because anthropologists also tend to apply 'mother formulas' as complex descriptive concepts in the process of making first-order interpretations. One such example are folklorists who subsume the experienced reality of contemporary Polish peasant culture under a self-confirming model of 'traditional peasant culture'. This means that its particular elements are treated as belonging to 'folklore', i.e. as being constitutive for a specific type of cultural system, for they are thought to be constitutive parts of what is modelled by ethnography as traditional culture (cf. Burszta 1992: ch. 6).

Examples such as these present us with the problem of how to shift from the content of common sense, which is culturally changeable, to its characteristics as a cultural system which are transculturally present. Geertz (1983: 92) points out that any attempt to demonstrate that common sense is a cultural system which is internally integrated and which can be empirically defined and conceptually formulated must itself have a peculiar character. On the one hand, this cannot be achieved through the usual classsification of all the contents, because in this respect the system is highly heterogeneous (the contents of common sense are not homogeneous even within the same community); on the other, there is no logical structure which can be said to be always reflected in common reason. Moreover, a simple summing-up of substantial conclusions is out of the question, since no such conclusions are drawn.

As a result, 'it is only in isolating what might be called its stylistic features, the marks of attitude that give it its peculiar stamp, that common sense (or indeed any of its sister genres) can be trans-culturally characterized' (ibid.: 85). Clearly enough, such an approach encounters serious theoretical/methodological difficul-ties, since there is no glossary of terms that could be used to describe the stylistic features, marks of attitudes or shades of tonality which define this genre of cultural expression. This is why Geertz has to employ terms which are usually used to describe common sense as 'natural', 'practical', 'immethodical', etc. How-ever, he gives each of them a meaning which is different from the commonly accepted one, treating them as quasi-qualities that make up the peculiar character of common sense. For Geertz (ibid.: 85) and others common sense is characterized, amongst other things, by 'naturalness', 'practicalness', 'thinness', 'im-methodicalness', 'accessibleness', features which can generally be ascribed to it as 'an everywhere-found cultural form'.

If, Geertz says, we take the first and perhaps the most fundamental of these quasi-qualities – naturalness – as an example, we will see clearly what kind of categories they are. Common sense shows some elements of reality to be exactly as its elements are in the usual course of events. However, the 'commonness' of these characterizations results from a peculiar air of 'of-courseness' that accompanies them (see ibid.: 85) rather than from the contents considered to be natural. This is why the essence of common sense has to be determined somewhat indirectly by referring to its commonly recognized 'tone' and 'temper' (ibid.: 92).

In fact, seen in this context, all these features are interrelated, and this reflects the very nature of cultural practices which are multifunctional. This is why common sense can be regarded as the hard core of general knowledge of all cultures: that part which deals with everyday reality first of all in a pragmatic way. Hence the need for discussions about common sense (as a kind of bridge-head between anthropologist's knowledge and social experience) to take into account some of the implications stemming from the recent controversies over the conventional character of knowledge and cognition.

THE CONSTRUCTION OF REALITY AND ANTHROPOLOGICAL COGNITION

What is also of crucial importance from the point of view of our considerations is the conventional account of knowledge as developed by the so-called 'strong programme' in the sociology of knowledge (B. Barnes, D. Bloor, *et al.*). These indicate that in no sense are beliefs for this or that purpose. Bodies of knowledge lack intrinsic features which would permit them to be described as 'pure' knowledge for predictive interests or 'ideologically biased' knowledge that serves for fulfilling needs for which common sense is a response. Consequently, common sense should be treated as an alternative mode of using a body of knowledge that is not necessarily in conflict with 'science'.

It seems that anthropologists are often inclined to neglect this multifunctionality of knowledge; for instance while during a search for native animal taxonomies researchers failed to distinguish between their knowledge of nature as 'objective' facts and as culturally produced facts. Such failures are responsible for what are considered the shortcomings in primitive thought, i.e. statements such as 'twins are parrots', or 'the cassowary is not a bird'. The latter of these (cf. Blumer 1967) is especially instructive: while trying to explain why, for the Karam, the cassowary occupies a special taxonomic status, the anthropologist relied on an assumed separation between effects that nature and culture have on Karam cognition. The answer to his problem is allegedly that cassowaries perform a special role in Karam culture as representations of cross-cousins. Men's relations with cassowaries are structured in isomorphism to their relations with cross-cousins, and this is a reason why the cassowary is given a special taxonomic status (the taxon *kobity* set apart from the taxon *yakt* of birds and bats).

For the sake of brevity, the details of this particular explanation must be set aside. However, the following should be noted: the extent that Karam knowledge corresponds to ours is intelligible by reference to nature, whilst the extent that it does not is intelligible by reference to culture. Reasoning of this type indicates that anthropologists used to disregard the multifunctional nature of cultural practices, being forced to choose what was believed to be a basic component of social cognition, i.e. a logocentric under-standing of cultural forms. Needless to say, the rationale for such a choice is taken from the common-sense system of his/her own culture in which he/she is immersed.

Therefore, if Geertz calls for comparative studies of common sense as a genre of cultural expression which is as genuine as science, art, ideology, etc. (see Geertz 1983: 92–3), the problem of linking this new form with 'the anthropological way of looking at things' and the difficulty of defining what this anthropological way of studying cultural phenomena should be (cf. Geertz 1985) are bound to recur. Geertz's suggestions about analysing common sense as category provide some hints, but also make us realize the difficulties with which the anthropologist is faced while attempting to follow these suggestions.

Keeping in mind what was said earlier, we can see that this attitude is closely connected with the broadly formulated criticism of the concept of culture as 'shared knowledge' or 'public behav-iour' (see, e.g., Keesing 1987), since it lays emphasis on the diversity, on the internal heterogeneity, or even on the 'competi-tiveness' of some forms of cultural knowledge – or, to quote Geertz's term again, on the 'localness' of cultural knowledge. The very notion of 'the culture of a community' is then in danger of being highly problematic, in that each concept, even in inter-personal communication between a researcher and a native, is subject to continuous change as far as creation of meaning is concerned. Here the significance of common sense as a shared experiential basis is unquestionable.

What follows from this is that the interpretations of the entan-gled, irregular networks of meanings, created and re-created by the interrogating anthropologist, also have to be rooted in the cultural practice of his/her own society. As a result, anthropo-logical knowledge has something of the nature of local knowledge; it is limited by the 'local frames of consciousness' of the anthropologist/researcher and permeated by an 'air of facticity' to the same extent as the knowledge of the investigated. We can therefore venture a thesis: that a description of other cultures is to some extent the projection of the common sense which is part of the researcher's own culture.

This may be the reason why anthropology enjoys growing popu-larity. It provides the opportunity of viewing and creating all sorts of imaginable worlds in a 'familiar' way. S.A. Tyler observes

(1986: 134) that contemporary (i.e. postmodern) anthropology 'is an enigmatic, paradoxical, and esoteric conjunction of reality and fantasy. . . . It departs from the common-sense world only in order to reconfirm it and to return us to it renewed and mindful of our renewal.'

Hence the ability of postmodern anthropology to evoke certain conditions which, however, are never expressed in an ethnographic text ('Ethnography evokes what can never be put into a text' – Tyler 1986: 138). Marilyn Strathern's comment is noteworthy here (1991: 14): '[thus] ethnographic evocation can be imagined as therapy . . . healing the alienating breach between self and other, subject and object, language and the world'.

This means that a specific choice should be made as to the ultimate goal of anthropology, other than the growth of knowledge or 'objective' representation of reality. The stress on the multifunctionality and conventional character of knowledge implies the necessity of giving up the ideal of seizing a state of identity between the conceptual system of the researcher and that of a community being studied. However, the anthropologist's job hardly boils down to answering the general question with which contemporary anthropology is faced: how can the researcher's self-control minimalize the 'darkening' of the picture of other cultures caused by the spectacles of our culture? (See Geertz 1988: 145.)

Does studying other cultures have to become a kind of personal confession of the intricate 'us–them' relationship? What really counts while trying to answer questions formulated in this way, which have bothered researchers for a long time (but which today seem to be putting restraints on accepted research practice), is shifting them towards writing anthropological texts.

Postmodernist slogans, especially those which American philosophy and literary criticism have produced, fall on eager ears because many anthropologists tilt in favour of literary rather than scientific discourse, and as with anthropologists' common sense a supposition prevails that anthropological knowledge is 'theoretically' distorted and is further transformed during the writing of 'culture' in a book. As a result researchers such as Clifford, Marcus, Pratt or Taussig are interested not in culture as the problem of an object to be adequately characterized, but in the question of how anthropologists' imaginings of culture are put into a text which, subsequently, functions in its own right in 'anthropologists' culture'.

Unlike Geertz, his more radically thinking followers would also question any objectivist base of their own discipline, and that would simply mean the end of anthropology understood as a 'mirror for cultures'. Instead, the main problem for anthropology would be a response to the proposition that the object of anthropological explanation should be its inability to explain. But does this mean that the anthropologist is bound to remain within 'local knowledge' and within the common sense of his/her own culture?

Our answer has to be negative, lest anthropology is to depart from the common-sense world 'only in order to reconfirm it'. We should reject such a position, while accepting the claim Geertz has made for broadening the human discourse as the ultimate aim of anthropology. At the same time it must be accepted that it should retain the basic concern for the study of human action in its most mundane expressions.

Since all the categories anthropologists are dealing with seem to be conventional orderings, it follows that concept application in a particular culture must be studied as the contingent activity (mainly linguistic, but not only) of those using the concept or imagining. Because concepts are employed open-endedly, there is a need for such an understanding that could make sense of the creative extension of cultural usages as well as help properly appreciate what is involved in the most routine examples of concept and category application. An adequate characterization of what is routine appears to be the central problem of the human sciences in general. Relations between mundane routine practices and common sense are easily discerned since in both spheres unthinking, unreflexive identifications are a real basis of cultural reality, which is actual but contingent and corrigible. Here the ability to enrich the anthropologist's own cultural experience by meeting cultural 'others' is of crucial importance.

The tendency is to decline the objectivist concept of cognition and, following in Bourdieu's footsteps, to assume that the so-called ethnographic facts are a hybrid effect of the anthropologist's encounter with the subjects he/she is studying, and therefore are not a record of a 'pure' experiencing of the others. The person who is investigated first has to learn to explicate his own culture and to objectivize the world he lives in. The researcher and the researched develop shared concepts on a strictly conventionalist basis; sometimes this is called developing common symbols by means of which they communicate during the research (cf. Rabinow 1977: 152–3).

This is a must: otherwise hidden under the cover of so-called 'object language' (or, as Davidson put it, the first-order language) anthropological common sense will be reproducing the figments of an anthropological myth which is deeply at variance with the facts of cultural reality in an alien, but at the same time a common world. Such meditation needs proper implementation; the above discussion, for instance, implies the emptiness of the notion of perfect translation. The anthropological knowledge of another culture is something different both from the anthropologist's cultural knowledge and from a native representation. The consequences of this fact have been widely discussed (e.g. Hastrup 1990), and their detailed analysis is out of the scope of this chapter. However, by tackling problems such as the common-sense component of cognition, anthropology can pursue genuinely universal problems of each human culture, whether modern (scientific) or 'savage'.

CONCLUSIONS

The above discussion has made clear why for a long time anthropology was indifferent towards intellectual trends elsewhere which, for instance in sociology, have brought about an unconditional linking of the foundations of social knowledge with the realm of common sense. To put it as simply as possible, for a long time anthropologists have been reluctant to admit that they are able to share the social experience of their 'natives' (either 'at home', or 'abroad') only by use of the system of reference called common sense, which consists in a symbolic frame referring to reality in the most 'down-to-earth' way; the frame being in a sense universal, though its content varies radically from one culture to the next. Needless to say, Geertz's elaboration of this category is only a first step in the right direction, for it reveals some traps the anthropologist encounters while trying to match representation with reality, the particular with the universal.

ACKNOWLEDGMENTS

We are indebted to Marilyn Strathern, Kirsten Hastrup and Peter Hervik for their comments on earlier versions of this paper. One of them was presented to the departmental seminar at the Social Anthropology Department, University of Manchester in February 1993.

REFERENCES

Ardener, E. (1985) 'Social anthropology and the decline of modernism', in J. Overning, ed., *Reason and Morality*, London: Tavistock.

Barnes, J.A. (1974) *Scientific Knowledge and Sociological Theory*, London: Routledge & Kegan Paul.

—— (1981) 'On the conventional character of knowledge and cognition', *Philosophy of the Social Sciences* 11: 303–33.

—— (1982) 'On the extensions of concepts and the growth of knowledge', *Sociological Review* 30, 1: 23–44.

Bloor, D. (1976) *Knowledge and Social Imagery*, London: Routledge.

—— (1984) 'A sociological theory of objectivity', in S.C. Brown, ed., *Objectivity and Cultural Divergence*, Cambridge: Cambridge University Press.

Blumer, R. (1967) 'Why is the cassowary not a bird?', *Man*, n.s. 2: 5–25.

Boudon, R. and Lazarsfield, P. (1965) *La vocabulaire des sciences sociales*, Paris-La Haye: Mouton & Co. and Mason des Sciences de l'Homme.

Bourdieu, P. (1990) *The Logic of Practice*, Cambridge: Polity Press.

Burszta, W.J. (1992) *Wymiary antropologicznego poznania kultury*, Poznan: Adam Mickiewicz University Press.

Clifford J. (1988) *The Predicament of Culture*, Cambridge, Mass.: Harvard University Press.

Derrida, J. (1972) 'Structure, sign, and play in the discourse of the human sciences', in R. Macksey and E. Donato, eds, *The Structuralist Controversy*, Baltimore, Md: Johns Hopkins University Press.

Geertz, C. (1973) *The Interpretation of Cultures*, New York: Basic Books.

—— (1983) *Local Knowledge: Further Essays in Interpretive Anthropology*, New York: Basic Books.

—— (1985) 'Waddling in', *Times Literary Supplement*, 7 June.

—— (1988) *Works and Lives*, Stanford, Calif.: Stanford University Press.

Hastrup, K. (1987) 'The challenge of the unreal', *Culture and History* 1: 50–62.

—— (1990) 'The ethnographic present: a reinvention', *Cultural Anthropology* 5, 1: 45–61.

Keesing, R. (1987) 'Anthropology as interpretive quest', *Current Anthropology* 28, 2: 161–76.

Malinowski, B. (1922) *Argonauts of the Western Pacific*, London: G. Routledge.

Marcus, G.E., and Cushman, D. (1982) 'Ethnographies as texts', *Annual Review of Anthropology* 11: 25–69.

Ortner, S.B. (1984) 'Theory in anthropology since the sixties', *Comparative Studies in Society and History* 26: 126–66.

Overing, J., ed. (1985) *Reason and Morality*, London: Tavistock.

Pratt, M.L. (1986) 'Fieldwork in common places', in J. Clifford and G.E. Marcus, eds, *Writing Culture: The Poetics and Politics of Ethnography*, Berkeley: University of California Press.

Rabinow, P. (1977) *Reflections on Fieldwork in Morocco*, Berkeley: University of California Press.

—— (1985) 'Fantasia dans la bibliothèque. Les representations sont des faits sociaux: modernité et post-modernité en anthropologie', *Études rurales* 97–8: 91–114.

Rorty, R. (1979) *Philosophy and the Mirror of Nature*, New York: Blackwell.

—— (1989) *Contingency, Irony, and Solidarity*, Cambridge: Cambridge University Press.

Saussure, F. de (1945) *Course in General Linguistics*, New York: McGraw-Hill.

Scholte, B. (1983) 'Cultural anthropology and the paradigm-concept: a brief history of their recent convergence', *Sociology of the Sciences* 7: 229–87.

Sperber, D. (1985) *On Anthropological Knowledge*, Cambridge: Cambridge University Press.

Stomma, L. (1986) *Antropologia kultury wsi polskiej XIX wieku*, Warsaw: Pax.

Strathern, M. (1991) *Partial Connections*, Savage, Md: Rowman & Littlefield.

Taussig, M. (1993) *Mimesis and Alterity*, London: Routledge.

Thornton, R.J. (1988) 'The rhetoric of ethnographic holism', *Cultural Anthropology* 3: 285–303.

Tyler, S.A. (1986) 'Post-modern ethnography: from document of the occult to occult document', in J. Clifford and G.E. Marcus, eds, *Writing Culture: The Poetics and Politics of Ethnography*, Berkeley: University of California Press.

Wittgenstein, L. (1953) *Philosophical Investigations*, New York: Macmillan.

Chapter 8

Where the community reveals itself
Reflexivity and moral judgment in Karpathos, Greece

Pavlos Kavouras

In the mid-1930s the patrons of a coffee-house in Olymbos, a large
mountain village on the Greek island of Karpathos, witnessed an
odd event.[1] The local rural guard, Nikolis, entered the coffee-
house carrying a leg of lamb on his shoulder, approached his co-
villager Manolis, who was in a carefree mood, and struck him on
the face with the leg of lamb without saying anything. Infuriated,
Manolis reported the assault to the local constabulary immediately.[2] To defend himself, Nikolis said to the chief constable:
'I struck him because he was spreading rumours in the community
that Sophila's newborn bastard was mine while it's his.' Manolis
was taken by surprise. He did not expect that Nikolis, in his effort
to discredit him as a slanderous person, would go so far as to
report to the authorities a community problem such as a moral
crime, to accuse him of being an adulterer. Much depressed,
Manolis admitted his affair with Sophila. Although many
Olymbians had suspected him to be the father of Sophila's newborn, only the *trimistiro* Nikolis dared to expose the moral
offender publicly.

The above story was narrated to me in the summer of 1989 by
one of the witnesses of the assault. As I enquired into the local
usages of *trimistiro* (the characterization attached to Nikolis by the
story-teller) I discovered that this notion pertained to a category of
persons who exercised unofficial social control by publicly criticiz-
ing the moral behaviour of their co-villagers. Despite being a
native speaker of Greek and a trained anthropologist studying the
Olymbos culture for about two years, the concept of *trimistiro* and
its sociocultural connotations had until then escaped my attention
almost entirely.[3]

This chapter reflects the process of my own understanding of *trimistiro* as a hidden aspect of Olymbos culture which involves the transformation of social experience into critical knowledge.[4] I shall argue that any person who is characterized as a *trimistiro* is a strategic user of reflexivity, who aims at legitimizing the moral judgments he or she makes about others, as well as about him/ herself, through rhetorically manipulating social experience and community knowledge. I shall refer to the persons embodying the notion of *trimistiro* as social critics and to their practices as enactments of social criticism, because by denouncing specific co-villagers as moral offenders they implicitly reprehend the social structures these people represent. I shall also use the term 'critical' as an analytical construct with the rhetorical connotation of skilful contrivance to account for the process and the results of the strategic manipulation of reflexivity by the *trimistiro*. Hence, in the story cited above, Nikolis' strategy of exposure may be viewed as a critical practice whereby he rhetorically manipulates the contexts of interpretation by juxtaposing Manolis' image with his own as offender and punisher alternately.

THE NOTION OF *TRIMISTIRO*: FOLK USAGES AND DEFINITIONS

Trimistiro is a Greek dialectal expression used only in Karpathos. According to the folklorist and historian Mihail Mihailidhis-Nouaros (1972: 382), the term applies chiefly to children, meaning cunning and naughty; a compound formed by the numerical adverb *tris* (thrice) and the noun *mistirio* (mystery), the word *trimistiro* signifies a child 'who is strange (*paradhoxo*), latent (*krifo*) and wondrous (*katapliktiko*) like any mystery'. Yet the contemporary usages of *trimistiro* in Karpathos are not limited to children. Olymbians also speak of middle-aged or older men and women as being *trimistira* (plural form of *trimistiro*): an unruly child, an adult thief, a grouchy old man or a capricious old woman are all typical examples of the polysemic significance of this expression.

The etymology of the word *trimistiro* sheds light on central aspects of its social meanings. The numerical adverb *tris* means in a threefold manner or degree, implying, loosely, in a repeated way or superlatively. As a superlative qualifier the prefix *tri-* expresses that the degree of the manner denoted by the word *mistirio* is exaggerated or excessive. Olymbians use the term to refer to the transgressors of sociocultural boundaries, especially to those exhibiting any kind of excessive, immoderate, inordinate, extravagant or exorbitant behaviour. The transgressors/*trimistira* are morally assessed in terms of their success or failure in transcending the limits of social experience and hence of community knowledge within a particular context of thought or action. Olympians praise transgressions as socially successful and, eventually, morally ideal practices if they are transcendental in character, censuring those that are trivial and transient as instances of immorality. For example, a mason whose craftsmanship is particularly ingenious, who instead of the conventional rectangular house-openings makes arched ones, will be publicly honoured as a *trimistiro* in construction.

In modern Olymbos, however, the negative connotations of *trimistiro* have prevailed over the positive ones. To most contemporary Olympians, *trimistiro* is an offensive expression, an insult. They use it to represent the extremely shrewd and intriguing individual who employs any means of communication, but chiefly the spoken word, to impose his or her views on other people. Olympians believe that the *trimistira* are strategic users of such sly methods of action as adulation, hypocrisy, slander and irony, and that they aim at asserting themselves by socially stigmatizing their adversaries. Other insulting nuances in the usage of *trimistiro* refer to a person's social behaviour that is locally perceived as capricious, malicious, deceitful or vulgar.

Reflecting upon its various connotations, the idea of *trimistiro* should be understood in relation to the specific contexts of its usage. Hence, the following working definition: *trimistiro* is a sociocultural category Olympians apply to co-villagers who seem to be extremely enigmatic, that is, mysterious in the sense of exciting wonder, curiosity or surprise, as well as baffling all attempted explanation; they also imply that the *trimistira* are inscrutable in that they defy all efforts to understand them, leaving one feeling hopeless or defeated.

Perhaps the most significant local conception of the *trimistiro* is that he or she is the embodiment of an unofficial modality of sociocultural control. This view is held by a notable minority of contemporary Olympians, a few *trimistira* and several astute observers and analysts of Olymbos culture, who all portray modern Olymbos in their narratives as being in a state of cultural crisis, attributing their anxieties about the destruction of the 'traditional' way of life to *modernismos* (modernism).[5] A young Olymbian exemplified this problem with a succinct but powerful statement: 'Olymbos leans on her *trimistira* for its survival.'

The local critics view *trimistira* as social catalysts facilitating or hindering cultural change. They ascribe this form of power to a *trimistiro*'s rhetorical manipulation of commonly available information concerning the moral reputation of each person's genealogical history. By constructing personal historical narratives about other community members, *trimistira* restructure folk knowledge, imposing upon their audiences their own interpretative perspectives. Olymbians are vocal in their anxiety about falling upon a *trimistiro* in a public place, as they fear his or her shaming reaction should he or she misconstrue their words and deeds. As a middle-aged Olymbian man put it, 'everybody is afraid of the *trimistira*; while people reproach *trimistira*, they neither renounce nor justify them'.

Therefore the *trimistira* appear to be the protagonists of moral and social criticism in Olymbos. They express reasoned opinions on any matter of concern to the community (for example a wedding arrangement), and pass judgment on its social value. The *trimistira*-critics judge social structures or institutions as embodied activities, assessing their value in relation to the moral worth of the persons engaged in them. To explore the rhetorical strategies of these critics I shall examine their intentions, ideas and actions as narrative structures of power. I shall begin with the premise that the *trimistira* are social actors who cast moral judgment on the basis of a practical rationality used by everybody in the community, suggesting that without this tradition-bound rationality it would be impossible for these critics to render their verdicts in a manner intelligible to their audiences (MacIntyre 1988: 1–12, 389–403). This view implies that the community context of rationalized moral criticism is the most significant dimension of the social existence of a *trimistiro*.

SOCIAL EXPERIENCE, NARRATIVE AND REFLEXIVITY

A theoretical framework that seems to be quite pertinent to the analysis of the folk notions of *trimistiro* is the dramaturgical approach of Erving Goffman.[6] What the *trimistira* of the Olymbian accounts and Goffman's social actors have in common

is that they 'stage' their behaviour in face-to-face social interactions in such a way as to manipulate their audiences' exercise of
thought or judgment – their reflexivity – and, eventually, the
definition of the situation. However, as the moral philosopher
Alasdair MacIntyre (1984: 115–17) has shown, Goffman's
approach is not applicable to tradition-bound social interactions
because of its modernist bias of emotivism. Alternatively,
MacIntyre's concept of 'characters' as ideal social figures (ibid.:
27–31) is closer to the notion of *trimistiro* than Goffman's perspective of the emotivist self.

My analysis of the *trimistiro* as a manipulator of reflexivity in
tradition-bound situations of moral and social criticism builds
upon both Goffman's idea of 'staging' and MacIntyre's concept of
'characters'. Far from being a theoretical hybrid, such a methodological blending of heterogeneous perspectives reflects a major
tendency in recent ethnographic practice (Ortner 1984; Clifford
and Marcus 1986; Marcus and Fischer 1986). Ethnographers writing in this vein have succeeded in accounting for the systems of
knowledge and patterns of experience of other people by making
the latter co-authors to such representations rather than treating
them as mere objects of study (e.g. Rabinow 1977; Crapanzano
1980; Herzfeld 1985). Some ethnographers have achieved this
sharing relationship by focusing on the stories people tell of themselves and for themselves, as metaphors of social existence.[7] In
their discourses, narrators construct rather than describe their
cultural realities, contesting the world-views of other people, as
well as their own (Crapanzano 1980; Rosaldo 1986: 97–8;
Myerhoff 1986: 261–2).[8]

The *trimistira* are masters of narrative.[9] By relating stories or
giving accounts of events intelligible to the community they construct discourses involving plot, setting and characterization which
they use as a controlled referential background for 'staging' social
criticism. Any such discourse has a personal narrative structure
which is based on a strategic juxtaposition of the life-histories of
the critic and the criticized.

The anthropological literature on narrative is quite extensive.[10]
To account for the rhetorical strategies of the *trimistiro* I shall rely
mostly on MacIntyre's (1984: 204–25) sociohistorical approach to
narrative analysis. MacIntyre (ibid.: 208) argues that in order to
understand a personal narrative one must situate the actor's
intentions in causal and temporal order in the context of his or her

personal history, as well as the history of the setting or settings (institutions, practices, milieux) to which these intentions belong.[11]

So far I have discussed the notion of *trimistiro* by summing up the Olymbos folk knowledge of it. I have also considered some theoretical problems pertaining to the analytical representation of the *trimistiro* as a rhetorical strategist and social critic. Now I shall examine the intentions, ideas and actions of an actual *trimistiro*, an Olymbian woman whom I shall call Kalitsa, by enquiring into her discourses and practices.

JUXTAPOSING REALITIES: THE SOCIAL AND NARRATIVE ACTION OF THE *TRIMISTIRO*

My first encounter with Kalitsa took place in her house in Olymbos. I set up this meeting very carefully. As I was aware of the capricious manner of this category of persons, I asked a community notable, Mihalis, a man related by marriage to Kalitsa's family, to let her know of my impending visit. At first Kalitsa was rather hostile towards me. She wanted to know why I wanted to hear her life history. I suddenly realized that my enquiring strategy was wrong. In the tradition-bound society of Olymbos life histories were sources of community knowledge and, therefore, sources of social power for a *trimistiro*. Thus I decided to tell her the purpose of my visit:

—Mihalis sends me to you. I want to ask you about the *trimistira*, who are they and what do they do?
—The *trimistira*, eh? That's me! Everyone in the village knows me as an irritable and irascible person (*arathimi*). As I've no vices of my own, I never put up with other people's.

 Listen to this story and you'll understand what a true *trimistiro* does. I'd been in deep mourning for seven years, for my brother who died of consumption at 31, when one day, on the last Sunday of Carnival, my father urged me to attend that evening's dance so as to forget my troubles. Reluctantly I agreed. I put on a black mantle, covered my head with its hood, and went to the dancing place. There I sat with the chaperones [to the girl dancers]. To honour my appearance, the dancers began singing praises of my niece, my late brother's only child. Among the dancers was Minas, a distant relative of mine and renowned musician and singer, who, on seeing me, asked a man to bring him some water. The man soon returned with a pitcher. Then, as Minas was dancing right behind me, he snatched the pitcher and emptied its contents on me, making me all wet. Enraged, I sprang up and attacked him fiercely. Oh, if only you'd been there to hear what I told him. I called him by his grandmother's father's name, Kostaras. I said: 'Oh you, Kostara![12] Oh you, Kostara with the *pikalami!*'[13] – He was a fisherman and used a fishing rod to catch fish. – 'Aren't you ashamed of yourself?' I couldn't stop myself. I kept on insulting him: 'You scoundrel! You insensitive man! You ass! You rotter! Like your *yenia* (lineage), you're all worthless.' Minas couldn't stand the insults and soon left the dance. Next morning, he went to see my father to complain about my defaming conduct. When my father said he'd no right to wet me at the dance, Minas replied that he did what he'd done for my own good. He explained he hadn't wanted to mock me or my family but simply my clothing, and that he'd wet me in order to urge me to end my mourning. But what he'd done was unacceptable. He could have told me what he intended to do; he could have asked me nicely to uncover my face. And I'd have told him – because I'd no intention of getting into trouble with him – to leave me alone, not to talk to me, to stop meddling in my affairs. But he didn't. So he got what he deserved.

Kalitsa's narrative helps raise several methodological questions about the comprehensive study of the transformation of social experience into critical knowledge in Olymbos.[14] One such question concerns the distinction between anthropology and folklore especially, the epistemological boundaries of any anthropological enquiry based on a body of information gained and preserved by folk knowledge (Herzfeld 1987: 64–7; Cowan 1990: 58–9; Stewart 1991: 122–30).[15] If one tried to understand Kalitsa's narrative through such a framework of analysis, one would certainly identify her as a *trimistiro* on the basis of her irascible and audacious social behaviour but would be unable to follow her rhetorical strategies aimed at shaming Minas. A second question, related to the first one, is whether the local folk knowledge about *trimistiro* is a lived ideology, that is, an actually experienced and uncritically enacted form of consciousness. This view suggests that Olymbians, in the accounts they give of the *trimistira*, may be mystifying, intentionally or unintentionally, the hegemonic structures of power in their society.[16] Finally, there is a question concerning the narrative realities of Kalitsa's text. Are the characters represented in her text mere references reflecting the 'objective' reality of the incident or, rather, the concrete symbolic embodiments of certain community ideas about morality and cultural hegemony strategically juxtaposed by Kalitsa through narration?

With the above questions in mind, let me turn to the analysis of Kalitsa's narrative. One way of exploring this narrative is to view it, following Crapanzano (1980: 5), not only as a fragment of the narrator's personal history but also as a part of her autobiography.[17] I shall begin by presenting Kalitsa's and Minas' personal histories in a genealogical context of action; next I shall explore the broader historical background of the hegemonic power relations in Olymbos in the period from the mid-1910s and early 1920s (the time in which Kalitsa and Minas were born) until the 1950s (when the conflict between the two of them occurred); then I shall discuss the ceremonial situations in which Olymbians express themselves as a symbolic community; and, finally, I shall interpret Kalitsa's story, situating the various nuances of her social and narrative action in specific 'personal historical' contexts.

NARRATING KALITSA: EVENTS, SITUATIONS AND CONTEXTS IN HISTORICAL PERSPECTIVE

Kalitsa is an illiterate Olymbian woman aged 77 years. She is unmarried and lives alone in a spacious and untidy house of her own in Olymbos. She comes from a traditional family of shepherds and talented poet–singers like her father Filipis and brother Orgis.

Kalitsa's autobiographical motive may be resolved into two components, her unmarried status and Orgis' life and death. On several occasions Kalitsa stressed to me that she remained single because she became a second mother to her niece, Orgis' only child, looking after her until the girl was married. To understand the significance of Orgis' life and death to Kalitsa herself one must approach this relationship from the perspective of Orgis' marriage and its social implications. Orgis was married in Olymbos in the mid-1940s. His wedding was controversial. He married up, being one of the first shepherds to take as wife a *kanakaria*, that is a first-born daughter from a family of *kanakaridhes*, the powerful and prestigious landowners of Olymbos (Capetanakis 1979;

Philippides 1973; Vernier 1984; Daskalopoulou-Kapetanaki 1987; Kavouras 1991; Skiada 1991). Although richly dowered and morally virtuous, the young *kanakaria* was not a perfect bride as she was socially defective in a very particular way. She carried the genealogical stigma of 'consumption', as both her sisters and mother had died of the disease. That Orgis died also of consumption two years after the wedding is a tragic coincidence of especial symbolic significance to Kalitsa.

In her narrative, Kalitsa associates Orgis' physical death and misfortune in marriage with her own social death and poor marital status, reversing the causal relationship between Orgis' death and unlucky marriage to account for her own unfortunate status as a mature unmarried woman in Olymbos.[18] On the one hand, Orgis' normatively successful marriage was ended by an unpreventable physical cause (an incurable disease) and, on the other, the cultural effect of this event on Kalitsa's life caused her own social death – she mourned her brother's loss for many years and became a second mother to Orgis' orphan girl. By connecting the two worlds in causal and temporal terms Kalitsa creates the dramatic background of her social and narrative contexts of action. Her inscrutability may be partly understood in relation to her commuting freely between these two worlds. Moreover, the symbolic association with the world of her dead brother enables Kalitsa to justify in practically rational terms her living a private and, eventually, paradoxical life in Olymbos.

To understand why Orgis' marriage was controversial, beyond the point of the genealogical stigmatization of the bride as a 'consumptive', one should approach this event as a manifestation of the dramatic sociocultural developments that occurred in Olymbos in the years of the Italian Occupation (1912–43). One such major institutional transition was the substitution of the Italian market economy for the long-standing tributary system of the Ottomans (Philippides 1973: 36–9; Vernier 1977). In the ensuing context of radical socioeconomic change, several repatriated rich emigrants from Olymbos became economically more powerful than the *kanakaridhes* (the landowners) and challenged the latter's political and symbolic hegemony. They spent a lot of money on community feasts and in donations to the Church, aiming at surpassing the *kanakaridhes* in social prestige (Vernier 1984; Kavouras 1992).

The process of the social reproduction of the hegemonic culture of the *kanakaridhes* is reflected in the customary inheritance system of Karpathos (Mihailidhis-Nouaros 1984; Vernier 1984). The long-standing practice of bilateral primogeniture ensured the indisputable continuation of the social hierarchy of the *kanakaridhes*, as nuptial candidates should be equally ranked in order to be acceptably married. As is typical in most kin-based hierarchical societies, in pre-war Olymbos the reproduction and legitimization of the existing power structures rested on marriage arrangements (cf. Campbell 1964: 263–8; Vernier 1984; Kavouras 1992). Any cross-marriages between people of different social rank were censured by the *kanakaridhes* as immoral relations, and the fallen protagonists were punished by disinheritance. Such was the social domination of the *kanakaridhes* until the 1910s (when several rich emigrants returned to Olymbos) that nobody could challenge their hegemonic practices. Furthermore, the community culture reflected the ideology of the *kanakaridhes* by reproducing and legitimizing their traditional hegemony. In the 1920s, for the first time in Olymbian history, several emigrants without land but with plenty of money married *kanakaries* (plural for *kanakaria*). Orgis' marriage, however, is a different case, for Orgis was not a rich emigrant but an ordinary shepherd. Although a socially unequal arrangement, this marriage reflects the *rapprochement*, albeit occasional and selective, of the *kanakaridhes* with the shepherds (their long-standing socioeconomic adversaries and cultural partners in pre-Italian Olymbos) in a common front against the modernist innovators, the returned emigrants (Philippides 1973: 42–7; Halkias 1980: 82–91; Kavouras 1992).

In the period between the early 1920s and the 1940s, when Orgis' wedding occurred, several rich repatriated Olymbians, whose wealth arose from commerce or business but not land, became controversially prestigious figures. They acquired prestige by exploiting the coincidence of circumstances that emerged in connection with a series of new laws and policies implemented by the Italian administrators. In the years between 1924 and 1939 Olymbians suffered considerably when the Italians tightened their grip on the Dodecanese. In a concerted effort to Italianize the islanders, the Italian rulers used various strategies of cultural imperialism: they suppressed traditional authority by appointing local confidants as mayors; they attempted to control school teachers and Orthodox Christian priests through paying them wages; they changed the teaching of language at school by substituting Italian for Greek; and they strictly censored all mail (Mihailidhis-Nouaros 1951: 9–18).

The fear of assimilation and the misery of a famine in the early 1940s caused the Karpathians much distress. To survive the famine the rich repatriated migrants sold their gold valuables for the barley and olive oil of the *kanakaridhes* on the local black market. The famine also had a significant side-effect. It enabled the *kanakaridhes* to declare that landownership was more valuable and, therefore, prestigious than the possession of any other commodity, including money and jewellery (Mihailidhis-Nouaros 1951: 15–18; Vernier 1977; Skiada 1991: 233–5). Hence, Orgis' marriage bridges temporally, and to a certain extent causally, the successive interrelations of power among the various social ranks in Olymbos in the period of the Italian Occupation. It is essential to note at this juncture that the body of folk knowledge pertaining to the sociocultural background of Orgis' marriage is available to everybody in the Olymbos community. It is this availability of community knowledge that Kalitsa exploits when she uses commonly known information for the purpose of contextualizing her social and narrative actions in readily intelligible terms. Allusion and irony based on community knowledge are Kalitsa's favourite rhetorical methods for manipulating the reflexivity of her audience.

THE SOCIAL PROCESS OF GENEALOGICAL STIGMATIZATION IN OLYMBOS: THE CASE OF MINAS

Minas is a literate Olymbian man aged 70 years. He is married and has several children. Although Olymbians praise Minas as an accomplished musician and exceptional poet–singer, they are usually ambivalent about him. To understand Minas as a controversial figure it is necessary to situate his social existence in a genealogical context of morality.

Minas carries a social stigma from his father, Annis, who was the first-born son of the prominent *kanakaris* Minatsis. In the 1910s, Minatsis disinherited Annis for marrying a girl of very low rank. Annis' wife, Ernia, was the offspring of a mixed marriage between an Olymbian man and a 'foreign' woman (*xeni*) from another Karpathian village. Ernia's parents were poor; both

her father and her maternal grandfather were fishermen. In the
Olymbos of the *kanakaridhes*, fishing was considered as the
socially lowest mode of making a living. Indeed, Annis' relatives
strongly opposed this marriage because of Ernia's compounded
low status as 'foreigner' and 'poor'. Minatsis' refusal to bless this
wedding forced Annis to elope with his sweetheart and get married
without his father's consent. Enraged by his son's disobedience,
Minatsis disinherited him. Annis had no choice but to emigrate in
order to ensure a living. In the period between the 1920s and the
1960s, he pursued a very successful career as a construction worker
and foreman in various countries, including Morocco and Persia.[20]
While Annis was abroad, Ernia raised her children alone in
Olymbos with her husband's remittances. Minatsis did not retract
from his decision to disinherit his son, and treated his daughter-in-
law as both a cultural and a family stranger; he ignored her.

Minas grew up as an independent person, making a sharp
contrast to most of his social peers in Olymbos. His civil manners
and elegant Western attire differentiated him immediately from
his conservative and traditionally dressed co-villagers. In the 1940s
Minas acquired notoriety for his liberal conduct. As a member of a
group of six young men who were the first-borns of successful
emigrants, Minas systematically challenged the conservative ethos
of the Olymbos culture (Kavouras 1991: 387–9). The liberal individualism of the young modernists, however, was not limited to
practices reflecting opposition to conventional opinions, views and
policies. It also extended to showing or revealing a spirit of giving
freely and without limit. The young modernists exhibited such
generosity by conspicuously spending a lot of money at local
festivities. Although both *kanakaridhes* and emigrants were generous at community festivals, they used generosity for opposite
sociopolitical ends: while the former aimed at reproducing and
legitimizing their hegemonic power, the latter challenged the
social domination of the *kanakaridhes*.

WHERE THE COMMUNITY REVEALS ITSELF:
THE SETTINGS OF THE *GLENDI* AND THE
PAROUSIA

Kalitsa's clash with Minas happened at a community dance in the
early 1950s. This form of conflict is not typical of gender confrontations in Olymbos, as it does not reflect the conventional public

cation of the formation under investigation). They remain, however, at the extreme periphery with regard to the capitalist centres and thereby form the underclass of the social formation. They only emerge as an ethnic group by consequence of being ethnicized. This ethnicization serves as a means to enshrine them in their subordinate position.

As the Kalahari debate proceeded, historical reconstruction of the detailed succession of events became the focus of the debate. When framed in the format of a map, these reconstructions reduce to a naturalistic spatial presentation typical of an historical atlas. And, indeed, the latest stage in the debate is a comparison of maps depicting the routes of traders and explorers representing the beginning of the influence of the world economic system on the culture and socioeconomic organization of various 'San' groups (see Lee and Guenther 1991). In the context of the historical argument the spatial dimension is reduced to a matter of scale and distance. If the availability and reliability of historical sources on the myriad of individual movements were our only point of consideration, we would be bound to accept a reduction of these movements into arrows of varying thickness on our map of history. These arrows can then be read as processes of gradual marginalization of an originally autonomous group governed and confined by a forager ethos – or as the formation of an underclass in the larger social formation following the economic interests of the dominant group. The two conflicting approaches in the debate have become to a certain degree compatible, as historical and geographical diversity is increasingly accepted (Kent 1992). In this diversity the *social experience* of 'Bushmen', represented either as marginalized pristine hunter–gatherers or as a peripheral underclass, is assumed to be very similar in all cases or at least to be non-problematic for the argument. In either scenario 'Bushmen' who engage in inter-ethnic relations suffer from domination and exploitation at the hands of cattle-owners.

At the same time the two approaches are no longer contradictory because they are more or less applicable as aspects valid in all instances that have been discussed. It therefore has to be questioned whether history will solve anthropology's problem of explaining the diversity of social constellations found on the ground (see Barnard 1992: 86). It appears that the historical record constitutes a necessary and welcome supplement for anthropological research into socioeconomic change among southern African foragers, but that ethnographic research into the continuing process of integration and interethnic interaction still has an important role to play. Temporal sequence is not a sufficient guide to causal succession. But the relationship between spatial distance and social space involving power politics, and social hierarchy still needs to be clarified.[4] To identify social space with natural space or to assume that the link between the two is arbitrary is not a helpful point of departure. More promising are those points in the Kalahari debate where a number of simultaneous transitions are recognized. Lee writes about the 'locus' of political power being shifted 'to agencies *external* to the Dobe area' while hunting and gathering as well as herding are intensified (1979: 403). Wilmsen grants that in western Botswana agropastoralism was being 'transferred' to Khoisan peoples while the hegemony of Bantu-speaking groups was already a reality in eastern Botswana (Wilmsen 1989: 75). As I want to demonstrate in the second half of this chapter, it is the anthropology of social experience in particular that opens up a dimension of the Kalahari debate which has been overshadowed in discussions about historical and archaeological evidence.

Nevertheless, it is a positive result of the Kalahari debate that the task set out by Fabian, as pointed out above, has been accomplished. The ethnography of southern Africa's foragers is firmly connected with livestock-holding, long-distance trade and market integration as hallmarks of 'our' time and space. At least the intellectual groundwork has been done to set irreversibly in motion a new phase of regional ethnography.[5] Most isolationists in their field research encountered interethnic trade, wage labour, serfdom, livestock-herding, livestock-ownership and their effects. The recent debate has provided room in anthropological discourse to account for these experiences and to link them to other aspects of anthropological research. The internal anthropological question, mentioned earlier, of reconciling field experience and anthropological discourse has surfaced and can be dealt with.

However, the issue of social experience versus anthropological description has not been tackled in the debate. The main issues of the debate have not been discussed in the light of the question as to how the !Kung, G/wi, Hai‖om, Nharo, and others *experienced* the *rapprochement* with neighbouring groups in either scenario. It is not only diversity that needs further explanation. There is insufficient linkage between the level of changing *conditions* of social experience on the one hand, and the level of social experience itself in the context of these changing conditions on the other. In what follows I consider the process whereby foragers are dealing with livestock-herding and ownership. I attempt to recapture the full spectrum of social experience as contained in the ethnography, as well as the linkage between the two levels mentioned.

THE SOCIAL PRACTICE OF EXCORPORATION AS A REACTION TO THE SOCIAL EXPERIENCE OF INCORPORATION

The advent and incorporation of cattle into the 'San' economy is at the very centre of the Kalahari debate. Single archaeological and archival records relating to the distribution of cattle have been examined in depth in order to establish whether they support the integrationist or the isolationist view (see Lee and Guenther 1991; Solway and Lee 1990; Wilmsen and Denbow 1990; Hitchcock 1990). Whether an early bone discovery is a hint towards the presence of cattle or of game, whether 'oxen' or 'onions' is the correct reading of an early document, were more than just sidetracks in the debate. Unfortunately the detailed and necessary discussion of these sources was not followed by an equally thorough argument as to what are the social implications for a group of hunter–gatherers who share a place with livestock, be they their own or those of others. It seems unlikely that the essence of social relations, or of ethnic identity for that matter, can be derived from the mere existence of cattle in an area, even if that existence can be proved.

A central ethnographic feature discussed in the context of the social implications of livestock (mainly cattle but also goats) entering the Kalahari is the so-called *mafisa* system. It has been repeatedly reported as *the* characteristic feature for the patron–client relationship between 'Bushmen' and neighbouring pastoralists (especially Tswana and Herero). In the *mafisa* system these Bantu-speaking cattle-owners come into a remote area with their cattle and leave them there for the 'San' or other minority groups that do not own cattle (such as the Kgalagadi) to look after. In its best-known form the herdsmen are allowed to use the milk and, if a cow dies, also the meat for their consumption while the owner is away. On the owner's return they might be paid a calf or two (Lee 1979: 407).[6]

Among the Hai‖om in neighbouring Namibia we find what may be called an inverse *mafisa* system. Here it is often the case that those Hai‖om who own a few heads of goats or even cattle (which is exceptional) leave their animals with the dominant Owambo agropastoralists to look after. The Owambo are allowed to use whatever the animal produces, including the offspring (although this is often a matter of debate and conflict between Hai‖om and Owambo).

However, what at first glance appear to be two opposite practices follow the same underlying dynamics of '*excorporation*'.[7] The 'traditional *mafisa*', as documented for !Kung–Tswana relations, and the 'inverse *mafisa*' among Hai‖om and Owambo are two examples, but by no means the only ones, of strategies of dealing with livestock as a form of delayed return that becomes available to foragers in their interaction with neighbouring groups. The *mafisa* system provides a regular surplus of milk (and sometimes meat). The techniques of cattle-tending are readily incorporated and to some degree provide an alternative to hunting and gathering. By contrast to this, the underlying strategy which requires the need to accumulate, to appropriate and to secure delayed return in the way agropastoralists do is *excorporated* because it remains in the hands of the pastoralists. The consumption of the products of a delayed-return activity (such as cattle-keeping) is controlled and channelled from outside the corporate group, which effectively turns cattle-herding into an immediate-return activity.

As a consequence far-reaching changes in the arrangement of internal social relations which are required by delayed-return systems (see Woodburn 1988; Woodburn and Barnard 1988) are prevented or at least subdued: for example, exclusive ownership and controlled channels of exchange, authoritative control of economic returns, the abandoning of sharing obligations. Consequently those 'San' who acquire livestock suffer under this social constellation. For example, they are excluded from social solidarity and become the objects of gossip and witchcraft accusations. The problems such people face when an attempt is made to take up an independent herder existence are well known (see, e.g., Lee 1979: 413). The Hai‖om inverse *mafisa* is also a form of *excorporation* because only in this way can general rules of sharing and exchange (guided by kinship) be maintained while still retaining some means of accumulation and provision for delayed consumption. Although it is not recognized as a system by the actors, it is an institutionalized *excorporation* practice. Externally, individuals are free to move, either seasonally or more permanently, especially to work on commercial farms further to the south, or to visit relatives – whether they own cattle and goats or not. Internally, Hai‖om who acquire livestock can still maintain sharing practices with various kinsmen because the pressure to slaughter and to share the animals immediately is taken off their shoulders, owing to the placing of the animals with the Owambo. Maintaining relations of exchange and of sharing as well as entitlement to social support bears directly on the identity of any individual. Individual appropriation of economic assets is directly associated with non-Hai‖om behaviour, typical of the Owambo and other farmers and herders.

There are other economic dynamics at work. Risk reduction is a relevant aspect not just for rich cattle-owners who want to disperse their cattle as a protection against taxation or decimation due to disease and raiding. It is also, in a less institutionalized manner, relevant for any cattle-holder who seeks security in mutual cattle-lending with a friend or in moving to the cattlepost of a more powerful cattle-owner (Schapera 1938: 253). Economic efficiency is another factor, since labour shortage discourages cattle-owners from herding a few head of cattle independently. Similarly the changes in water availability (because of the changing legal status of borehole-ownership) has been shown to effect incorporation and exclusion of marginal cattle-holders with respect to a large local herd (Peters 1984). Other motivations play a role as well.[8]

All these factors (and this is not a complete list) show that *mafisa* and inverse *mafisa* do *not* constitute two 'systems' which can be easily opposed and delimited from the diversity of cases. As Lee has pointed out for the *mafisa* system between !Kung and Tswana, it is not always absent landlords who place their cattle in this way. Resident Herero and Tswana cattle-owners may make similar arrangements, either long-term or short-term, with local !Kung (Lee 1979: 407).

Similarly among the Hai‖om, in some cases livestock are kept in cooperation with Owambo, and occasionally Hai‖om without cattle engage in herding for Owambo cattle-owners. Finally, in both cases there are individual !Kung and Hai‖om who keep their own livestock without engaging in a *mafisa* or reverse *mafisa* arrangement (partly through outside support: see Marshall and Ritchie 1984: 123ff.).

Diversity does not only occur in interethnic contact but is already prevalent in the internal practices of cattle-lending and cattle-herding among pastoralists. Among the Tswana, cattle are lent out to lower-status kinsmen but also to higher-status persons such as husbands and fathers (Schapera 1938: 220). In some cases this is said to help the cattle recipient to build up his own herd (Schapera 1930: 294). This was common for cattle-lending among Nama or Boers (see Russel 1976: 192). In other cases it is presented as a strategy to keep low-status people in their position (Comaroff 1985: 69; Wilmsen 1989: 99). This seems to have been common practice in the highly stratified Tswana society of the nineteenth and the present centuries.[9] We find contradictory reports as to whether the 'San' themselves thought the *mafisa* was favourable for them or not (Marshall and Ritchie 1984: 123; cf. Solway and Lee 1990: 117). The existence of a *mafisa* or inverse *mafisa*-type arrangement in itself gives no clue as to whether the practice is benevolent for the non-cattle-owners involved. In either case the cattle-owning party may use the arrangement to create political and economic dependence, but the cattle-receiving party, as well, may try to outwit the cattle-givers (Schapera 1938: 248).

It seems that economic considerations of the actors cannot account for the full diversity of possible constellations. Woodburn's immediate–delayed return opposition (Woodburn 1980) allows us to predict some of the difficulties that are likely to occur in changes from one system to the other. Foragers with an immediate-return economy can be expected to find it more difficult to change into cattle-owners than into cattle–herders. It is not the novelty of subsistence techniques associated with pastoralism (or agriculture) that causes problems, but the social implications involved. With no personal authority to control the exchange and redistribution of economic assets (such as livestock) over time, and with strong egalitarian values working against the establishment of such an authority, the accumulation of economic assets is restrained.

However, the idea of 'San' economy as an immediate-return system seems a necessary but not sufficient element to explain the complex situation. Immediate-return systems which operate in close connection with neighbouring delayed-return systems adopt delayed-return elements in ways that cannot be explained by referring to the time and investment aspects alone. A complementary explanation for interethnic settings must focus on the social experience involved, because delayed-return features are not absent or categorically excluded. Rather, we find patterns of *excorporating* these features in individual and institutionalized strategies which are employed in a range of social constellations.

It is worthwhile to recall at this point that a shift of *inner* experiences does not provide a satisfactory explanation either. In terms of inner experience we could construct a 'hunting complex' for 'San' foragers in parallel to the well-known 'cattle complex' among pastoralists like the Tswana (see Kuper 1982: 13). In both cases the predominant economic activities, hunting and cattle-keeping, are culturally elaborated and give room for intensive inner experiences in the sense outlined by Edward Bruner (1986) for the men involved. But the way 'Bushmen' as well as cattle-owners switch between the social practices of cattle-herding and game-hunting (Owambo and Tswana are keen hunters as well) cannot be accounted for by the inner experiences involved. Furthermore, any explanation that is based exclusively on the notion of inner experience is subject to frequent abuse by local pastoralists (amongst others). The stereotypical view holds that 'Bushmen' do not as a rule keep livestock (a) because they do not look after domesticated animals since they do not value them, (b) because their longing for meat forces them to slaughter within a short period, and (c) because they do not plan ahead (see Guenther 1977: 200). I maintain that this pattern of explanation can only be freed from its psychologistic, biologistic and racist overtones by focusing on patterns of social experience instead.

It appears that the various strategies for dealing with a livestock economy must have a social grounding in order to allow not just cattle-herding but also livestock-ownership among southern African foragers. The strategies for achieving social grounding are numerous. Among the Hai‖om with whom I worked during field research, there is only one individual who owned several (at the time seven) head of cattle, which were mostly herded together with the cattle of the neighbouring Owambo, by either Owambo or Hai‖om boys (or a mixed group).[10] Two ways of grounding made this development possible. First, local Hai‖om and Owambo stress their kinship relationship which is constituted by the fact that the Owambo clan name translates into the Hai‖om surname; for both sides this suggests mutual assistance and acceptance.[11] Second, a daughter of the Hai‖om man is married to an Owambo, not as a second wife or as a concubine, as is often the case, but apparently in regular wedlock. The Hai‖om man even maintained that a cow was given as bridewealth.

These two strategies of social grounding, based on regular practices in Hai‖om and Owambo society, are carried over into the interethnic relationship and allow for cattle-keeping across ethnic lines. Close association with the Owambo allows the Hai‖om man to keep his cattle without alienating the Hai‖om in neighbouring places, although it forces him to exploit this Owambo connection to a degree by being generous towards fellow-Hai‖om. The Owambo provides a gun and ammunition for the Hai‖om man's hunt. The game is shared according to traditional Hai‖om conventions, at times leaving the hunter with no meat at all when the kill is consumed by the members of the neighbouring local group.

In this case the establishment of common ground with a neighbouring Owambo was particularly successful and lasting. In all other cases observed, such an individual accumulation of livestock-ownership could not be sustained because the common ground of Hai‖om identity in contrast to Owambo identity, continually invoked by the Hai‖om, relies critically on the notion of Hai‖om sharing and being in need, as opposed to Owambo bargaining, accumulating riches and being self-sustaining and independent. Livestock-ownership only becomes tolerable and viable when it is excorporated from Hai‖om common ground into Owambo socioeconomic organization. This is not the product of an economic mechanism, but it follows continual negotiations of social values among Hai‖om and is therefore subject to change.

Forms of social grounding follow a variety of paths, and they are exploited in a number of ways. For a Hai‖om to lend out livestock, as in the inverse *mafisa* system, allows for saving up, and for evasion of pressure to share without threatening social bonds of mutual assistance. For a !Kung to engage in herding at a Tswana cattlepost may improve the ground for elaborate exchange relations with other !Kung. For the Owambo farmer to accept a goat from a Hai‖om not only provides the prospect of offspring or meat, but it also creates some obligation for the Hai‖om to spend some time with the Owambo as a worker (paid in kind) when needed. Hence it becomes a tool in social grounding itself. For the Tswana cattle-owner to lend out cattle to a !Kung can prevent cattle theft because it turns the well-being of the herd into a common interest for the parties involved. To construct dependent clientship as a herder (be it in the Owambo or in the Herero context) appears to be a successful attempt by the cattle-owner to make the cattleless person accept status positions implicit in the social grounding.

Economic factors and even ecological factors such as the availability of other food resources and of alternative cattle-owners to choose from are likely to influence whether such a social ground is accepted or not. But the kind of common ground partners create relies also on the nature of earlier social practices. If, for instance, cattle-owners are accepted as foster-parents for Hai‖om children, it often follows that the whole family engages in herding for the fostering Owambo. If stigmatization prevents this kind of social grounding, permanent residence and herding services are much less likely. The ethnography suggests that stigmatization itself does not primarily rely on physical differences or on the difference between Khoisan and Bantu languages, but on practices such as cattle-keeping (Silberbauer and Kuper 1966: 177–8). Grounding and practices such as the lending/herding of cattle are causally linked, but it is not always possible to distinguish cause and effect, since most relationships have a history of long-standing interaction. There is, however, a recurring pattern: the attempt to construct, maintain and manipulate social ground as a prerequisite of social interaction.

We are now in a better position to see how ethnic identity and interethnic relations are constructed, maintained and transformed. The Kalahari debate seemed to have left us with two alternatives: southern African foragers as a product either of the wider social formation that has ethnicized them, or of an intrinsic ethnic difference that has not changed in its core. The focus was on the outside forces and stimuli that triggered changes in the construction of identity. This was so partly because of the nature of historical data, which focused on responses to outside changes. In cases where the outside stimulus, such as the advent of cattle, is variable and does not entail a specific response but offers a number of possible arrangements, current field research opens up opportunities for investigation usually not given by historical data. With regard to the advent of cattle on 'San' land, investigations into social experience allow us to see not only how events are received but how they are actively constructed. It reveals the active role 'San' groups play in the shaping of social relations and ethnic identity. Individual motives and strategies can be accounted for. The fact that practices of social grounding contain conventional and individual options explains the amount of unpredictability contained in the ethnography. However, the contexts of individual actions reveal patterned social arrangements and practices, since individual experience is not arbitrary but is closely related to institutionalized practices. Ethnic identity is open to political manipulation and it is not static. Nor is it necessarily a process of ethnogenesis and increasing ethnic differentiation, as it apparently is in the case of Tswana and Europeans who fostered ethnic difference while appropriating 'San' land for their cattle. The 'traumatic experience of cattle acquisition' by hunter–gatherers (ten Raa 1986) may in other circumstances lead to ethnolysis. In the example from eastern Africa given by ten Raa, aggressors exploit increased immobility of poor cattle-owners and their decreased ability to hide. The institutionalized practices of social grounding among the Hai‖om, too, can blur boundaries between ethnic groups when common ground is established and shared with Owambo agropastoralists for the purpose of keeping livestock (and other forms of using delayed returns). With regard to the increasing incorporation of 'Bushmen' into Owambo communities over centuries (see Williams 1991) ethnolysis seems to have been no exceptional outcome, depending on the particular processes of grounding institutionalized.

SOCIAL EXPERIENCE AND INTERDISCIPLINARY RESEARCH IN COGNITIVE ANTHROPOLOGY

In the case of southern African forager ethnography an investigation into social experience has led us to issues of ethnic identity and of the definition and handling of attributes that distinguish insiders from outsiders – issues that reach into the field of cognition and inner experience.

In the ethnographic example I have discussed, there is a clearcut perceived dichotomization constructed by the Hai‖om between a 'Bushman we' of victims in need, who have nobody but their fellow-sufferers to share food and other things with them, and a 'them' of rich livestock-owning providers, who are defined by their stinginess and their unwillingness to share. This dichotomy of cognitive categories goes together with a lexical dichotomization which is invoked in conversation. There are indications that parallel dichotomies are to be found among other forager groups.[12] But it is far from clear how cognitive and linguistic factors in connection with social practice bear on questions of the experience of social identity. In my conclusion I want to consider how the diversity found in the ethnography of the experience of southern African foragers who are being incorporated into pastoral life contributes to interdisciplinary research on cognition.

It seems that in cognitive science researchers find it difficult to render to anthropology anything more than the position of a provider of cross-cultural data. A vague notion of anthropology providing the cultural context for cognitive processes exists, but the data anthropologists provide are far from influencing the premises of research in the field of interdisciplinary cognitive science. Cognitive anthropology is primarily understood no longer as a subdiscipline of anthropology, but an interdisciplinary field shared by anthropologists, linguists and psychologists. In the past, cognitive anthropology as a subdiscipline took its theory and research methods from the 'more advanced' formal branches of disciplines dealing with cognition. Social practice as an aspect of analysis does not enter the research process to any relevant degree. It is marginal in the collection of data and hardly appears in data analysis. However, cognitive anthropology as an inter-disciplinary field opens up new opportunities for a holistic anthro-pological theory of social practice and experience. In the past, discussions of the relation between cognition and language did not regard 'culture' or 'social practice' as an independent variable. Culture was subsumed either under cognition (culture as knowledge) or under language (culture as a sign system). Early approaches in cognitive anthropology focused on componential analysis and on taxonomies which operationalized culture for the purposes of psychology and in particular linguistics at that point in time (see Renner 1983; Kokot 1988 and 1993; Wassmann 1993). While these structuralist methods worked fairly well for ethno-botany and for aspects of the kinship system, they did not solve the problems of understanding 'social experience' in its com-plexity. In effect, investigators of the link between the psycho-logical and the cultural dimensions of experience seem to have felt justified in restricting themselves to a phenomenological study of inner experience. The meaning of social implications was derived completely from the sense endowed by the individual subject or by the culture as a personified subject. Recent developments in the field of cognition and linguistics indicate ways to supersede both the phenomenological and the structuralist restrictions. It appears that cognitive processes cannot be located fully within the individual but have to be looked for in the 'domain of externalized cognition' in objects, social interaction and language usage (Gumperz and Levinson 1991: 615; see Lave 1988 for earlier reflections on 'cognition in practice'). A full analysis of social experience would therefore look not only at how cognitive concepts and linguistic categories influence experience, but also at social practice in a specific time and place.

With regard to cognition, conceptual coordination is a prerequisite for social interaction, that is, social actors rely on a common conceptual ground. With regard to language, a degree of lexical coordination has to be established when interlocutors want to do anything by means of language (Clark, in press). But as the ethnographic example presented in this paper shows, coordination of social action is also necessary for people in order to establish continued social interaction or, to put it bluntly, in order to live together. In most cases all three aspects are hardly separable, as they are intertwined. Social experience not only relies on shared concepts and shared modes of linguistic interaction but also relies on preceding actions and experiences. This becomes particularly clear in those cases where cognitive and linguistic features cannot account for an apparent diversity in social practice. The social experience and construction of southern African forager group identity needs to be explained with regard to the coordination of past and future practices of herding, owning and lending cattle. Common identity is shaped in the process of reconciling access to goods and resources that need some form of accumulation with a continuing practice of sharing and mutual solidarity by the means of *excorporation*. To subsume 'culture' under either cognition or language is to obscure the ways in which this is done in different social settings.

The task for research in cognitive anthropology as an interdisciplinary field then is to see how social practice, language and cognition interconnect, and to work out correspondences and correlations, if they are to be found. In this way some of the essence of ethnographic research, and not just isolated exotic cross-cultural details, can enter the interdisciplinary discussion. Anthropological ethnographies have more knowledge to offer than the providing of what Fabian called just a 'convenient Other' in cross-cultural research (Fabian 1983: x).

NOTES

This chapter contains preliminary results of my Ph.D. project in progress at the London School of Economics and Political Science (University of London). Field research with the Hai‖om of Namibia (1990–2) was funded by a University of London Studentship, the University of London Central Research Fund and the Swan Fund. In the post-fieldwork period the project is supported by the Max-Planck Research Group in Cognitive Anthropology, Nijmegen. This support is gratefully acknowledged.

An earlier draft of this paper was presented to the workshop 'Social experience and anthropological knowledge', second EASA conference, Prague, August 1992. I am thankful to the conveners, Kirsten Hastrup and Peter Hervik, as well as to Alan Barnard, Eve Danziger, Johnny Parry, Eric Pederson, James Woodburn and fellow-participants at the post-fieldwork seminar, Department of Anthropology at LSE, for their critical comments.

1 In recent years the interest in issues of space has risen considerably. In political philosophy Henri Lefebvre (1991, originally in French 1974) has suggested a comprehensive theory of space, while 'social space' has become a central concept in the sociology of Pierre Bourdieu (1985, 1987), who also stimulated new interest in the symbolism of domestic space (1977). In geography GIS (Geographic Information Systems) was developed, and was subsequently adopted by archaeology (Allen *et al.* 1990). Architects and town-planners have developed an analytic, descriptive theory of space (Hillier and Hanson 1984), and linguists focus on space as an aspect of pragmatics (Levinson 1992; Senft 1992). A large number of highly varied anthropological contributions deal with spatial conceptualizations in ethnography, e.g. Moore 1986; Pinxten *et al.* 1983; Stoller 1989; Thornton 1980; and Weiner 1991. For a recent contribution on southwestern Africa, see Noyes 1992. Using this background, my paper focuses on spatial concepts in anthropological theory and conceptualizations of space in ethnography rather than on the temporal dimension of theory and ethnography that preoccupied Fabian.

2 All these terms are problematic. While 'Barsawa' is virtually unknown in Namibia, most Hai‖om do not like to be called 'Bushman' or 'San'. I have used these terms in quotation marks when referring to discussions in which they are used. Otherwise I have used the ethnonyms used by the groups themselves in their conventional spelling, e.g. Hai‖om and !Kung (|, ≠, ‖ are signs representing click sounds).

3 For a comprehensive bibliography and summary of the debate, see Barnard 1992. Most contributions are found in *Current Anthropology* 1990–2. One of the latest contributions to the debate is Kuper 1992.

4 My definition of 'social space' as a technical term relates closely to that of Lefebvre, who defines it as the outcome of past actions that permit 'fresh actions to occur, while suggesting others and prohibiting yet others' (Lefebvre 1991: 73), for example, the way(s) in which foragers deal with livestock.

5 Earlier important ethnographic work is not devalued by anything said in the course of the debate. The theoretical and programmatic contributions to the debate have to some degree overshadowed the way in which empirical work has continued to enrich our knowledge before and during the debate and as the debate peters out. Furthermore in many research outputs the opposed programmatic aims merge to some degree. With regard to the documentation of experience, only two works should be named. In the isolationist strand an account of life-experience in the format of a life history (Shostak 1981) replaced the traditional format of ethnography. The most recent piece of work, which can be broadly placed in the integrationist strand, aims at historical differentiation by incorporating unpublished archival sources into an account of how colonizers and colonized 'Bushmen' experienced the colonial encounter, and its violent conflicts (Gordon 1992).

6 It should be noted that *mafisa* arrangements are declining and that it was an institution primarily among Bantu-speaking pastoralists rather than interethnically between pastoralists and foragers. 'San' watching over cattle may refer to this cattle as *mafisa*, although typical institutionalized aspects of the *mafisa* of earlier times may not be included (Hitchcock 1990: 130; see also Schapera 1938: 247). For more details on *mafisa* arrangements, see Schapera 1938: 246ff.; Gibson 1962: 629; Wilmsen 1989: 99. A more detailed discussion of different types of Hai‖om cattle-holding will be included in my forthcoming Ph.D. thesis.

7 I introduce the term 'excorporation' here to emphasize that economic accumulation is not entirely *excluded* in the sense of being erased. It is only placed outside the corporate group. Furthermore it is not necessarily *externalized* and eliminated permanently but may be reincorporated at some stage of the politicoeconomic process.

8 A case in point is the fact that some Hai‖om were more or less forced to leave their goats with local Owambo when the army presence and armed conflict in the area drove them away from their land beyond the cattle disease fence which prohibits the movement of livestock to the south.

9 Note that the *mafisa* worked well for impoverished Herero war refugees to Botswana to build up herds for themselves (Gibson 1962: 629), while the 'Bushmen' under the same ecological conditions and with long-standing *mafisa* arrangements had far too few head of cattle to qualify for support from the (Tswana-dominated) administration (Guenther 1986: 310). I take this to be another indication of the importance of social grounding not only in *mafisa* arrangements but also in nation–state politics.

10 I was told that there are also some goats which are permanently looked after by a relative of the neighbouring Owambo at a distant place.

11 The full implications and subtleties of the practice of linking Hai‖om surnames with Owambo clan names is developed and discussed in full detail in my forthcoming Ph.D. thesis.

12 See Guenther on the notion of 'sheta' among Nharo of the Ghanzi block (1986: 50), and their expressions of collective ethnic inferiority (1977: 199).

REFERENCES

Allen, K., Green, S., and Zubrow, E. (1990) *Interpreting Space: GIS and Archaeology*, London: Taylor & Francis.

Barnard, A. (1992) *The Kalahari Debate: A Bibliographical Essay* (Centre of African Studies, Edinburgh University, Occasional Papers 35), Edinburgh.

Bourdieu, P. (1977) *Outline of a Theory of Practice*, Cambridge: Cambridge University Press.

—— (1985) 'The social space and the genesis of groups', *Theory and Society* 14, 6: 723–44.

—— (1987) *Choses dites*, Paris: Éditions de Minuit.

Bruner, E. (1986) 'Introduction', in V. Turner and E. Bruner, eds *The Anthropology of Experience*, Urbana: University of Illinois Press.

Clark, H. (in press) 'Common ground, communalities and community', in J. Gumperz and S. Levinson, eds, *Rethinking Linguistic Relativity*, Cambridge: Cambridge University Press.

Comaroff, J. (1985) *Body of Power, Spirit of Resistance: The Culture and History of a South African People*, Chicago: University of Chicago Press.

Fabian, J. (1983) *Time and the Other: How Anthropology Makes Its Object*, New York: Columbia University Press.

Gibson, G. (1962) 'Bridewealth and other forms of exchange among the Herero', in P. Bohannan and G. Dalton, eds, *Markets in Africa*, Evanston, Ill.: Northwestern University Press.

Gordon, R. (1992) *The Bushman Myth: The Making of a Namibian Underclass*, Boulder, Colo.: Westview Press.

Guenther, M. (1977) 'Bushman hunters as farm labourers', *Canadian Journal of African Studies* 11, 2: 195–203.

—— (1986) *The Nharo Bushmen of Botswana: Tradition and Change*, (Quellen zur Khoisan-Forschung 3), Hamburg: Buske.

Gumperz, J., and Levinson, S. (1991) 'Rethinking linguistic relativity', *Current Anthropology* 32, 5: 613–23.

Hillier, B. and Hanson, J. (1984) *The Social Logic of Space*, Cambridge: Cambridge University Press.

Hitchcock, R. (1990) [Comments on S. Solway and R. Lee], *Current Anthropology* 31, 2: 129–30.

Kent, S. (1992) 'The current forager controversy: real versus ideal views of hunter-gatherers', *Man* 27: 45–70.

Kokot, W. (1988) 'Kognitive Ethnologie', in H. Fischer, ed., *Ethnologie. Einführung und Uberblick*, Berlin: Reimer.

—— (1993) 'Kognition als Gegenstand der Ethnologie', in T. Schweitzer, M. Schweitzer and W. Kokot, eds, *Handbuch der Ethnologie*, Berlin: Reimer.

Kuper, A. (1982) *Wives for Cattle: Bridewealth and Marriage in Southern Africa*, London: Routledge & Kegan Paul.

—— (1992) 'Postmodernism, Cambridge and the great Kalahari debate', *Social Anthropology* 1, 1A: 57–71.

Lave, J. (1988) *Cognition in Practice: Mind, Mathematics, and Culture in Everyday Life*, Cambridge: Cambridge University Press.

Lee, R. (1979) *The !Kung San: Men, Women, and Work in a Foraging Society*, Cambridge: Cambridge University Press.

Lee, R., and Guenther, M. (1991) 'Oxen or onions? The search for trade (and truth) in the Kalahari', *Current Anthropology* 32: 592–601.

Lefebvre, H. (1991) *The Production of Space*, Oxford: Blackwell.

Levinson, S. (1992) 'Primer for the field investigation of spatial description and conception', *Pragmatics* 271: 5–47.

Marshall, J., and Ritchie, C. (1984) *Where are the Ju wasi of Nyae Nyae? Changes in a Bushman Society: 1958–1981* (Centre for African Studies Communications 9), Cape Town: University of Cape Town.

Moore, H. (1986) *Space, Text and Gender: An Anthropological Study of the Marakwet of Kenya*, Cambridge: Cambridge University Press.

Noyes, J. (1992) *Colonial Space: Spatiality, Subjectivity and Society in the Colonial Discourse of German South West Africa 1884–1915*, Chur: Harwood Academic Publishers.

Peters, P. (1984) 'Struggles over water, struggles over meaning: cattle, water and the state in Botswana', *Africa* 54: 29–49.

Pinxten, R., Van Dooren, I., and Harvey, F. (1983) *Anthropology of Space: Explorations into the Natural Philosophy and Semantics of the Navajo*, Philadelphia: University of Pennsylvania Press.

Renner, E. (1983) 'Die Grundlagen der kognitiven Forschung', in Hans Fischer, ed., *Ethnologie. Eine Einführung*, Berlin: Reimer.

Russel, M. (1976) 'Slaves or workers? Relations between Bushmen, Tswana, and Boers in the Kalahari', *Journal of Southern African Studies* 2: 178–97.

Schapera, I. (1930) *The Khoisan Peoples of South Africa: Bushmen and Hottentots*, London: Routledge & Sons.

—— (1938) *A Handbook of Tswana Law and Custom*, London: Oxford University Press.

Senft, G. (1992) *Everything We Always Thought We Knew About Space – But Did Not Bother to Question . . .* (Cognitive Anthropology Research Group Nijmegen, Working Paper 10), Nijmegen: Mimeo.

Shostak, M. (1981) *Nisa: The Life and Works of a !Kung Woman*, Harmondsworth: Penguin.

Silberbauer, G., and Kuper, A. (1966) 'Kgalagari masters and Bushman serfs: some observations', *African Studies* 25, 4: 171–9.

Solway, J. and Lee, R. (1990) 'Foragers, genuine or spurious? Situating the Kalahari San in history', *Current Anthropology* 31: 109–46.

Stoller, P. (1989) *The Taste of Ethnographic Things: The Senses in Anthropology*, Philadelphia: University of Pennsylvania Press.

ten Raa, E. (1986) 'The acquisition of cattle by hunter-gatherers: a traumatic experience in cultural change', *Sprache und Geschichte in Afrika* 7, 2.

Thornton, R. (1980) *Space, Time, and Culture among the Iraqw of Tanzania*, New York: Academic Press.

Wassmann, J. (1993) 'Der kognitive Aufbruch in der Ethnologie', in J. Wassmann and P. Dasen, eds, *Alltagswissen: der kognitive Ansatz im interdisziplinären Dialog*, Frieburg (Schweiz): Universitätsverlag.

Weiner, J. (1991) *The Empty Place: Poetry, Space, and Being among the Foi of Papua New Guinea*, Bloomington: University of Indiana Press.

Williams, F. (1991) *Precolonial Communities of Southwestern Africa: A History of Owambo Kingdoms 1600–1920*, Windhoek: National Archives of Namibia.

Wilmsen, E. (1989) *Land Filled with Flies: A Political Economy of the Kalahari*, Chicago: University of Chicago Press.

Wilmsen, E., and Denbow, J. (1990) 'Paradigmatic history of San-speaking peoples and current attempts at revision', *Current Anthropology* 31: 489–524.

Woodburn, J. (1980) 'Hunters and gatherers today and reconstructions of the past', in E. Gellner, ed., *Soviet and Western Anthropology*, London: Duckworth.

—— (1988) 'African hunter-gatherer social organization: is it best understood as a product of encapsulation?', in T. Ingold, D. Riches, and J. Woodburn, eds, *Hunters and Gatherers*, vol. I, Oxford: Berg.

Woodburn, J., and Barnard, A. (1988) 'Introduction', in T. Ingold, D. Riches, and J. Woodburn, eds, *Hunters and Gatherers*, vol. I. Oxford: Berg.

Chapter 11

Events and processes
Marriages in Libya, 1932–79

John Davis

The word 'experience' in the title of this volume makes me suspicious. I am quite sure that experience is the touchstone of good anthropology. If you are confronted with two pieces of ethnography, one of which bears no relation to the experience of the ethnographer or of the people they write about, and the other of which does bear some sort of relation, you are in no doubt about which is better. And, similarly, if you compare a theory which proposes to explain, say, gift-giving in terms of a market, and one which invokes reciprocity, you will try to come to a view of what your informants' experience is, before adopting one or the other explanatory device. In those cases, 'experience' is a crucial evaluative concept in anthropology. But the word also stands as an emblem for the demand that anthropologists should recreate experience (either their own or other people's) so that it is directly accessible to readers (and occasionally viewers of their movies). That is a tall order: poets sometimes achieve it, although in one restricted area of life at a time; and we can imagine that it is not always their own experience that they conjure, but occasionally that of third parties. Actors, painters, musicians and movie directors also sometimes provide us not just with occasions for heightened understanding of our own lives, but with the sensation that we can live other lives. Of course, some of us are uneasy about the reality of that (do we experience Toscanini, or Verdi or Falstaff? Even, some people fear, do we just experience ourselves?). Even so, we agree that it is heady, exhilarating, memorable and rare.

It seems to me to be rather unreasonable to ask of anthropologists that we should create and use techniques which regularly and predictably allow us to convey the experience of life of an exotic people (several hundred, or several hundred thousand people) in a directly accessible way: we do not have the skills to represent whole lives, and it is fantasy to ask of us that we should aim to produce a kind of virtual reality for our readers (and viewers). How interesting that two of the contributors to this volume should write about meals! No doubt, the experience of that particular company is irrecoverable, and that day in that setting will remain elusive; but meals have menus, and dishes have recipes – you need rosemary, a suckling lamb, pepper, oil, garlic (and so on), and if you do the right things with them you can recreate some part of the sensation and experience of a *pasquetta* picnic in your own kitchens. Well, perhaps so. But what recipes do we have for Mount Hagen genders or Kachin religiosity? And what room do we use to recreate them in?

Other people's experience is inaccessible, except in momentary and partial glimpses, but it is still a touchstone. The point I wish to make is that this should not be an invitation to write operas, not even novels: apart from anything else, we do not have the skills to practise those crafts as well as our own. On the other hand, we do know that every scrap of information we include in our monographs is part of some person's experience, and that to lose sight of that is in one way or another to diminish the value of our work. This is so even when the work is banal and unpoetic stuff, based for instance on archives and statistics. Indeed, I want to demonstrate in this chapter that we can use computers and statistics in a way which captures something of what life has been like: I cannot create a total representation which directly matches a total social fact, but I can recover something, note how that has changed and (using my imagination) become aware of what it is that I am leaving out – get some sort of appreciation of the difference between life as it was lived and the representation I make of it.

In 1979 I was allowed to take photographs of the shariʿa archives in Kufra and Ajdabiya in eastern Libya. For various reasons I had limited time and film, and I decided to copy marriage and divorce records. I think the Kufra records are complete, 1932–79; but the Ajdabiya archive was much larger, and I had to settle for incomplete copying. I photographed each odd-numbered register: and then (under increasing pressure of limited resources) each third volume. I ended up with copies of about 14,000 records: these are my effective archive (henceforth 'archive' for short). The work of analysing them continues, and it is that which I want to describe and discuss.

What is a record? Figure 11.1 shows one. On 13 February 1974 Muftah Musbah Mahmud married ʿAza Al-Haj ʿAbdulnabi Saʿid. He was a 'worker' aged 32, she was 21 and a housewife, and was represented by Muhammad Saʿid Yunis, who was almost certainly her father's brother. Since the marriage document declares her to be a woman rather than a virgin, she had almost certainly been married before. Her husband probably had as well. They had both been born in Ajdabiya (a town in Cyrenaica, near the sea, about 100 miles from Benghazi). The document declares that the *sidaq* (*mahr*, a sort of bridewealth) consisted of 280 Libyan dinars, some gold and silver ornaments, and some clothing. The ornaments and clothing were prompt *sidaq*, handed over that day; the cash was deferred, in practice indefinitely, but constituting a claim against him should he divorce his bride. The witnesses were Bu Bakr Salah Muhammad the ward leader (*mukhtar mahalla*), aged 36; and ʿAtiya Muhammad Yussuf, a clerk aged 32. That was an event. It is recorded in the archives of the shariʿa registry in Ajdabiya, stamped and signed by the marriage officer in volume 41 at page 11.

The document itself is quite interesting. For instance, it is a printed form with spaces for the marriage officer to fill in, alternatives for him to delete. It is made out in triplicate – one carbon for the groom, another for the bride's representative, and the top copy for the registry – and is headed 'Libyan Arab Republic'. It is taxed using the Italian method of sticking on tax-tokens. The document is an official form therefore, and it combines religious formulas with state ones: spaces for men's names, for instance, are preceded by the word Brother (ʿ*Akhu*) which, used when English-speakers might use Mister, is revolutionary good form, more or less equivalent to 'Comrade'.[1]

It is also interesting because it allows me to reconstruct a relationship: Muftah and ʿAza were married to each other from 1974 until they divorced, or until the end of the archive. For that period those two and their families were in a relationship of a particular kind – even though in practice domestic and family life is fairly variable, what marriage entails is formally quite distinctive among relationships. ʿAza at least could not marry anyone else, which had consequences for perhaps quite unconnected men and women who were looking for spouses after February 1974. The

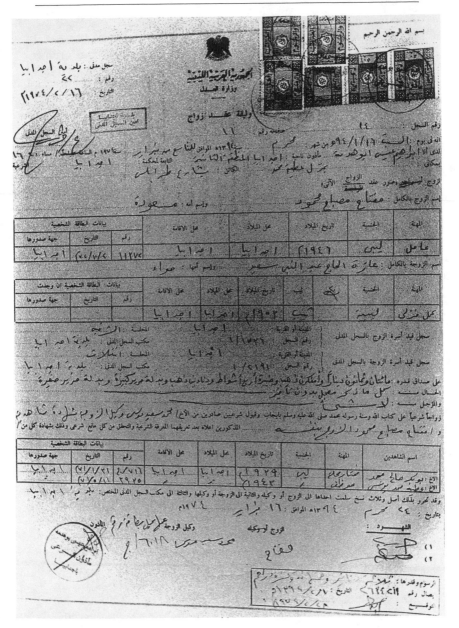

Figure 11.1 The marriage certificate of Muftah and 'Aza, February 13 1974, at Ajdabiya

marriage was therefore an event with consequences, and I can use the document to indicate in a broad way what those might be. Of course the document is a thin and incomplete record, a crumb from the party, a fragmentary residue produced and deposited in a bureaucratic office under state supervision: an event-dropping, like the mouse-droppings also found there. But it is a contemporary record and contains more information than any of the parties to it are likely to have remembered a year later.

The event also presupposes a number of precedent decisions. The people have asked themselves: Shall I marry? Whom shall I marry? When? Where? How much *sidaq*? Who should be the bride's guardian? Who should be witnesses? Should we have special conditions set in the contract? What sort of party should we have? Who shall dance? Who shall drum? Who will be master of ceremonies? Getting married is a complex business with a lot of options, and requires decisions by ten or twenty people. Let us say, for the purposes of illustration only, that it takes fifty decisions to produce an event such as a marriage or a divorce. The record – sometimes no more than half a small page of manuscript – is not only an artefact, a culturally specific representation of an event, and not only an indicator of changed relationships and possibilities. It also implies precedent decisions by a significant number of people: the archive as a whole implies, let us say, three-quarters of a million decisions taken by, say, a couple of hundred thousand persons.[2]

That is a very crude and positivist way of putting the matter. The word 'decision' serves for a variety of different ways of settling issues: although a young girl had little choice about who her representative should be, a woman of 25, a divorcée, did have a choice, within limits. My reason for putting this in such a crude way is to make the point that whether or not you wish to call them 'decisions' the documents point to, imply, a vast number of settlings of issues which were all part of the experience of marrying in Libya 1932–79. Most of them are not recoverable. We shall never know what the issues were, the range of possibilities considered when the spouses chose their witnesses. In some cases we know the outcome (guardians, witnesses, *sidaq* and, indeed, choice of marriage partner). In others – Who shall dance? – the archive is quite silent, although we do know that in the vast majority of cases such a decision was made. So the records imply what I call decisions, but which may not have been quite like that in any particular case. They are a very limited set of crumbs. Nevertheless, it is useful to imagine these unrecoverable discussions because in this way we can remind ourselves that the record is not simply interesting in itself, but is also a pointer to the dynamic processes of social life, of the room for manoeuvre available to Libyans, and of the use which Libyans made of that room.

Marriage and divorce are matters of Islamic law, and you have seen from the document how the state insists on registering and taxing marriages and divorces. In fact, however, apart from greater administrative control, the law of marriage and divorce in Libya did not substantially change in the period covered by the archive. So we are not dealing with the consequences of the exercise of centralized power, but with what Mann (1986) usefully suggests we should call 'diffuse' power. The decisions which people take in the course of their lives are consequential, control the options for others and can initiate or maintain patterns of social behaviour, and can hence shape and mould social practice, creating patterns which are distinctively Libyan. People exercise power over others cumulatively in the conduct of their daily lives, without any centralized locus of power or authority. This is at least as consequential as the legiferous activities of Qaddafi or Pericles.[3] In short, I mean to argue that patterns of marriage and divorce, and changes in those patterns, are the outcome of those 750,000 or so decisions which are implicit in the documents. We cannot recover most of them, but we have to imagine them, and to recognize the records as reminders of them: turdish *aides-mémoire*, no doubt, but as it happens more complete and detailed than any other records over such a time-span for a Muslim population.

DESCRIPTION OF THE ARCHIVE AND OF OTHER MATERIAL

So the information available for analysis consists in the first place of the documents. I also have a genealogy taken down by dictation from various sources in 1978–9. And maps of houses and shops, lists of licences issued by government offices, and lists of members of popular committees, and so on: all relatively systematic material in the sense that it is fairly uniform and more or less complete. This is in turn related to other sources of information:

fieldnotes, memories, and work by other people such as Peters
(e.g. 1991), Evans-Pritchard (1945) and Mason (1977) who published on the area. That is not systematic in the same sense,
although it is probably greater in quantity and at least as analytically useful as the systematic information. A single document on
its own is quite interesting; but a collection of ten thousand
documents is not ten thousand times more interesting unless it is
shaped and formed, unless the documents can be compared to
each other, and unless they are linked in the first instance to each
other, and then to the other systematic and non-systematic information. For instance, the groom was eleven years older than the
bride. Was that an average age-difference? She had been married
before: does the archive contain her marriage and divorce papers
from that previous marriage? The bridewealth was valued at about
400 Libyan dinars. Was that a lot or a little? And was it affected by
the previous marriage of the bride? By the status of the bride's
father? How had bridewealth changed in the previous forty years?
To answer this kind of question requires a computer. When I
analysed the form used for a marriage registration I found that
there are potentially 170 items of significant information which
may be recorded on a particular document: for divorces it is
slightly less. Some of the official forms do not have all the blanks
filled in; and about half the documents are not on official forms,
but are written free-style in account books, school exercise books
and the like. These sometimes have very scanty information
compared to the full details required by the modern state.
Nevertheless, you can reckon on somewhere around two million
items of information which are useful for anthropological analysis;
and for coping with this a machine is essential.

A computer representation of a document is not the document
itself. Apart from the fact that I have left out some of the information available on the document, electronic storage is different
from paper storage. At the moment I regard this as an advantage:
it is much easier to count and compare electronic records than
paper ones. But there are differences: an electronic record could
not be used to establish a claim to a widow's pension, for instance;
and the electronic version of the archive is one step further away
from the reality of Libyan experience and use.

When you come to link the archive with the other sources you
have to take into account the fact that they are not all the same
kind of information. The computer version of the document is a

partial representation of a representation; and the genealogy is a model which I made of the selective and variable information supplied by Zuwaya. I do not think I have misrepresented facts, which I checked and counter-checked, but I have written them down in a form which few Libyans used. And Libyans gave different versions of the genealogy: people in different places and in different lineages gave different versions; and no doubt if someone were to ask for the same information now or in twenty years' time they would discover that the versions changed in time as well. The genealogy, moreover, is a model built in 1978–9; it is my account of what was said to me then about the relationships of people. The documents in the archive are contemporary with the events they describe. Since I intend to try to relate the genealogy to the documents,[4] it is important to remember that they are not quite the same kind of thing. Adding documentary and genealogical and other information together does not necessarily improve the quality of my representation. It certainly makes it more complex, but fitting slightly inconsistent materials together can introduce new distortions: unrealities may not cancel each out, but multiply when they are put together. Nevertheless, it is worth trying to bring them into relation, for the documents contain no information about relations between parties to a marriage or divorce. If I can add that, I can join in discussions of a traditional anthropological kind, for instance about marriage between close kin (Holy 1989; Peters 1967; Hammel and Goldberg 1971; Hammel and Hutchinson 1973); I can also, I think, recapture something of the different textures of experience.

I think it is important at this point to mention some of the difficulties, technical and theoretical, which are present in this kind of work. The technical ones are chiefly concerned with what is known as record matching (Macfarlane 1980), which really means in this case being sure that a person who appears in one document is the same as one who appears in another. It is essential to know that, in order to be able to talk for instance about the duration of marriages, or about polygyny.

The naming system used by Libyans generally is fairly helpful in this respect: people are called by their own name, their father's, and their father's father's name, as in Muftah Musbah Mahmud, or ʿAza ʿAbdulhadi Said. That allows for fairly precise triangulation: in the genealogy 1,100 people are called Muhammad, 600 of them were sons of people called Muhammad, but only 2 of them were also grandsons of a Muhammad. So, although 11,000 or so people share only 70 or so names, they permute and combine them in a way which avoids confusion. Difficulties arise because marriage officers do not always use the formal naming system (they can use nicknames, for instance, or lineage instead of personal names, or diminutives or dialect forms). In short, in more than 2,000 cases so far names are sufficiently similar to raise the question that two references might be to the same person, but not to resolve the issue conclusively.

The problem is solved if (as in many of the modern documents) the clerk has recorded the identity-card details of the individual. But older documents, some of them from the period before ID cards, sometimes miss that information out: I have to rely on other indicators. There are seven items of information on a perfect record which could match, and which suggest with varying degrees of confidence that the references are to the same person. For instance, dates can establish non-identity definitely: if the divorce record is earlier than the marriage record, the documents cannot be directly related. Date of birth, place of birth, occupation can all increase confidence, and so on. These are often matters which can be expressed as Boolean tests and assessed by computer. The computer can also assign a degree of confidence to the linkage between documents, so that later calculations and constructions can be made using only cases of certainty, or those plus the more uncertain ones, and so on.

A further technical problem which may be of interest is that the genealogy, which is the chief source of information about the kinship relations between spouses and others, is incomplete. By my reckoning some 3,000 or 4,000 women are missing from the genealogy, and about 1,500 of them are likely to appear in the marriage and divorce records. Some women in the registers have no place in the genealogy – an American, for instance, clearly; but also men and women who belong on the genealogies of other groups. Even so, I think I shall have to invent 1,000 or so women on the genealogy, in order to accommodate people who appear in the documents. The procedure is essentially the same as that for matching records: if I know that a person in the records was born in such and such a place, and I know the father, brother, mother, sister and can find those people in the genealogy, then I can (with some degree of confidence) create a new person for the genealogy. But it is a slightly unnerving thing to do, and of course it adds to the confusion of different sorts of reality: the genealogy becomes an amalgam of a fairly close representation of what Zuwaya said about their relations, and of some additions of what I believe to be the case, using information of a different kind, driven by a need to construct a particular kind of analysis.

Some people imagine that creating a database is a smooth and objective process which results in real data. But in fact a database is just as much an act of creativity as a description of a cycle of rituals. You have to solve problems of representation, combine different sorts of information, and compromise between conflicting sources in both cases. And the solutions you find have consequences for the rest of your work. Some of the problems arise because I use a computer; but, again, only with a computer can I answer some of the most interesting questions. People make a conventional distinction between quantitative and qualitative social scientists. Qualitative people are reproached for, among other things, producing work which is (statistically) unrepresentative and fails to talk of distributions. In fact I believe that even the most determinedly postmodernist constitutist makes judgments about both these issues and is not arbitrary.[5] I personally do not want to reproach them, but if you do it should be on the ground that they do not make their fundamentally statistical judgments explicit, and expect us to take them on trust. Similarly, we all accept that quantitative people make judgments about what is interesting or useful to use statistics for, and that this is a value-laden activity which is usually left inexplicit. My point is additional: making a database is a creative act, constrained by cultural interests and shaped by the demands of the technology. Both these issues are usually underemphasized by practitioners. But none of this leads me to believe in a principled difference between the two alleged sorts of social science.[6]

MANIPULATIONS

That is the database, and it is as it is. I think that it allows me to recapture some of the experience of being a Libyan in the period 1932–79; and of explaining some of the changes which have happened. I want now to describe three kinds of things to do with the database.

The first is person orientated: we try to link the events to other events which involve the same people, and to represent some part of experience. To do this I want to abandon the conventional family-tree genealogy, and to adopt the kernmantel model proposed by my colleague Nick Allen. A kernmantel rope is made of strands which are not twisted but parallel, and are enclosed in a knitted skin. It is useful to climbers because it does not kink as twisted-cable ropes do. It is useful to anthropologists because

> genealogical diagrams reduce individuals to punctate elements in a network of relations. . . . We need a diagram which shows people as life-spans. Let us therefore envisage society as consisting of life-spans of varying length, starting at different points of time and running parallel to each other. One can use the image of a kernmantel rope.
>
> (Allen 1989: 49)

Of course, you would discard the enclosing skin, too suggestive of a bounded and confined 'society'. But Allen's invention is extremely valuable because it allows us to represent three important aspects of experience. So we can start with a line which we call Muftah. The line begins at a date (1942) and ends effectively in 1979, because that is when information ceases. Between 1974 and 1979 Muftah's line is linked to that of ʿAza (which begins in 1953). This is Figure 11.2. You will want to specify the quality of the experience further (what it felt like); but at least you know when it was and how long it lasted, and have a visual representation of it: one which encourages you more than a genealogy does to think about the meaning of relationships during the course of a lifetime.

The second representation is of accumulated experience: ʿAza and Muftah have a lived-in past, and have accumulated knowledge, understanding, expectations, prejudices which they bring to their current lives. Of course, we have all always known that this is true of all people everywhere; but our conventional diagrams do not stimulate us to think about that as much as Allen's kernmantel model does.

You can add to the diagram: at some time in the past ʿAza's line was similarly linked to another line, as yet unidentified. ʿAza and Muftah were each brought up in households, experienced other marriages in other roles; and they have friends, witnesses, guardians. All these can be added, as in Figure 11.3. It is important to be clear what this is. It is a diagram which partially rep-

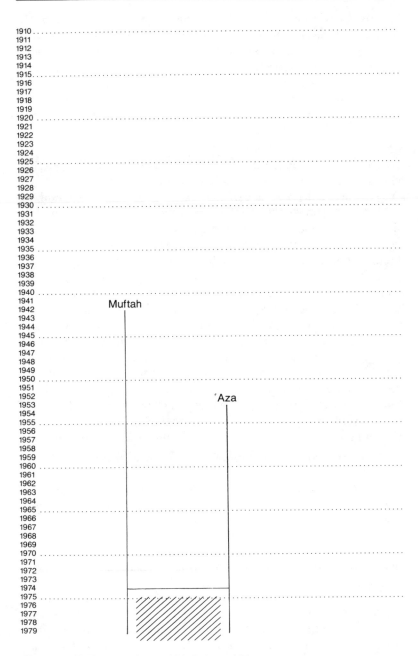

Figure 11.2 The marriage of Muftah and ʿAza

resents relationships among the people who participated directly or indirectly in an event, in Ajdabiya on 13 February 1974. It is derived from the information in an official document which does not mention the party, the ceremonies, the aunts and uncles and sisters and cousins who also took part in one way or another. It does not mention the gifts which were exchanged, apart from the legally obligatory *sidaq*. It is silent about connections with other records – marriages, divorces, remarriages with the same or different people. But to some extent these may be recoverable and can be added to the diagram. Finally, it is silent about the bureaucratically irrelevant relationships between the people concerned: Atiya, one of the witnesses, was a friend of the groom, and we could try to represent this with a patterned link between them, like the marriage one. From the genealogical information available you can add the patrilineal connections between people, and place them in the model which they had of their membership of their *qabila*, and you can add further information about occupations and residence. All these add further connections of different kinds to other people who may themselves be married and divorced.

The result would be a diagram of extreme complexity, representing a number of partial realities, and in my view not much use. It begins to get very complex as you add in other kinds of relationship, and I guess that this is about the sensible limit of a monochrome, two-dimensional diagram. Nevertheless, by combining archival evidence, genealogy and other ethnographic information you can imagine how you could build up a complex, though no doubt still incomplete, representation of the relationships and experience of a population. I think it is too complex to do, but it is good to imagine.

So the third aspect of experience represented in a kernmantel diagram is change. First, it is quite clear that exclusive relationships alter the field for everyone else: I have mentioned that when a couple marry, the options available to everyone else alter. This and similar consequences of actions are accessible from a kernmantel diagram. Second, the patterns of relationships extant in 1975 are not the same as those of 1932. The duration of marriages of young people is shorter; the number of plural marriages is much smaller, and so on. Again, I do not claim that nobody ever perceived this before, but I do think that the kernmantel diagram brings this much closer to the foreground of perception, and reminds us that changes are located in the experience of lives.

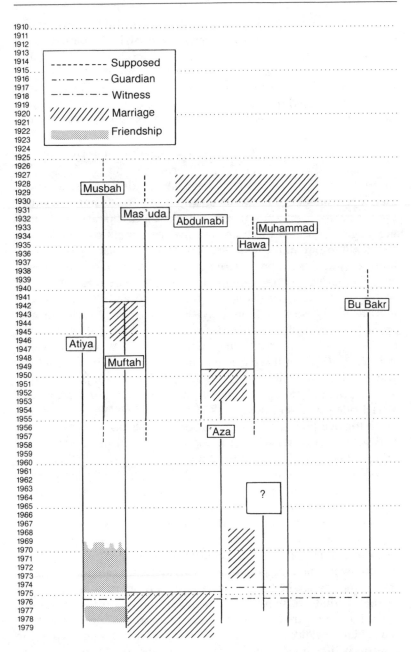

Figure 11.3 Elaboration of the diagram of the marriage of Muftah and
ʿAza

So the second kind of manipulation of information takes particular topics and tries to discover and explain the patterns. For instance, I have fairly good information about how old spouses were when they got married. So I can work out, year by year, the mean age at marriage of those spouses who appear in the documents, the mean difference in age between spouses, and the range of variation. The pattern is fairly clear: in the early 1930s women married at 16 or earlier, men as much as fifteen or twenty years later. In the later period women married rather later (17 or 18), and men rather younger (25). Information about duration of marriages is less systematic. I have no death records, and so a marriage which ends in the ideal way, at death, is not accessible. Divorce records may not be complete, and I cannot assume that all marriages for which there are no divorce papers continued until the death of one of the spouses. Nevertheless, I can match known marriages against known divorces year by year and, with proper caution, derive an approximate divorce rate. The rate varies, and so too do the kind of divorce which is used and the duration of marriages. These variations may themselves vary with the geographical and kinship distance between the spouses' households of origin, or for instance with the amount of bridewealth retained as deferred *sidaq*. But those calculations are very much in the future, and it is very difficult to arrive at any preliminary impression.

These are all attempts to answer questions about more and less. Was bridewealth more in 1979 than in 1932? Was bridewealth more for rich people than for poor ones? Was it more for virgins? Did some categories of people marry close kin more often than others? Did any of this change between 1932 and 1979? Did rates of polygyny remain constant in those years? Did polygynists divorce more than others? Did people who married close kin, or married with more costly bridewealth, divorce more or less than others? And did any of that alter during the fifty years?

These questions produce answers which are essentially lines on a two-dimensional graph: in themselves they contain no explanation, even when the population is divided into categories (e.g. of those who married close kin and those who did not) and the rates of this or that are plotted for each. Graphs serve two purposes. They indicate a trend against which I can assess the typicality of particular instances. Second, when trends are juxtaposed I can approach the threshold of explanation, and begin to talk about social processes.

relations between men and women (Caraveli 1986; Skiada 1991: 316–49; cf. Campbell 1964: 278–91; Dubisch 1986). Olymbos is a strictly sex-segregated society. While men spend time with other men, mainly in the coffee-houses and at community gatherings, women socialize with other women at various work sites such as the house, the village gardens and the fields. In these gender-specific places men and women discuss separately from each other personal and community matters, gossip about co-villagers or engage in verbal confrontations with persons of their own gender.

A notable exception to the norm of sex segregation is the Olymbos dance. The dance is the last phase of a community ritual known as the *glendi*, a complex ceremony of drinking, playing of music, singing and dancing (Caraveli 1985; Kavouras 1991: 200–85). The *glendi* is basically a male affair; women participate actively only in the phase of the dance. Olymbians view this ritual *rapprochement* of the sexes as a process which is conducive to the formation of a community body; and they call the symbolic space of the dance the *parousia*, literally the presence or appearance (of the community), that is the place where the community 'reveals itself' (Kavouras 1991 and 1992).

The *parousia* inspires Olymbians with profound awe and reverence. In this setting, participants behave with extreme caution because their reputation is threatened with serious damage if their words and deeds are misconstrued by the dancers and onlookers. A heightened aspect of the *parousia* is experienced during the *glendi* phase of the slow dance (*kato horos*) in which the male dancers sing praises, or sometimes censures, of the girl dancers (Kavouras 1992). Olymbians revere the *kato horos* as the most brilliant facet of the *parousia* and consider it to be the culmination of the *glendi* process. The ritual estimation and ranking of a girl's personality in the dance involves the assessment of her social worth on the basis of the evaluation of her conduct in the – familiar for the community – framework of the girl's genealogical history of morality. All statements and arguments concerning the girl dancers are expressed in the form of extempore fifteen-syllable rhyming couplets known as the *mandinadhes* (Caraveli 1985; Kavouras 1991: 244–72; Kavouras 1992; cf. Herzfeld 1985). Such poetic exchanges are conducive to creating a community dialogue in which every male participant is expected (in the sense of being both entitled and obliged) to contribute to the assessing and evaluating process. Olymbians view the *glendi* as a salient symbol of their culture. They distinguish those excelling in singing, playing of music and dancing from the ordinary participants by honorifically dubbing the former *meraklidhes* (Caraveli 1985: 264; Kavouras 1991: 217–22). For example, a clever and ingenious poet–singer is addressed as *meraklis* (singular of *meraklidhes*), and if he transcends a certain level of mental quickness and resourcefulness in singing he is called a *protomeraklis*, a principal *meraklis*. By being the motive force of the *glendi*, *meraklidhes* have the indisputable authority to restrain any participants from transgressing its rules or the moral boundaries of the *parousia* in general.

Let me return to Kalitsa and Minas. As a principal *meraklis* Minas has a normative jurisdiction to cast judgment openly on anybody's conduct in the *parousia*. On the other hand, Kalitsa is in a disadvantageous position as her reaction to Minas' offence is bounded not only by Minas' supreme authority but also by her gender, which constrains her to remain silent.

Now I come to the final phase of the analysis of Kalitsa's narrative text. With the help of the preceding information about the *trimistiro* and the clarifications concerning Kalitsa's allusions to aspects of the changing culture of Olymbos, I shall interpret Kalitsa's own account of her clash with Minas by examining step by step the various interrelationships between the intentional, the social and the historical contexts of her narration.[21]

INTERPRETING KALITSA'S NARRATIVE

By introducing herself as a *trimistiro* Kalitsa contradicts the prevailing view that this expression is insulting. However narrow the definition of herself as a *trimistiro* may be, it nonetheless contains ambiguous connotations – the characterization *arathimi* (irritable and irascible) does not suggest an ideal personality. Kalitsa aims at depicting herself as a paradoxical person in the particular sense of being impatient and of having an extremely excitable temperament. To avoid, however, the slur of irrationality she hastens to transcend the nuances of capriciousness in the expression *arathimi* by suggesting that her impatience and anger are not manifested without due or sufficient cause. In a very comprehensive statement about her intentionality as a *trimistiro* she portrays herself as a righteous person acting as an unofficial yet impartial 'justice' in Olymbos.

Kalitsa employs kinship to create a dramatic context of narration. She establishes a practically rational framework of action pertaining to her relations with her father Filipis and brother Orgis. This framework enables Kalitsa not only to defend her righteousness but also to account for herself as an honourable person. She saves her own morality by annihilating the surmise of social stigmatization, attributing her unmarried status to the death of her brother. Furthermore, she alludes to her honourable status by referring to the presence of her father and brother as principal *meraklidhes* at the *parousia*, implying that any maiden from Olymbos would be proud to be represented in the community dances by such esteemed poet–singers as Filipis and Orgis.

As indicated, Kalitsa uses her relationship to her brother to rationalize her paradoxical conduct. Yet seven years of mourning is too long a period of seclusion even for a conservative Olymbian woman like herself lamenting the death of her beloved brother. Thus, the excessive period of mourning reflects Kalitsa's tendency as a *trimistiro* to exaggerate, as well as to transcend, the local limits of social normality.

Kalitsa also uses the figure of her father, Filipis, as both an excuse and a catalyst for her own actions by depicting him as urging her to attend a community dance. Her purpose is evident; she aims at morally justifying her decision to go to the dance as a rational and socially appropriate choice, in spite of its apparently offensive character, as she was still in mourning. To transcend the social boundaries of mourning she strategically juxtaposes her position to that of her father, whose grief for the loss of his son, an esteemed poet–singer like himself, was considered to be the greatest possible in the community. Thus, she transfers the burden of responsibility for going to the dance from herself to her father, implicitly admitting Filipis' superior authority as her parent.

This is an allegorical tactic. Kalitsa's explicit deference to her father's authority alludes to her conformity with the customs and morals of her community. She therefore employs this stratagem to lead her audience to accept her contention that since she demonstrated her reverence for the Olymbos culture by showing deference to her father she should be viewed as an irreproachable figure.

Let me now examine the dance event and its significance for Kalitsa's rhetorical strategizing. In her narrative she mentions in passing that the community dance she attended was held on Carnival Sunday. She knows, of course, that this particular dance is not an ordinary feast. In pre-World War II Olymbos the end of Carnival also marked the end of the wedding season, and the Carnival Sunday dance was the last opportunity Olymbians had before Lent to celebrate a marriage or announce a wedding arrangement. Kalitsa elaborates the dramatic framework of her social and narrative action by juxtaposing two apparently incompatible situations: the death of her brother and the Carnival Sunday dance. While Orgis' death symbolizes Kalitsa's social death as a mature unmarried woman, the Carnival Sunday dance is a glorification of marriage. Once again, she resorts to hyperbole to transform ordinary interactions into archetypal contradictions.

To avoid any slurs on her social reputation Kalitsa went to the dance dressed all in black. Her clothing conveyed a non-verbal message: 'I'm here only as an onlooker, not as an active participant.' Yet, as any observer might contend, her appearance was so extremely absurd – an apparition – especially in the context of the dance, that it made her look ridiculous and pitiable. In her narrative, however, she handles this unfavourable situation strategically. While she admits to being criticized in the dance, she hastens to annihilate the slurring implications of the criticism by accounting for it as a socially isolated, individual reaction. She refers to the male dancers by dividing them into a large majority honouring her through singing praises for her niece and only one person, Minas, who ridicules her. In portraying Minas, Kalitsa reveals how a *trimistiro* uses language to transform social experience into critical knowledge. She begins by introducing him not only as a principal poet–singer but also as her relative. By this strategic move she alludes to Minas as a normatively ideal guardian to herself in the *parousia*, substituting in this role her absent father and brother. In depicting her adversary in socially ideal terms she intends not to praise him, but instead to lead her audience to detach themselves from Minas' actual conduct in the dance by situating his behaviour and personality in an archetypal context of morality. By means of this perspectival shift, Kalitsa aims at deflecting the audience's attention from Minas' own interpretation of the situation, which reflects not only his own views but, to some extent, also the opinion of the community of participants in the Carnival Sunday dance.[22] Therefore she individualizes the incident by pre-empting any interpretations based on Minas' actual context of action, by re-contextualizing him as an ideal character. This conceptual transformation enables Kalitsa not only to avoid stigmatization, but also to act as a community critic casting judgment on the impending moral crime in an exemplary manner.

Kalitsa accounts for Minas' paradoxical behaviour by resorting to his genealogical history. This method of action is not a rhetorical device contrived by Kalitsa, but a customary tactic employed by any adult Olymbian confronting an unexpected social situation. It is generally believed that a person's morality depends on the morality of his/her family, and that a person's moral traits are not culturally acquired but hereditary. This framework enables Olymbians to rationalize a person's behaviour in terms of his/her genealogical history. In any event, the thrust of this kind of hereditary determinism is not sociobiological but symbolic. In the kin-based society of Olymbos those persons who attain the ideal personality of a character are singled out not as socially isolated individuals but as paradigmatic figures of their lineages (cf. Campbell 1964: 274–97; MacIntyre 1984: 27–9).

Let me now return to the conflict between Kalitsa and Minas. Kalitsa begins her account of this event by portraying herself as equal in ruthlessness to Minas, juxtaposing her verbal severity to his physical ferocity: she dishonours him for drenching her at the *parousia*. Kalitsa, however, does not handle the incident as a personal confrontation between herself and Minas. She contends that Minas' behaviour is allegorical and that his target is not simply herself or her family but something far more significant. Her judgment of Minas is neither emotivist nor criterionless, but rests on a practical rationality shared by everybody in the audience. Minas is known to the community not only as a celebrated poet–singer, but also as a notorious allegorist who has ridiculed the families of certain girls through mocking the latter in the dance.

Kalitsa's sole purpose is to shame Minas.[23] She is, of course, aware of the extreme difficulty of her task, because Minas as a principal *meraklis* has absolute authority at the *parousia* of the *glendi*. Therefore, her strategy is to show that Minas is ultimately a vicious man who uses his poetic talents in a self-serving way. To prove this contention she shows that Minas, instead of leading the *glendi* participants to experience a sense of their community as he ought to be doing were he an authentic *meraklis*, deceives them by misleading everybody into forming wrong opinions about herself and her family as being strange people. Since she cannot confront Minas in his own context of action, she fights him in the archetypal context of genealogical traditions. In contrast to Minas' non-verbal strategy of ridicule, Kalitsa uses explicitly offensive language to punish her adversary in an exemplary manner. In essence, Kalitsa reverses Minas' rhetorical strategy and turns it against him: while Minas mocks Kalitsa with the intention of ridiculing her family, Kalitsa shames Minas by disgracing his.

By juxtaposing Minas' contradictory personae as ideal social character and as base offender Kalitsa implicitly poses a rhetorical question to her audience: how could such a normatively esteemed person as Minas commit such an unethical act? However, she does not let her audience form an independent opinion about the event, but leads them instead to admit that Minas is a deceitful character, justifying her judgment on the common knowledge that Minas' family was socially stigmatized. She expresses this association powerfully by addressing Minas twice as 'Kostara', (the vocative case of 'Kostaras'), a derogatory augmentative of Minas' maternal grandfather's Christian name, Kostis. By this tactical move she reminds everybody in the audience that Minas is not an authentic Olympian but the offspring of a mixed marriage. This reminder aims at suggesting that, despite his admittedly great talents in singing, Minas should not be allowed to pass judgment on the personal or family matters of other Olympians as he is not, properly speaking, a member of the Olympian community.

This is a well-calculated move. In associating Minas with his maternal grandfather, Kalitsa has a twofold purpose. The explicit first aim has been accounted for already: she wants to shame Minas by showing that he is not an authentic Olympian. To understand the implicit second target one should begin by noting that Kalitsa omits to mention in her narrative the conflict between Minas' father, Annis, and his father, Minatsis, over Annis' marriage. That Kalitsa refrains from mentioning Annis' family conflict does not mean that her audience will not make this association. In fact, this is precisely what she expects them to do; and in order to facilitate this line of reasoning she ends her offensive characterizations of Minas with the statement: 'Like your *yenia* (lineage), you're all worthless.'

At this juncture Kalitsa reveals herself as an ingenious mythopoeist. She re-contextualizes the figures of Minas and herself by portraying them as archetypal embodiments of two antagonistic sociocultural modalities. She suggests that her confrontation with Minas reflects the juxtaposition of the traditional conservatism of the *kanakaridhes* with the liberal individualism of the emigrants.

To support this view she explicitly focuses on Minas' genealogical image. In leading her audience to focus on Minas' family in her own specific context of examination, she knows that two figures will be singled out for consideration: the prominent *kanakaris* Minatsis and his son, the successful emigrant Annis. At this phase of her narration, Kalitsa rhetorically manipulates the coincidence of circumstances concerning Minas' family tensions by reducing all contexts into one: the conflict between the landowners and the emigrants. The father–first son relationship between Minatsis and Annis qualifies it as the strongest possible bond in the kin-based society of Olymbos, alluding also to the hegemony of the *kanakaridhes*. However, it is also generally known that Annis' marriage destroyed this relationship, turning it into a life-long separation. What Kalitsa implies therefore is that the separation of Minas' family should be considered as a symptom of the fragmentation of the Olymbos community resulting from the prevalence of the emigrants over the *kanakaridhes*.

In the early 1950s (when Kalitsa's clash with Minas happened) Olymbians knew that the hegemony of the *kanakaridhes* was irrevocably over. However, since the socioeconomic infrastructure of Karpathos did not change significantly until the early 1970s, any liberties taken by the repatriated emigrants and their descendants were censured by the community (Vernier 1977; Karagheorghi-Halkia 1981; Kavouras 1992). While Olymbians supported the new rationality, which was categorically against the oligarchic authority of the *kanakaridhes*, they strongly opposed any attempt at substituting the modernist idea of progress for their traditional way of life. In the 1950s Olymbians were already concerned about losing their cultural identity; and they expressed their anxieties by attributing the loss of their customs to the alienating influence of the adoption of foreign practices.

Kalitsa's strategy now becomes clear. She intends to represent the incident in the dance as a timely expression of the cultural crisis in Olymbos. By portraying Minas' genealogical history as representing the conflict between authentic and non-authentic existence in Olymbos, Kalitsa portrays Minas as an archetypal figure embodying the emotivist ethos of liberal individualism. One should not forget, however, that the time in which the incident occurred and the time of the narration are only two moments in Kalitsa's life separated by a temporal interval of about forty years. They are, however, significant instances because it is the weaving-together of these two fragments of Kalitsa's personal history that defines the main thrust of her social and narrative action.

Kalitsa sends to her community audience an allusive yet clear message: Minas embodies the alienating force threatening contemporary Olymbos with destruction. Once this connection is established Kalitsa's own rationalization of the incident evolves unimpeded. Her view is that in soaking her at the *parousia* Minas intended not simply to mock herself and her family, but rather to ridicule the traditional culture of Olymbos. By defining Minas' offence to herself as an inconceivable hubris against the community Kalitsa closes the hermeneutic circle by explaining to her audience that this shameless act is the rightful product of the offender's inauthentic existence.

The connotations of Kalitsa's allusions to Minas' genealogical history in the context of the cultural crisis in Olymbos were readily understood by everybody in the audience; and they could not be refuted. Minas had no choice but to leave the *parousia* utterly dishonoured.

REFLEXIVITY AND MORAL JUDGMENT AS VEHICLES FOR SOCIAL CRITICISM

The *trimistira* are special characters. Although they do not embody any particular values and ideas of morality, they express social criticism through judging the moral conduct of their peers. The *trimistira* evaluate and assess publicly any significant actions and ideas of other community members by demonstrating how specific persons inhabit particular moral characters. This tactic enables them to situate the behaviour and personalities of the adjudged figures in a community context in which the perception of one's genealogical background is critical. To be able to act as arbiters of justice in the community the *trimistira* must persuade their audiences that they are morally irreproachable.

The *trimistira* may not be characters *in themselves*, but their projected righteousness gives them the community pretext for using the symbolic space of moral characters to launch their social criticism. They are not, however, entirely free to act as they like, as they must respect not only the community standards of morality but also be consistent in – to use Barbara Myerhoff's phrase (Bruner 1986: 12) – 'authoring themselves' as critical social characters through their punitive narratives. Hence, the moral–

characterological restraints that the *trimistira* enforce upon their own behaviour and personalities may appear to come from the outside social world but are actually socially legitimized projections of their own conscience. Therefore the *trimistira* do not simply inhabit but create their moral universes. In the resulting cosmological formations the community symbolizes the conscience of the *trimistiro*. This arrangement explains why the *trimistira* define the moral boundaries of their social and narrative action in terms of certain community standards of morality, which they specifically and concretely articulate before their audiences. The symbolic relationship between community and conscience implies that the *trimistira* are both character-constituted and character-constitutive social actors.

As characters of social criticism the *trimistira* employ a three-fold framework of action. First, they defend their proclaimed righteousness by affirming their morally consistent behaviour and personality. Second, they transcend the moral boundaries of personal or family dispute by rendering an account of their conflict with their adversaries in socially archetypal terms. And, third, they publicly censure those who dispute their integrity by manifesting the latter's injustice as a cultural symptom of lower social existence.

The *trimistira* are strategists. They manipulate their audiences by rhetorically persuading them to believe in their own interpretation of a social situation. They construct their critical narratives with a rhetorical coherence that enables them, under the pretext of logical consistency, to define the community context of interpretation. Their rhetoric of morality is based on their ability to de-contextualize and then re-contextualize community inferences concerning individual activity. By critically contextualizing referential evidence the rhetorical strategists manipulate the reflexivity of their audiences through broadening the latter's perceptual horizons. This is exemplified by any social situation involving negotiations between families, as for instance a wedding arrangement. Although Olympians feel ambivalence as to whether they should let any *trimistira* interfere in the wedding negotiations, they attribute any rapid and irrevocable influence of the outcome to the catalytic interpretation of the genealogical histories of the prospective bride and groom provided by any concerned *trimistira*.

As characters of social criticism the *trimistira* transcend the cultural boundaries of gender distinction. In the strongly sex-segregated society of Olymbos the female *trimistira* are just as powerful as the male ones. This aspect of structural transcendence of institutionalized gender distinctions reflects the tradition-bound nature of Olymbos culture. Moreover, that the female *trimistiro* Kalitsa must 'lower herself' by using vituperation to confront the poet–singer Minas should be interpreted not as a sign of her inability as a woman to compete with a man in poetry, but rather as a characteristic idiom of any *trimistiro*. Criticalness, like harshness, defines the whole process of judging by a *trimistiro*, involving not only the judgment but also the methods used in casting it.

In a recent volume on the 'anthropology of experience', the editor, Edward Bruner (1986: 5–6), epitomized the contributors' views by arguing that human beings transcend the limitations of individual experience through interpreting expressions. He defines this transcendence as constituting a hermeneutic circle, a process whereby 'experience structures expressions and expressions structure experience'. Although, as Bruner contends, every human being is engaged in this hermeneutic process, such categories of persons as the *trimistira* of Olymbos manipulate this faculty by transforming social experience into critical knowledge through everyday language; and they employ the emergent context of knowledge as a reflexive vehicle for their social criticism. The practice of rhetorical strategizing should not lead one to consider the *trimistira* in dramaturgical terms, as being socially isolated, individual performers of identity roles. By manipulating the hermeneutic circle the *trimistira* are actually engaged in a self-reflexive process of informing and thereby defining a tradition-constituted and tradition-constitutive mode of being in the world. Far from being mere performers of criterionless judgment, the *trimistira* stand out as self-reflexive critics, being the socially concrete, embodied manifestations of cultural resistance to alienation.

ACKNOWLEDGMENT

Besides Kirsten Hastrup and Peter Hervik, and the other participants in the 1992 EASA workshop *Social Experience and Anthropological Knowledge* of which this volume is the outcome, I wish to thank Virginia Skiada, Alex Doumas, Diane Mueller, Nikiforos Diamandouros, Ineke van Wetering and Charles

Stewart for their valuable criticisms of earlier drafts of this article. A special debt of gratitude is due to my Greek compatriots, the people of Olymbos, as well as other Karpathians, for their hospitality, friendship and practical help.

NOTES

Besides Kirtsne Hastrup and Peter Hervik, and the other participants in the 1992 EASA workshop *Social Experience and Anthropological Knowledge* of which this volume is the outcome, I wish to thank Virginia Skiada, Alex Doumas, Diane Mueller, Nikiforos Diamandouros, Ineke van Wetering and Charles Stewart for their valuable criticisms of earlier drafts of this article. A special debt of gratitude is due to my Greek compatriots, the people of Olymbos, as well as other Karpathians, for their hospitality, friendship and practical help.

1 Karpathos is the second largest island of the Dodecanese, with a population of about 5,000 permanent residents and a great diaspora. It is estimated that there are about 3,500 Olymbians of whom only 600 live in Karpathos and the rest are in Baltimore, Rhodes and Piraeus. In the mid 1930s the population of Olymbos reached the peak of 2,200, the largest ever in Karpathos since 1890 (Philippides 1973: 30–3; Aghapitidis 1987: 165–70; National Greek Census).

2 In the mid 1930s the constables of Karpathos were Italian nationals, as the Dodecanese were under Italian rule from 1912 until 1943.

3 I conducted fieldwork in Karpathos between 1986 and 1989. The results of that research appear in my doctoral dissertation (1991) and in an article on the Olymbos dance (1992).

4 There are no references to the concept of *trimistiro* in ethnographic writings about Greece or in folklore studies about Karpathos (Kamilakis 1979). However, the anthropological literature on honour and shame offers a conceptual, although analytically problematic, framework for considering morality (which is the *trimistiro*'s arena of criticism) from a sociocultural perspective (Campbell 1964; Herzfeld 1980; Gilmore 1987).

5 By traditional I mean customary and conventional, referring to certain aspects of the Olymbos culture which acquired hegemonic significance in the period between the early 1880s and late 1940s (Kavouras 1991: 375–412). For a critical discussion of the usages of 'tradition' and 'traditional' in Olymbos see Kavouras (1992).

6 Goffman's work is the forerunner of 'practice' approaches in sociology (Rossi 1983: 309–24) and anthropology (Ortner 1984). Goffman explores the constitutive and situational aspects of social interaction and meaning by drawing on symbolic interactionism, sociological phenomenology and ethnomethodology (1959; 1969; 1971; 1974).

7 I use the word metaphor from a poetic and rhetorical perspective. My purpose in using metaphor in that sense is not to argue that reflexivity

is embedded in language but to emphasize the *trimistiro*'s manipulation of social experience through discourse. For cognitive and symbolic approaches to metaphor as a cultural trope see Fernandez (1991).

8 I use discourse as a cover term meaning any kind of active and framed
verbal communication. In dealing with the discursive activities of the
trimistiro as 'communicative events' (Hymes 1974: 4), I explore the
performative strategies employed by the *trimistiro* in his or her attempt
to render any such event in socially meaningful terms. Despite their
discursive character, such strategies are processes of social interaction
cutting across communciative (verbal or not), political and cultural
boundaries (Finnegan 1992: 42–4).

9 By narrative I mean any temporally framed linguistic expression,
especially the practice of relating stories whether they are anecdotal in
nature or more meticulous in their attention to consecutive details. It
follows that, thus defined, narrative is a special form of discourse.
Also, to emphasize the individual artistry and experience of a narrator
I refer to his or her narratives as personal ones.

10 The 'ethnography of speaking' and its specific developments such as
discourse analysis, performance theory and ethnopoetics offer valuable insights into the status of narrative in relation to social experience
and reflexivity (Finnegan 1992: 42–5).

11 By personal history MacIntyre means the narratives people construct
of their intentions, ideas and actions from an evaluative perspective as
successes and failures in their lifetime (1984: 3).

12 The vocative case of Kostaras.

13 A makeshift fishing rod made of cane.

14 By critical knowledge I mean any process of understanding which is
based on the exercise of social-through-moral judgment upon matters
of crucial significance to the persons involved.

15 By folk knowledge I mean any sum of information that is handed down
from generation to generation in a particular society; especially, any
'orally transmitted tradition' (Finnegan 1992: 11–13). Therefore, I
examine critical knowledge (which by definition is based on social
experience) as a special form of folk knowledge encountered in
tradition-bound cultures. Hence, in my anthropological analysis of the
trimistiro, I explore the processes and situations mediated by this
figure whereby folk knowledge becomes the critical one and vice
versa.

16 I use Gramsci's (1971: 12–14) concept of hegemony to account for
culture as a homogenizing process, legitimizing and reproducing sociopolitical inequality.

17 The contextual discernment between the textual realities of personal
history and autobiography helps to examine any particular narrative at
a referential, reflexive and self-reflexive level of analysis.

18 Women are the main agents of death rituals in Olymbos. The cultural
space of death enables women to use poetry and rhetoric in the form of
lamentations to express social criticism (Caraveli 1986; Kavouras 1991:
100–37; see also Seremetakis 1991).

19 Although Annis' father's Christian name was Minas, I shall refer to

him as Minatsis, using this dialectical derivative so as to distinguish old Minas from his grandson Minas, the main figure in Kalitsa's narrative.

20 The history of migration in Olymbos is divided into three phases, seasonal, long-term and permanent, each involving a distinct pattern of expatriation with respect to the migrants' duration of stay abroad (Philippides 1973: 34–6; Kavouras 1991: 52–66).

21 It would be quite illuminating to juxtapose Kalitsa's narrative with the accounts given of the same event by other Olymbians. I shall not attempt such a comparison, however, since my main focus in this chapter is the constructive strategies used by a *trimistiro* in expressing social criticism.

22 My analysis of Kalitsa's narrative tactics raises conceptual as well as epistemological issues regarding the degree of subjective or objective understanding of Olymbians and non-native anthropologists have of the methods of procedure used by the *trimistira* in situations of social criticism. To avoid falling into an analytical double-bind I have taken a practice-based approach (Ortner 1984) instead of a purely interpretive one. Following this view I have reached the conclusion that Kalitsa's strategies are, despite their seemingly impulsive character, deliberate practices.

23 Ridicule was the customary form of paradigmatic punishment in pre-war Olymbos. Although the Italian authorities endeavored to substitute judicial law for customary punishment, they did not succeed in abolishing the shaming practice of ridicule (Konsolas 1963: 264; Kavouras 1991: 339–74).

24 A consistent theme in the folk poetry of Olymbians is the experience of *xenitia* (exile, expatriation), the estrangement not only from one's geographical home but one's very being (Kavouras 1991).

REFERENCES

Aghapitidhis, S. (1987) «Ο πληθυσμός της Καρπάθου» ('The population of Karpathos'), *Καρπαθιακαι Μελεται* 4: 165–70.

Bruner, E. (1986) Introduction: 'Experience and its Expressions', in Victor Turner and Edward Bruner, eds, *The Anthropology of Experience*, Chicago: University of Illinois Press.

Campbell, J.K. (1964) *Honour, Family and Patronage*, Oxford: Clarendon Press.

Caraveli, A. (1985) 'The symbolic village: community born in performance', *Journal of American Folklore* 98: 259–86.

— (1986) 'The bitter wounding: the lament as social protest in rural Greece', in Jill Dubisch, ed., *Gender & Power in Rural Greece*, Princeton, NJ: Princeton University Press.

Clifford, J., and Marcus, G., eds (1986) *Writing Culture: The Poetics and Politics of Ethnography*, Berkeley: University of California Press.

Cowan, J. (1990) *Dance and the Body Politic in Northern Greece*, Princeton, NJ: Princeton University Press.

Crapanzano, V. (1980) *Tuhami: Portrait of a Moroccan*, Chicago: University of Chicago Press.

Daskalopoulou-Kapetanaki, S. (1987) «Ερμηνεία της συγγενειακής οργάνωσης σε σχέση με την ιδιοποίηση της γης» ('An interpretation of the parental structure in relation to the appropriation of land'), Ελληνική Κοινωνία 1: 67–79.

Dubisch, J. (1986) 'Introduction', in Jill Dubisch, ed., Gender & Power in Rural Greece, Princeton, NJ: Princeton University Press.

Fernandez, J., ed. (1991) Beyond Metaphor: The Theory of Tropes in Anthropology, Stanford, Calif.: Stanford University Press.

Finnegan, R. (1992) Oral Traditions and the Verbal Arts: A Guide to Research Practices, London: Routledge.

Gilmore, D., ed. (1987) Honor and Shame and the Unity of the Mediterranean, Washington, DC: Special Publication of the American Anthropological Association 22.

Goffman, E. (1959) The Presentation of Self in Everyday Life, New York: Anchor.

—— (1969) Strategic Interaction, Philadelphia: University of Pennsylvania Press.

—— (1971) Relations in Public, New York: Harper & Row.

—— (1974) Frame Analysis, New York: Harper & Row.

Gramsci, A. (1971) Selections from the Prison Notebooks, trans. and ed. Q. Hoare and G. Nowell Smith, London: Lawrence & Wishart.

Halkias, Y. (1980) Μούσα Ολύμπου Καρπάθου (The Muse of Olymbos, Karpathos), Athens.

Herzfeld, M. (1980) 'Honor and shame: problems in the comparative analysis of moral systems', Man 15: 339–51.

—— (1985) The Poetics of Manhood: Contest and Identity in a Cretan Mountain Village, Princeton, NJ: Princeton University Press.

—— (1987) Anthropology through the Looking Glass: Critical Ethnography in the Margins of Europe, Cambridge: Cambridge University Press.

Hymes, D. (1974) Foundations in Sociolinguistics: An Ethnographic Approach, Philadelphia: University of Pennsylvania Press.

Kamilakis, P. (1979) «Λαογραφική και γλωσσολογική βιβλιογραφία Καρπάθου και Κάσου των Δωδεκανήσων» ('Folklore and linguistic literature on Karpathos and Kassos, Dodecanese'), Καρπαθιακαί Μελέται 1: 267–367.

Karagheorghi-Halkia, F. (1981) «Κοινωνική και οικονομική ανάπτυξη νήσου Καρπάθου» ('Social and economic development of Karpathos'), Καρπαθιακαί Μελέται 2: 253–88.

Kavouras, P. (1991) 'Glendi and xenitia: the poetics of exile in rural Greece (Olymbos, Karpathos)', doctoral dissertation, The New School for Social Research. Ann Arbor, Mich.: U.M.I.

—— (1992) 'The dance at Olymbos, Karpathos: cultural change and political confrontations', Ethnographica (The Peloponnesian Folklore Foundation) 8: 173–90.

Konsolas, N. (1963) «Λαογραφικά Ολύμπου Καρπάθου» ('Elements of folklore from Olymbos, Karpathos'), Λαογραφία 21: 215–68.

MacIntyre, A. (1984) After Virtue: A Study in Moral Theory, Notre Dame, Ind.: University of Notre Dame Press.

—— (1988) *Whose Justice? Which Rationality?*, Notre Dame, Ind.: University of Notre Dame Press.

Marcus, G., and Fischer, M., eds (1986) *Anthropology as Cultural Critique*, Chicago: University of Chicago Press.

Mihailidhis-Nouaros, M. (1951) Χρονικόν της Νήσου Καρπάθου (A Chronicle of Karpathos Island), Pittsburgh Pa.

—— (1972) Λεξικόν της Καρπαθιακής διαλέκτου (Dictionary of the Karpathian Dialect), Athens.

Mihailidhis-Nouros, Y. (1984) «Παρατηρήσεις στο κληρονομικό έθιμο της Καρπάθου» ('Reflections on the Karpathos inheritance custom'), *Καρπαθιακαί Μελέται* 3: 7–27.

Myerhoff, B. (1980) *Number Our Days*, New York: Simon & Schuster.

—— (1986) 'Life not death in Venice: its second life', in Victor Turner and Edward Bruner, eds, *The Anthropology of Experience*, Chicago: University of Illinois Press.

Ortner, S. (1984) 'Theory in anthropology since the sixties', *Comparative Studies in Society and History* 26: 126–66.

Philippides, D. (1973) 'The vernacular design system of Elymbos: a rural spatial system in Greece', doctoral dissertation, University of Michigan. Ann Arbor, Mich.: U.M.I.

Rabinow, P. (1977) *Reflection on Fieldwork in Morocco*, Berkeley: University of California Press.

Rosaldo, R. (1986) 'Illongot hunting as story and experience', in Victor Turner and Edward Bruner, eds, *The Anthropology of Experience*, Chicago: University of Illinois Press.

Rossi, I. (1983) *From the Sociology of Symbols to the Sociology of Signs: Toward a Dialectical Sociology*, New York: Columbia University Press.

Seremetakis, C.N. (1991) *The Last Word: Women, Death, and Divination in Inner Mani*, Chicago: University of Chicago Press.

Skiada, V. (1991) 'Gender and material culture: the social history of wealth in Olymbos, a Greek insular village', doctoral dissertation, The New School for Social Research. Ann Arbor, Mich.: U.M.I.

Stewart, J. (1991) *Demons and the Devil*, Princeton, NJ: Princeton University Press.

Turner, V., and Bruner, E., eds (1986) *The Anthropology of Experience*, Chicago: University of Illinois Press.

Vernier, B. (1977) 'Emigration et derèglement du marche matrimonial', *Actes de la recherche en sciences sociales* 15: 31–58. (There is a Greek translation of this article in *Σκούπα* 3: 60–73.)

—— (1984) 'Putting kin and kinship to good use: the circulation of goods, labour and names on Karpathos (Greece)', in H. Medick and D.W. Sabean, eds, *Interest and Emotion*, Cambridge: Cambridge University Press.

Chapter 9

Time, ritual and social experience

Andre Gingrich

The present chapter is concerned with social experience and the anthropological knowledge of temporality. It sets out first to identify anthropology's conventional notions of time within the context of a modern heritage. Then it argues that in non-secular societies basic notions of temporality are encompassed by mythic rationality and religious principles. These principles influence temporal experience in so far as they are socialized and internalized by way of concepts and rituals.

The renewed interest of the social sciences in 'pluritemporalism' and 'heterochronous' conceptions raises a topic that anthropology has been dealing with for a long time. It is shown that religious ideology constructs connected, hierarchical orders of temporal concepts, which shape and influence temporal experience of mind and body. Explicit and verbalized concepts and structures do influence the experience of time. But, simultaneously, there are forms of temporal experience beyond words that are essential for the verbalized experience of time. An ethnographic case from north-western Yemen is presented to illustrate this point.

The social production of a nameless emotional process may be functionally indispensable for the preparation of those very rituals that socialize temporal concepts. Practice and verbalized concepts therefore shape the experience of time to a certain extent only. Anthropological knowledge cannot marginalize the fact that time experience beyond words is embodied and acted out in the reproduction of temporal conceptions as well. We face the paradox to have to speak about the unspoken, and to work through the explicit spheres of temporality in order to explain also those beyond words.

TIME AND ANTHROPOLOGY'S MODERN HERITAGE

Time and space are fundamental notions in the history of Western thought in general, and of modern Western social theory in particular. In the most common form, time and space are presented as categories that first of all were abstract, quantifiable and distinct from each other; only second were they perceived as interrelated entities. This prevailing conception was decisively shaped by the Newtonian view of the physical universe and, to lesser degrees, by the Cartesian and Kantian views of the human mind.

Since Newton and Kant, axiomatic notions of modern Western thought have taken time and space as fundamental forms of matter belonging to the empirical world, and as the human mind's basic forms of perception. The developments of science and philosophy in the last ten or twelve decades have not merely modified, but decisively transformed, the modern, Newtonian heritage. But the transformation of Western thought mainly has been accepted for the understanding of micro- and macrocosmological problems, while interhuman relations have been touched only marginally and gradually (Hawking 1988; Forum für Philosophie 1992; Adam 1990 and 1992; Nowotny 1989). Anthropology was one of the first disciplines among the human and social sciences to point out that notions of time and space are not universally shaped as those distinct and abstract categories that Western thought had taken for granted (Hubert and Mauss 1909; Durkheim 1912). But the theoretical reflection of those rich ethnographic varieties of time and space conceptions rarely stimulated extensive debates in other disciplines, not even in sociology after the publication of Sorokin and Merton's work (1937). And among anthropologists themselves the topic was usually incorporated into one or another of the existing theoretical frameworks, without too much consideration of the potential for questioning basic theoretical assumptions.

This process of incorporation, of 'digesting' the space–time dimensions, sometimes seemed to be an easier task for cultural relativism. At least this was the superficial impression that cultural relativism had to produce, for obvious reasons: if each culture can only be understood in its own social and cognitive terms, then time and space simply are part and parcel of these specific cultural terms. Yet how ethnographic fieldwork and anthropological knowledge could ever manage to understand and to translate the cultural specificities of time and space conceptions remains un-answered by the relativist position (Zerubavel 1981, Levine 1988).

I believe that the less relativist and more comparative ap-proaches of European anthropology have often taken the task more seriously, by their search for the reasons behind difference and similarity. Within their heterogeneous discourse, the main structuralist, functionalist and neo-Marxist approaches seem to have upheld, until the mid-1970s, one common assumption, which could be formulated with regard to time conceptions like this: however differing and varying the ethnographic, cultural forms of time conceptions may be, the basic human perception of time (and of space) is the same; what differ are the social and cultural forms by which duration and succession, direction and extension are measured, experienced or evaluated (e.g. Bloch 1977).

The advantage of this position *vis-à-vis* the relativist tradition was that it left room for enquiries into both differences and similarities of time and space experience, and that it related their conceptions to social structure. The modernist heritage in anthro-pology and social theory, however, remained unchallenged by this position. Anthropological theory continued to regard time and space as distinct and abstract categories in the two discrete worlds of mind and matter, by separating a universal, homogeneous world of empirical perception from a heterogeneous world of cultural classifications and social construction.

This view of a separate, homogeneous world of perception became questionable already when it was shown that perception itself depends upon sociocultural differences that no physiological or psychological theory alone can sufficiently explain (Gregory 1972). In this and other ways, at least some psychological and sociological approaches were forced to discover their own 'anthro-pological naivety'. At the same time, anthropologists' attention became directed towards conceptualization, practice and experi-ence, and began to transcend the abstract dichotomies of subjecti-vism and objectivism. Recent years of anthropological research and discourse have thus displayed a more profound reconsider-ation of time and space conceptions. Fabian's *Time and the Other* (1983) contributed to this process of reconsideration, although I think that the discussion and criticism to which the book was subjected were as important as some of its main hypotheses, such as Fabian's valuable demonstration that anthropological literature itself creates distance towards the 'other'. However, this cannot hide the fact that fieldwork first of all juxtaposes differences between self and other during a process of interaction across cultural border areas. During this process, the participants' basic assumptions on time and space are pragmatically tested and questioned. The anthropologist's cosmology itself becomes more explicit in the light of fieldwork interaction, when implicit and self-understood attitudes are characterized by others as different.

Some branches of postmodern anthropology do not go further than that; too often they are satisfied with celebrating these experiences of 'self'. However, a thorough and critical form of social self-reflection can only be one step within the overall interaction, a step which by itself is necessary but not sufficient. It is merely a precondition for critically relating the anthropologist's theory and practice to those 'other' conceptions and forms of life. The necessity of self-reflection is no argument against, but rather is supporting a better understanding of, 'other times and spaces'.

A host of both early and recent studies[1] have helped to identify basic differences between Western and other conceptions of time and space. The inequalities and contrasts have to be considered on a theoretical level, if anthropological knowledge attempts to relate the differences beyond individual cases of ethnographic fieldwork on a comparative basis. It has thus become clear that outside Euro-American cultural influence, time and space conceptions are rarely constituted as abstract categories, but are deeply and concretely embedded within the totality of sociocultural cosmovision. It cannot be assumed a priori that these time and space conceptions are absolutely distinct from each other, or that one of them usually prevails over the other. While it might be difficult to neglect the dominance of time over space in Western everyday life (Young and Schuller 1988), this dominance cannot be taken for granted in the anthropological knowledge of non-Western societies – or, as a matter of fact, in all corners and spheres of Western societies (Hastrup 1992).

Time and space conceptions are interwoven and embedded, while in most Western social theories they are seen as distinct and abstract. This is one prerequisite to theorizing the difference.

RITUALS AS PRODUCERS AND MARKERS OF TIME(S)

Within theories of times, an important dimension of investigation concerns the relations between cultural concepts and the continuous experiences of time and space. An earlier position (exemplified in the presentation and dicussion of Turton and Ruggles 1978) confused perception and experience. Experience itself was regarded as universal, and difference was mainly related to measurement of duration and extension. This perspective separated the subjective and the objective to an untenable extent. We now realize that experience shapes and influences concepts as much as cultural concepts attempt to channel, organize and interpret experience. Time and space are also basic dimensions of bodily and emotional experience, not merely on particular occasions like, say, hunger or tension, but in the daily routine of each life-phase as well.

Consciously and subconsciously, the interrelation between concepts and experience of time and space is permanent and omnipresent; it is uniquely ubiquitous. The explicit side of the relationship ties verbalized concepts to identified forms of experience. Concepts and experience then are articulated in a self-confirming relation of mutual correspondence. The other, implicit side of the relationship is non-correspondence: it often implies verbalized concepts without any counterpart in social experience, but it may also imply social experience without and beyond words and concepts.

If anthropological knowledge attempts to use these distinctions within 'other' social contexts, a basic problem arises. Most non-Western societies, at their local levels at least, are non-secular. Their general notions of time and space have not been transformed by processes of *Entzauberung*; they are encompassed by mythic rationality. In short, these notions first of all have to be understood within their religious context.

I have argued elsewhere (Gingrich 1991) that the temporal structuring of experience by concepts displays specific features in non-secular societies and cosmovisions. These time conceptions are explicitly heterogeneous (Hernadi 1992), concrete, and ordered in hierarchies of priorities and contexts. Rituals provide an essential social mechanism for shaping the relation between these heterochronous concepts and social experience. Embedded in religious cosmovision and interwoven with spatial conceptions as they are, time conceptions become socialized and routinized by means of a society's central rituals. Ritual events themselves socialize certain time conceptions, which thereby become more important than others. Non-time, or eternity, is combined with a hierarchy of other temporal conceptions, be they circular, linear, convoluted or twisted.

Rituals have their own temporal (and spatial) order and dramaturgy, which need not necessarily correspond to the hierarchy of times in their symbolic contents. This 'social time' of ritual's dramaturgical order can thus be distinguished from ritual's 'symbolic time', referred to in its verbalized contents. The hierarchy and plurality of symbolic times are socialized within each participant's mind and body by his/her inclusion in that dramaturgical, temporal and spatial inner order of rituals.

Apart from having their own inherent times, rituals also mark social time in events that connect and interrupt duration. Duration is experienced as movement from or towards ritual events, and the periods between these events to some extent routinize those important time concepts that have already been socialized during ritual events. Simultaneously, less important conceptions that are placed on lower levels of the cosmovision's hierarchy are applied in their everyday life contexts. These processes of ritual socialization and of routinization in everyday life shape and influence individual and collective experiences of time even in the form of general experiences of ageing, disease and decay. These sociocultural processes always precondition experience of time.

TIME WITHOUT WORDS

The implicit side of the relationship between concepts and experience is a sphere of non-correspondence. The experience of time is not exhausted by the verbalized and explicit forms of time concepts. Kirsten Hastrup (1991) has drawn our attention to those differences between the written, the verbal and the non-verbal that are especially important for anthropological knowledge of the permanent and omnipresent interrelation between concepts and experience of time. It cannot be understood if we follow the logic of words or of writing alone. What I have said so far about the socialization and routinization of time conceptions through rituals has dealt with one side of the relationship, namely with how these concepts may influence experience. In what follows I shall try to consider the other crucial direction, i.e. the ways by which we can identify non-verbalized experiences of time and their impact on temporal concepts and action.

Let me first illustrate this sphere of time experience beyond words, and its relationship to the words and writings on time, by an example from my ethnographic fieldwork among the Munebbih, a tribe of mountain peasants in north-western Yemen. Munebbih time conceptions are local variations of a wider, regional register of social temporalities. The overall hierarchy and heterogeneity of these time conceptions encompass the Muslim calendar, dynastic historiography, tribal genealogies, star calendars, social *rites de passage*, and other, less important elements. Each of these elements has its directional emphasis and is embedded in the overall cosmovision. The Muslim calendar is a fundamental coordinate of Islamic cosmology, which integrates and defines the whole register. Dynastic historiography is formulated in the terms of that calendar, as is the history of regional theocracies. As such, historiography is subordinated to the Muslim calendar. Tribal genealogies define a tribe's present social and political status by reference to a mythical, allegedly pre-Islamic past. But until the recent pre-republican past at least, this idiom of genealogical self-definition was prepared to accept the theocracy's superiority, and above it that of God.

Within this hierarchical order, star calendars play a crucial part, since they relate the temporal aspects of agricultural subsistence to the central value of tribal honour, an honour of living in fertile tribal land as a landowning, armed and male individual. The star calendars thus represent one among several tribal time conceptions, with specific emphasis on repetition and non-chronological rhythms, and with a clear reference to the 'natural time' of the solar year.

Elements of natural time are integrated into agricultural and ritual concepts to constitute a specific social temporality that exists in oral or in written versions. These two worlds of time conceptions in northern Yemen share a limited number of elements, but differ in most other aspects.

There are urban, written almanacs in Arabic (cf. Varisco 1982). By their material form alone they separate star concepts from their social context, and they present stellar time-reckoning in a way that is not applicable and experienced by tribal people. These almanacs depict homogeneous cycles of twenty-eight stellar risings and settings, a clear analogy to the mansion system of medieval Arabic literature. The almanacs include stellar events that are only conspicuous in certain places or for specialists, and they single out dates that have no relevance for any single mountain community. For the sake of order, proportion, homogeneity and broad analogy to dominant values of 'great' and literate tradition, the almanacs are largely useless in the tribal world. Western anthropologists relying on these almanacs would produce a gravely distorted image of local time conceptions.

By contrast, the orally transmitted star calendar of the Munebbih is not at all homogeneous and orderly, but fragmentary, irregular and interrupted. It comprises two large time-spans: the period of white stars, and that of the black (firmament) stars. The white-star period comprises several risings and settings during the moist seasons of the year; the black stars (lunar conjunctions with the Pleiades) are observed during the cooler and drier seasons. This central tribal time conception is socialized by the main rituals of circumcision ceremonies, weddings, and bull sacrifices for rain. Between these main rituals, the stellar calendars and other time conceptions are routinized and applied.

The two transitional periods between the cool, dry season of the black stars and the moist, warm season of the white stars are verbally presented as the clear-cut termination of one stellar period and the subsequent beginning of the other. In this sense the argument is very similar to the written almanacs, but not as explicitly dogmatic. The oral presentation depicts one period as if it would immediately follow the previous one. But in fact the two do not neatly follow each other, but either overlap (in spring), or leave a gap between them (in autumn). These periods of either 'gap' or 'overlap' are not designated by words; they have no name and do not correspond to any specific verbalized concepts that I know of. The two undesignated time-spans of gap and overlap are experienced as specific times beyond words.

I shall now focus on the overlapping period: it is experienced as insecure, dangerous and potentially evil. There is of course a certain meteorological insecurity as to when the drier season might end, and when the first signs of rain will come. There also is visual and optical insecurity, because both fragmentary time standards can be observed in the sky during these weeks. But the transitional experience of insecurity goes far beyond such practical observations and cannot be separated from the cosmovisional context. Will God withhold his gift, the essence of life? Has someone in the village or the tribal group behaved so badly that we are being punished by a drought? Have our enemies allied themselves with sorcerers, or are evil spirits going to obstruct our well-being?

This is the time of dark feelings about the past and the present. Intersubjectively, emotions flow together and stimulate each other during the overlapping period before the first rains. These emotions are rarely articulated, except in sudden outbursts or in secret whisperings. Practical concerns for field and crops combine with fear of God's anger, with tensions and anxiety with regard to enemies, evil spirits and black magic, and with feelings of guilt and suspicion about one's own mistakes. Emotional concern for man's relation to nature and cosmos is internalized and related to transcendent forces. These feelings of tension, anxiety, guilt, suspicion and fear grow and pile up as long as the rains do not come. If it rains in time, the dark emotional process dissolves in explosions of laughter and gratitude. If it does not rain, a ritual is performed. I shall not elaborate on ethnographic details here, but will merely emphasize the following point: the processual flow of dark emotions is the driving force behind the preparation and performance of the ritual, during which these emotions are virtually acted out. Negative and black feelings that have accumulated for weeks and even months are transformed in the ritual process by bodies and by words, by dancing and singing. Latent fears are translated into manifest and explicit forms of hope and desire. In a way, the ritual externalizes the unspoken fear about past and present events as outspoken hope for a new and better period.

In this way, the ritual functions as an emotional 'converter', as well as a means to influence the conceptual side of time experience: endurance and waiting (for the rains) have not yet been substituted by succession and discontinuity (during and after the rain). The ritual is a disruptive event in the experience of endurance that anticipates the actual rupture, namely rain. This anticipatory, disruptive event could not take place without the collective emotional potential that was built up before, in the phase of waiting and endurance.

Processes of emotional transformation have of course been described by many authors already, but this particular case illustrates a specific point: the unnamed period of overlapping is the social time of silent fears. These fears are an essential element of the transitional time experience of endurance, which local, verbalized concepts of time actually conceal. In spite of being disguised and hidden (and perhaps because of it), this 'black time' experience becomes the crucial driving force towards the ritual, where verbalization and externalization in body and mind attempt not only to create new, different emotions, but also to promote the disruptive construction of a new period: black emotions construct white time.

The dark emotional experience of the overlapping period is certainly not an independent variable. Agro-climatic factors, social tensions, and the belief in transcendental forces all contribute to the social production of these emotions. A nameless period provides the stage and the occasion for the silent performance of that black emotional product. The processual product, however, represents more than its component parts; it cannot be reduced to its 'productional factors'. Once the emotional process is set in motion, it gains a momentum of its own, and becomes a force that itself is capable of constructing something new and different. The explicit verbal concept of a white period cannot be understood without the unspoken dark experience of the nameless overlapping time.

The Munebbih case therefore illustrates that the experience of time is deeply rooted in bodies and emotions. By ritual socialization and by routinization in everyday life, explicit verbal time conceptions of a given culture influence these bodily sensations and emotional feelings. The Munebbih example therefore also testifies that culture and society to some extent appropriate the bodies and minds of their members in time and space. Michel Foucault's statement (1978) was far too narrow, when he claimed that it was a specificity of European societies since the sixteenth and seventeenth centuries to have morally and practically appropriated the body. I think that every culture is doing this to the extent that it sets up moral and practical rules for the body in time and space, which body and mind obey or transgress.

Foucault's statement was too narrow, however, in the other sense that this relationship is not unilateral. The process simultaneously, and very importantly, is effective in the other direction. Sensitivity and emotions are not helplessly exposed to explicit and verbalized conceptions of time; they can also become the essence of time experience, and the unspoken driving force for the constant construction and deconstruction of time.

THE PLURALITY OF TIMES

This chapter has dealt with social times and their connectedness to experience and ritual. The argument has demonstrated that the present enthusiasm for 'pluritemporalism' in various social science disciplines picks up a topic that is very familiar to social anthropology. I have tried to show, however, that social anthropology goes beyond that, by emphasizing that this heterogeneity of times is rarely unstructured, but rather is ordered in hierarchies of values and contexts. Non-Western cultures and societies rarely fragment and atomize their pluralities of times; they do not produce disconnected heaps of ecological, techno-economic, genealogical, mythical, historical and ritual times that coexist separately, as one author seems to imply (Izard 1991). These times are 'partially connected', embedded in ideology and society, and they are situated in ideological registers and orders that are inscribed into social structure. Temporality and structuration condition each other (Bourdieu 1972; Tcherkèzoff 1985).

These structures are not merely imposed on human agents, they simultaneously open up social space for their creativity and practice. The pluralities of times are constituted as conceptual symbols that refer to relationships between changes, as Elias (1984) has shown. But these changes do not occur by themselves; they need shared, intersubjective practice that produces events. Rituals represent a specific form of events, where fundamental values of cosmovision merge with practice. In this sense, ritual events can also construct concepts of time. The shared, intersubjective practice that prepares and performs a ritual event is in itself directed not merely by intentions and rules of behaviour. It was shown that social emotions are an indispensable power behind this practice, and that they are socially produced beyond the spheres of concepts and words.

However, and somewhat paradoxically, we cannot understand the experience of time beyond words by ignoring local words and concepts. There are no shortcuts to bodily and emotional words by way of anthropological theory. Some tendencies in ethnopsycho-analysis, which has gained some significance in the German-speaking countries and also in France, seem to imply this. I believe that such attempts must remain futile; the spheres of social experience beyond words cannot be understood without local words and concepts, e.g. by postulating universal mechanisms of the subconscious, regardless of cultural borderlines and differences. Explicit verbalization does shape bodies and emotions to a certain degree, and anthropological knowledge has to work through this sphere of verbalization and conceptualization in order to reach those spheres beyond words.

This would be to acknowledge the point that social experience beyond words is not itself a category of universal homogeneity, as many psychoanalytical and some psychological neopositivist theories would perhaps maintain. This form of experience is incorporated and embodied, and thus becomes habit-memory (Connerton 1989), which is applied to construct the future.

Anthropological reasoning has to recognize and to respect cultural difference in order to relate the differences socially without harmonizing them, and without marginalizing the unspoken. Marginalizing such emotional experiences of time as the nameless period of overlapping in the Munebbih world would distort and alienate anthropological knowledge itself. We have explicitly to live the paradox, to speak about the unspoken. For social experience to become knowledge it must be verbalized, yet never reduced to text.

NOTE

1 Apart from a number of earlier contributions (some of them discussed by Gellner 1987; Wendorff 1980; Aveni 1989; and Bergmann 1992), the works of authors like P. Bourdieu (1963, 1972) and N. Elias (1984), studies like those of S. Tcherkèzoff (1985) and B. Glowczewski (1991), and some of the writings of M. Bloch (e.g. 1974, and with J. Parry 1982) have decisively influenced the present debate in anthropology.

REFERENCES

Adam, Barbara (1990) *Time and Social Theory*, Cambridge: Polity Press.
—— (1992) 'Modern times: the technology connection and its implications for social theory', *Time and Society* 1, 2: 175–91.
Aveni, Anthony (1989) *Empires of Time: Calendars, Clocks and Cultures*, New York: Basic Books.
Bergmann, Werner (1992) 'The problem of time in sociology: an overview of the literature on the state of theory and research on the "sociology of time", 1900–82', *Time and Society* 1, 1: 81–134.
Bloch, Maurice (1974) 'Symbols, song, dance and features of articulation: is religion an extreme form of traditional authority?', *Archives européennes de sociologie* 15: 55–81.
—— (1977) 'The past and present in the present', *Man* 12: 278–92.

Bloch, Maurice, and Parry, Jonathan, eds (1982) *Death and the Regeneration of Life*, Cambridge: Cambridge University Press.

Bourdieu, Pierre (1963) 'The attitude of the Algerian peasant towards time', in Julian Pitt-Rivers, ed., *Mediterranean Countrymen*, Paris: Mouton.

—— (1972) *Esquisse d'une theorie de la pratique, précédé de trois études d'ethnologie kabyle*, Geneva: Droz.

Connerton, Paul (1989) *How Societies Remember*, Cambridge: Cambridge University Press.

Durkheim, Emile (1912) *Les Formes élémentaires de la vie religieuse*, Paris: F. Alcan.

Elias, Norbert (1984) *Über die Zeit*, Frankfurt/M.: Suhrkamp.

Fabian, Johannes (1983) *Time and the Other: How Anthropology Makes its Object*, New York: Columbia University Press.

Forum für Philosophie–Bad Homburg, eds (1992) *Zeiterfahrung und Personalität*, Frankfurt/M.: Suhrkamp, stw 986.

Foucault, Michel (1978) *The History of Sexuality*, vol. 1: *An Introduction*, New York: Pantheon.

Gellner, Ernest (1987) 'Time and theory in social anthropology', in *The Concept of Kinship and Other Essays*, Oxford: Blackwell.

Gingrich, André (1991) 'Ritual, Zeit und Identität: theoretische Anmerkungen aus sozialanthropologischer Sicht', opening lecture at the bi-annual meeting of Swiss, Austrian and German Anthropological Societies, Munich (to be published in *Vienna Contributions to Ethnology and Anthropology 6*).

Glowczewski, Barbara (1991) *Du Reve à la loi chez les Aborigines: Mythes, rites et organisation sociale en Australie*, Paris: PUF.

Gregory, R.L. (1972) 'Visual illusions', in B.M. Foss, ed., *New Horizons in Psychology*, Harmondsworth: Penguin.

Hastrup, Kirsten (1991), 'Beyond words: on the limits of writing in social anthropology', paper for 'The Multiplicity of Writing and Social Anthropology', Seminar at the Department and Museum of Social Anthropology, University of Oslo.

—— ed. (1992) *Other Histories*, London and New York: Routledge.

Hawking, Stephen W. (1988) *A Brief History of Time: From the Big Bang to Black Holes*, New York: Bantam.

Hernadi, Paul (1992) 'Objective, subjective, intersubjective times: guest editor's introduction', *Time and Society* 1, 2: 147–58.

Hubert, Henri, and Mauss, Marcel (1909) 'Etude sommaire de la représentation du temps dans la religion et la magie', in *Mélanges d'histoire des religions*, Paris: F. Alcan.

Izard, Michel (1991) 'Temps', in Pierre Bonte and Michel Izard, eds, *Dictionnaire de l'ethnologie et de l'anthropologie*, Paris: PUF.

Levine, R.V. (1988) 'The pace of life across cultures', in J.E. McGrath, ed., *The Social Psychology of Time: New Perspectives*, Beverly Hills, Calif.: Sage.

Nowotny, Helga (1989) *Eigenzeit. Entstehung und Strukturierung eines Zeitgefühls*, Frankfurt/M.: Suhrkamp.

Sorokin, Pitirim A., and Merton, Robert K. (1937) 'Social time: a methodological and functional analysis', *American Journal of Sociology* 42: 615–29.

Tcherkèzoff, Serge (1985) 'Black and white dual classification: hierarchy and ritual logic in Nyamwezi ideology', in R.H. Barnes, Daniel de Coppet, and Robert J. Parkin, eds, *Contexts and Levels: Anthropological Essays on Hierarchy* (*Journal of the Anthropological Society of Oxford*, Occasional Papers 4).

Turton, David, and Ruggles, Clive (1978) 'Agreeing to disagree: the measurement of duration in a southwestern Ethiopian community', *Current Anthropology* 19, 3: 585–600.

Varisco, David M. (1982) *The Adaptive Dynamics of Water Allocation in al-Ahjur, Yemen Arab Republic*. Ann Arbor: UMI.

Wendorff, Rudolf (1980) *Zeit und Kultur*, Wiesbaden: Westdeutscher Verlag.

Young, Michael, and Schuller, Tom, eds (1988) *The Rhythms of Society*, London and New York: Routledge.

Zerubavel, Eviatar (1981) *Hidden Rhythms: Schedules and Calendars in Social Life*, Chicago: University of Chicago Press.

Chapter 10

Space and the 'other'
Social experience and ethnography in the Kalahari debate

Thomas Widlok

Anthropological work on the life of the hunter–gatherers in the Kalahari has captured the attention of a number of disciplines concerned to understand the human condition. In the course of the recent 'Kalahari debate' the focus of anthropological research has shifted from studies of life in a harsh environment to research into the social process of interaction between hunter–gatherers and neighbouring agropastoralists. This chapter attempts to show how this newly focused ethnography of southern African foragers can contribute to recent explorations into the anthropology of social experience and to developing fields of interdisciplinary research.

INTRODUCTION

In his book *Time and the Other*, Johannes Fabian criticized the use of *time* in the history of anthropological discourse. He also noted that the discipline's treatment of *space* has been equally inadequate. He concluded that neither time nor space is adequately incorporated into anthropological knowledge as a constitutive dimension of social experience and practice. Spatial and temporal forms of description are used as modes of distancing in an attempt to push the 'other' into a different time and space. Fabian traces this strategy, which he calls the 'denial of coevalness' (1983: 31) across all major traditions of anthropology. Evolutionism, for example, spatialized time into typologies and taxonomies ordered as hierarchical trees of being; structuralism treats diachronic or spatial variants as entries in an all-encompassing taxonomy; relativism walls in cultures so that every culture has its own time (ibid.). In the first half of this chapter I examine the current debate on the anthropology of southern African foragers, giving special attention to the increased pre-occupation with 'space' in theory and ethnography.[1]

Fabian characterized the central problem of anthropology as a contradiction *within* anthropological knowledge between our experiences in the field and the scientific discourse of the discipline (ibid.: xi). The workshop at the 2nd EASA conference was entitled 'Social experience and anthropological knowledge', which indicates a step forward because it puts in the foreground the general tension between interactive social experience of any sort (and of any social actor including ourselves) on the one hand, and the full range of anthropological knowledge, whether manifest in fieldnotes, in ethnographic monographs, or in comparative analysis, on the other. Instead of implying a 'we and the other' dichotomy, the issue, as I understand it, is one of how to describe and investigate in an adequate manner immediate and holistic experience in any social context with the necessarily reductive methods of anthropology. In earlier contributions to this subject emphasis was laid on the question of how anthropology was to deal with *inner* experiences defined as 'how *individuals* actually experience their culture, that is how events are *received* by consciousness' (Bruner 1986: 4; my emphasis) rather than on *social* experience, that is, how social experiences effectively shape social relations and social practices and are in turn shaped by them, and how 'events' are shaped by interlinked cognitive and social processes. In the second half of this chapter I want to shift our attention to social experience as it is expressed (and can be observed) in social practice. Again time and particularly space as fundamental dimensions of social interaction are at the focus of my investigation. The argument is developed in the context of the ethnography of the diverse ways in which southern African foragers are dealing with the advent and presence of cattle-owners on their land. I show how a shift of focus can improve our understanding of the social experience of confrontation with the economy of communal and commercial cattle-holders. In my conclusion I explore the potential of this approach for anthropological contributions to interdisciplinary research on the cognitive dimensions of community construction.

SPATIAL AND TEMPORAL CONCEPTUALIZATIONS IN THE ANTHROPOLOGY OF SOUTHERN AFRICAN FORAGERS

The anthropology of southern African foragers, commonly called 'Bushmen', 'San' or 'Barsawa',[2] is at present characterized by a very lively debate between so-called 'isolationists' and 'integrationists'. In the traditional approach, groups of 'Bushmen' were studied as isolates, while their interaction and experience with outsiders were seen as phenomena of recent social change. The revisionist attack argued, with archaeological, historical and ethnographical data, that 'Bushmen' have for a long time been subjugated by other groups and are therefore best seen as the underclass of the Kalahari who only became ethnicized as 'San' in the course of this incorporation into the wider economy.[3]

At first the debate seems to be about time. Richard Lee has argued that only in the early 1970s (after his main field research) was there a major socioeconomic transition period in which external control was established over the economy of the !Kung that had gradually, though only partially, incorporated elements of herding and wage labour (Lee 1979: 403). Wilmsen, an opposing 'integrationist', maintains that indigenous Khoisan foragers were economically integrated and subordinated into a larger social hierarchy as early as the first millennium AD (Wilmsen 1989: 75). However, in both arguments the problem is also one of interpreting spatial proximity. The integrationists question whether spatial isolation that prevents major change is intact until white traders arrive on the scene or direct administrative interference is established. In response, the isolationists question whether the proximity between archaeological sites indicating forager presence and those exhibiting pastoralist settlements implies a relation of hierarchy and exploitation between two social groups. The scenarios of both sides can be depicted as follows.

The traditionalist scenario: traders, cattle, labour contracts, money and alcohol emanate from the centres, usually the European settlements close to the south Atlantic coast, and gradually reach 'San' groups which only then become marginalized in the new social formation. Owing to their remote location, some groups lived beyond this margin up to the recent past.

The revisionist scenario: 'Bushmen' are part and parcel of the political economy of the Kalahari (note the geographical qualifi-

The way to approach explanation is by putting trends together. This has two elements. The first is that they have to be trends – answers to questions about more or less, ideally but not necessarily arranged on a time scale. Of course in many cases we have no time-series, and cannot produce trends. In that case it is a good second-best to look at variation in space (rural–urban), or a good third-best to look at variation by one or more social categories (Black–white, upper–lower class, male–female). But these are second- and third-best ways of answering more or less questions: each is interesting, but each would be improved with a time series, which indeed I am lucky enough to have.

The second element is to perceive a pattern or connection. Essentially this is covariance, and modern statistical tests can suggest the degree to which a plurality of trends is interconnected.

The decision about which trends to put alongside others is not arbitrary, but is open to discussion and hence accountable. It is quite clear from my very preliminary work on the documents that the proportion of polygynists among all married men has declined considerably since 1932, as has the ratio of new polygynous marriages to new non-polygynous ones. It is quite easy to see that as confirming Huzayyin's implicit assumption: polygyny is commonest in rural areas with a high concentration of uneducated men and women. As men move to cities, and become more educated, so they become monogamous (Huzayyin 1981). It is a reassuring picture of a civilizing process in which the forces of modernization inexorably cause increasing justice, decency and freedom from oppression in Cairene domesticity, while unregenerated farmers and herders are left untouched by world-historical forces.

But perhaps that is a little too reassuring? We have not got many studies of marriage among people who have moved from country to town, but those which do exist suggest that women's lives are more restricted in town than in the country. Is that what we mean by modernization? Are we convinced that polygyny is an aboriginal practice that needs no explanation because it is a given? I shall return to the matter of Zuwaya polygny later; meanwhile I want to draw your attention to the way in which a measurement of two simultaneous states of affairs (rural polygyny, urban polygyny) has been converted to a process by making rural precede urban in some notional time; and then that wholly illusory 'trend' has been explained by fitting it up to an extremely rarefied notion of endogenous process. You may not have rules which tell you which are the best juxtapositions to make, but you do have rules which indicate which are better than others. The trends for instance should be of the same scale and order: it is not sensible to set a rural–urban scale against a time-scale, for instance. And similarly it is not sensible to set any trend in a local population (as it might be 'Egyptian polygynists') against a world-historical trend (as it might be 'the ineluctable march of domestic modernity'). That is because however good the evidence for a world-historical trend may be, it refers to processes on such a huge scale that it is difficult to assess what the connection could be between it and the more local phenomenon. Quite often I think it is mainly mystical optimism – 'Progress occurs necessarily, and *tiens* here it is at last in Bishla.'[7] In short the scales and orders of trends should be similar, although it is surprising how often they are not.

Third, I think that the Durkheimian principle still stands. You should juxtapose information about the same kinds of thing, at any rate in the first instance. As a rule of method we do not try to explain social trends with meteorological or psychological trends. And indeed I am inclined to believe that we should try to explain matrimonial and kinship trends within the general area of marriage and kinship and demography before turning to economics and politics. Of course 'the same kind of thing' is negotiable and arguable, but in general terms the Durkheimian rule of method seems to hold. In summary, you can approach explanation by juxtaposing trends; but the scales should be similar, the trends should refer to things of the same order, and they should refer to the same kind of thing in the first instance.

In my view the most difficult step is to link trends to external events. Let me mention some of the more striking events which occurred between 1932 and 1979 in Libya. The year 1932 saw the battle of Hawaria, just outside Kufra, in which Italian troops brought mechanized warfare, war on wheels, to the central Sahara for the first time, defeating tribal resistance conclusively after thirty-one years of intermittent efforts at colonial pacification: 450 men and boys were killed; many went into exile in Egypt, Sudan, Chad; a significant number went out of circulation because they were imprisoned, executed, and so on.[8] The Italians maintained an uneasy domination, attempting a settler colonization in the north, until 1939: seven years of *pax italica* (sp. *fascistica*), followed by World War II. The northern coast became one of the battlegrounds of the war.[9] Many refugees went south, to the oases of Kufra; some Long Range Desert Group patrols went through the oases, and a Free French force arrived in Kufra and tried to annex it for France. But otherwise the southerners had direct experience of war only when they went north; some of them joined the Sanusi Battalion. After the war the whole area was governed by the British Military Administration until 1952, when Libya became an independent monarchy. British and American companies discovered oil in 1956, which came on stream in the early 1960s; *per capita* incomes rose from about $25 to $1,000, then to $4,000, peaking at $12,000 in 1973–4 before falling to the current $8,000. In 1969 some army officers made a *coup d'état* and, after various experiments in government, instituted a revolutionary populist government in 1973.

It seems quite clear that these events and people's decisions about marriage and divorce were connected. It is really quite difficult to specify the ways in which they were connected, however. We can start by saying that the influence of external events was on individuals' decisions, on those decisions which are implicit in the records of the *shari'a* archive. Rather than ask 'How did the war affect the trend in age of marriage?', we should ask 'How would it have been to take a decision in those times?' The difference is perhaps not all that great, since those decisions create the trend; but it seems sensible to me to place the emphasis on human decision-making: for all its defects, we can imagine something about what it could have been like; it is very much more difficult to imagine how a trend decides to bend in one direction or another.

One example is the history of polygyny in the 1930s and early 1940s. From 1932 until about 1936 there was a higher rate of polygynous marriage than at any other time in the period covered by the archive. That is to say, on an impressionistic scanning of the documents, a number of women marrying for the first time became second or third or occasionally fourth wives; and a number of women marrying for the second or third time became second or third wives. In the next five years, up to 1941, a large proportion of them divorced. By 1950, the pattern seems to have become more or less set for the remaining twenty-nine years covered by the archive. In the early period, I estimate that as much as half the adult male population was out of circulation. In those circumstances, fathers and guardians decided that it was better to marry off their young daughters, even into polygynous households, than to try to control them: it was a second-best, a prophylaxis against sin. Similarly, women who were widowed or whose husbands went into exile found it sensible to attach themselves to a protecting household as wives. But five or ten years later, the young women had grown up: they had increased independence, they were aware of the conditions of second or third wife; the influx of refugees from the north played some part in rectifying the population imbalance. It is interesting to note, incidentally, that the majority of the cases of *khul'* divorce in the archive date from this period; and, as Layish has discovered, in a number of these the judges stretched the law to permit an easier way out of an awkward or oppressive marriage (Layish 1991).[10] This is, I may repeat, impressionistic and based on an incomplete analysis of the records, but it serves to illustrate one method of arriving at an explanation. An event (the Italian colonial war) produces demographic change; that produces circumstances in which more people take a decision which in normal circumstances is regarded as less than ideal. In the course of time young women grow, and are able to take decisions on their own account; and they are assisted in this by the influx of refugees from the north (another 'event'), which to some extent redresses the demographic imbalance. We know of the 'events' and of the trends in polygynous marriage and in divorce: I put them together by imagining what it would be like to be the Zuwaya father of a girl approaching marriageable age in Kufra in, say, 1935. It is extremely likely that this account will be different when I know more about associated trends: for instance about the closeness of these marriages, about the relative ages of all the spouses in the polygynous households, and about the relative divorce rates from polygynous and monogamous households in the late 1930s and early 1940s. So it is an interim illustration of procedures, and the conclusions are quite likely wrong. But I do think that it is a more plausible explanation than imagining that the 1932 figures for polygyny reflect an unchanging aboriginal condition which is affected by a general trend to greater civilization and modernity in the Italian Sahara between 1936 and 1942.

Hastrup (1993) and I (Davis 1992) have recently and independently reconsidered the boundary between events and social processes or structure. I think it is true to say that we think anthropologists and other social scientists have drawn the boundary arbitrarily: it is a way of putting certain kinds of thing into a category which is by definition inaccessible to explanation. Famine, plague, revolution, war have all at one time or another been designated 'events' and placed outside our competence, which is concerned with enduring structures or with social processes. Of course in our non-anthropological lives we know that war, for example, is a social product, and is not an extra-terrestrial cataclysm, just as famines that kill (de Waal 1989) do so as a result of social causes. But when in our professional lives we designate something as an event we are simply passing it over to historians, and making a professional act of renunciation.

Events are important because they are part of experience, even if some of our colleagues find it convenient to deny them the right to an anthropological explanation. Suppose, however, we do attribute them to social processes? We make them accessible to explanation.[11] The point here is that we can then look at issues of causation really quite coolly, even if, inexperienced as we are, the results are speculative.

For instance the major model of changes in family and kinship in Europe, even in its most modern recension, suggests that changes in national economy and political organization cause changes in family recruitment and activity. Is that always so? The Libyan revolutionary political order is one in which a surprisingly responsive official rhetoric emphasizes the importance of individual autonomy (the slogan is 'Representation is fraud!'), and assumes that the links among members of a nation are like those among members of a family: Qaddafi, as I have remarked elsewhere, is a Gellnerian in his model of segmentary organization, at least because he thinks that a nation (the most encompassing level of association) has only one kind of social bond. I do not think that the social processes which I perceive in the *shariʿa* archive can be said to have caused the Libyan revolution of 1969–73, but I do think that the shape and form of the political order that it established can be attributed to the sorts of movement and change which the documents reveal. In short, the choices and decisions which Zuwaya and other Libyans made about their matrimonial lives, the nature of the experience of kinship which they consequently created for themselves, resulted in local social orders which shaped the Revolutionary Command Council's choices and decisions about the political structure. Although Libya is often said to be an autocratic and arbitrary state, that is very often not the case; and in my view the leadership is in large measure responsive rather than dictatorial. That is partly because the leaders themselves belong to the same social milieu as is represented in the archives; and partly because, when they take steps to ensure that they remain in power, they choose to do things which accord with the experience (i.e. the accumulated wisdom, prejudice and understanding) of the citizenry, rather than otherwise. The hidden hand of multiple kinship decisions, in short, extends beyond kinship in the strict sense, and affects and explains political choices. That is a sketchy account of a complex and ramified explanation, which has to be much more qualified than it is. But it does suggest that within very carefully prescribed limits, we can find one case at least in which the standard European model of causation in family and domestic affairs is reversed. And it suggests too that there is some value in shifting the boundary between events and processes, to include rather more than some of our colleagues have done in the past.

We ought to think of other people's experience as ineffable, ungraspable and inexpressible. But in many cases, in order to explain social change, we can make lifetime-based models, of a kernmantel kind, which emphasize the experience of decision-makers, the shape of sectors of their social world, which may have a fairly close approximation to how it was experienced. Indeed, in this task, it may even be useful to use computers and statistics (those most unpoetical and roughshod tools of analysis) to help us identify the choices which people have in fact made, and to help us imagine the experience which influenced decisions.

NOTES

1 Mount (1983) has an interesting discussion of brotherhood as a rhetorical term. Referring to Hobsbawm (1975) Mount argues that the appeal to fictive kinship is an invitation to abandon spouse and children in the name of some more universalistic association. (He urges his readers to turn a deaf ear to such pleas since only the family is truly subversive of oppressive organizations like the state). 'Brothers!' may have different resonances for people who think of themselves as organized in patrilineages, and who know that the Sanusi order, controllers of the pre-revolutionary state, used Brother as a term of reference and address for initiates. The contemporary Libyan state uses kinship and family as an integral part of its justifying rhetoric (Davis, 1987: 211–16 – also below).

2 Some of whom appear more than once in the archive.

3 I think I should say that in spite of obvious similarities with Adam Smith's account of the hidden hand of self-interested decision-making, I do not propose an economistic model of rational matrimonial choice. On the one hand, I am neutral about the value of the outcome (Smith

was on the whole positive about the working of the hidden hand; I think that the consequences can be either good or bad). And on the other, I deny the reality of western rationalist economic models.

4 It is worth noting that the Zuwaya are about 90 per cent of the population of Kufra and about 25 per cent of Ajdabiya. Some documents cannot be related to the genealogy.

5 If I may try to summarize in three sentences, Strathern argues for example that 'individual' is a fluid and temporary category in Mount Hagen, constituted from time to time, deconstituted at others. Male and female are similarly inconstant characteristics of people. Underlying this powerful discussion she must have made some judgment about distribution (a sufficiently high proportion of skin-bags must have this experience) and about representativeness: if each skin-bag became a gendered individual for say one second a month, it would not be worth basing such an elaborated discussion on such an elusive experience. She would argue something else (Strathern, 1988).

6 Unprincipled differences include the fact that different people believe more in one kind than the other.

7 Huzayyin uses Bishla as his case of rural Egypt: I have not been able to locate it. Another defect of this implicit model, incidentally, is that it lacks economy. For the model of the march of progress, socialism, civilization is an organic one in which the seeds and blueprints of development are contained within the process. Such models may be nice to think about, but they do not help explanation. For if you have a trend to explain, and you look outside it for external factors to do the job, it is rather a cop-out if you choose an organic model which already contains seeds and blueprints. After all, if the trend you wish to explain is itself an example of blueprinted development, you would expect it to contain its own specific seeds rather than just to participate in the aura of the generic ones.

8 One of the reasons the archive exists is that tthe Italian authorities insisted on a record of transactions in the local court: before then, the documents issued were the property of the applicants to the court. The earliest, all-purpose register includes Italian translations of the Arabic records. This practice was discontinued after a few months, presumably when the powers realized that the proceedings were not subversive.

9 Ajdabiya changed hands between Axis and Allies four times before the Allies gained decisive control. This is reflected in the archive where the administrative officer who received the tax payment on register entries was sometimes Italian, sometimes British.

10 See Layish 1991. The essence of *khul* divorce is that the spouses agree before a judge that she will pay back some or all of the bridewealth, and in consideration of that he will then divorce her. But in the extremely unsettled times of the 1940s, many wives did not have the cash or goods to repay the bridewealth. The judges' easier way out was to allow wives to contract to repay the bridewealth with whatever they might receive in consideration of their next marriage. And the judges sanctioned this contract by stating that the current divorce and the

subsequent marriage would both be null and void unless the wife repaid the bridewealth. This stretches the principle of *shari'a* – a law that a divorce is a clean and irrevocable break: but I think I can see that it was a humane way of coping with exceptional circumstances.

11 One of the consequences of doing so is that we demote them, so to speak, from the status of unroutine to routine events. That requires us, in many cases, to think of social organization as routinely producing pain and injustice – common enough in sociology, less so in anthropology. It also requires us to abandon the distinction between micro and macro social processes since 'macro' is often a sort of asylum where we lodge uncomfortable facts. In this task, I find Mann's discussion quite helpful (Mann, 1986).

REFERENCES

Allen, N.J. (1989) 'Assimilation of alternate generations', *Journal of the Anthropological Society of Oxford* 20: 45–55.

Davis, J. (1987) *Libyan Politics: Tribe and Revolution. The Zuwaya and their Government*, London: I.B. Tauris.

—— (1992) 'The anthropology of suffering', *Journal of Refugee Studies* 5: 149–61.

de Waal, A. (1989) *Famine that Kills: Darfur, Sudan, 1984–1985*, Oxford: Clarendon Press.

Evans-Pritchard, E.E. (1945) 'The Sanusi of Cyrenaica', *Africa* 15: 61–78.

Hammel, E.A., and Goldberg, H. (1971) 'Parallel cousin marriage', *Man*, n.s. 6: 488.

Hammel, E.A., and Hutchinson, D. (1973) 'Two tests of microsimulation: the effect of an incest tabu on population viability, and the effect of age differences between spouses on the skewing of consanguineal relationships between them', in B.D. and J.W. MacCluer, eds, *Computer Simulation in Human Population Studies*, New York: Academic Press.

Hastrup, K. (1993) 'Hunger and the hardness of facts', *Man* 28, 4.

Hobsbawm, E.J. (1975) 'Fraternity', *New Society*, 27 Nov.

Holy, L. (1989) *Kinship, Honour and Solidarity: Cousin Marriage in the Middle East*, Manchester: Manchester University Press.

Huzayyin, S.A. (1981) 'Marriage and remarriage in Islam', in É. Hélin, J. Dupâquier, *et al.*, eds, *Marriage and Remarriage in Populations of the Past*, London: Academic Press.

Layish, A. (1991) *Divorce in the Libyan Family: A Study Based on the Sijills of the Shari'a Courts of Ajdabiya and Kufra*, New York: New York University Press.

Macfarlane, A. (1980) *The Origins of English Individualism*, Oxford: Basil Blackwell.

Mann, M. (1986) *The Sources of Social Power*, vol. 1: *A History of Power from the Beginning to AD 1760*, Cambridge: Cambridge University Press.

Mason, J.P. (1977) *Island of the Blest: Islam in a Libyan Oases Community*, Athens, Ohio: Ohio University Press.

Mount, F. (1983) *The Subversive Family: An Alternative History of Love and Marriage*, London: Jonathan Cape.

Peters, E.L. (1960) 'The proliferation of segments in the lineage of the Bedouin of Cyrenaica', *Journal of the Royal Anthropological Institute* 90: 29–53.

—— (1965) 'Aspects of the family among the Bedouin of Cyrenaica', in M.F. Nimkoff, ed., *Comparative Family Systems*, Boston, Mass.: Houghton Mifflin.

—— (1967) 'Some structural aspects of the feud among the camel-herding Bedouin of Cyrenaica', *Africa* 37: 261–82.

—— (1968) 'The tied and the free: an account of a type of patron–client relationship among the Bedouin pastoralists of Cyrenaica', in J.G. Peristiany, ed., *Contributions to Mediterranean Sociology*, The Hague: Mouton.

—— (1977) 'Patronage in Cyrenaica', in E. Gellner and J. Waterbury, eds, *Patrons and Clients in Mediterranean Societies*, London: Duckworth.

—— (1980) 'Aspects of Bedouin bridewealth among camel herders in Cyrenaica', in J.L. Comaroff, ed., *The Meaning of Marriage Payments*, London: Academic Press.

—— (1991) *The Bedouin of Cyrenaica: Studies in Personal and Corporate Power* (Cambridge Studies in Social and Cultural Anthropology), Cambridge: Cambridge University Press.

Strathern, M. (1988) *The Gender of the Gift: Problems with Women and Problems with Society in Melanesia* (Studies in Melanesian Anthropology), Berkeley: University of California Press.

Chapter 12

Anthropological knowledge incorporated
Discussion

Kirsten Hastrup

In the preceding chapters various routes from social experience to anthropological knowledge have been explored and discussed. In the process, both local and anthropological concepts have been questioned, and means of transcending the gap between them have been proposed. In the theoretical landscape created by the authors, the individual explorations have had the character of itineraries rather than maps, describing the actual experience of the traveller rather than encoding the abstract picture of the cartographer (cf. Certeau 1988: 118ff.). Maps and tours reflect different poles of experience; in this volume we have concentrated on the latter, because we wanted to stress process at the expense of structure, and knowledge as a creative field rather than as a solid construction.

If this seems to devalue our attempt at a reconstruction of the route to anthropological knowledge, this is owed to the refraction inherent in the visualist paradigm to which anthropology has been subject over the past centuries (Salmond 1982; Fabian 1983; Hastrup 1986). Descartes deemed sight 'the noblest and most comprehensive of the senses' upon which the conduct of our life entirely depends (Descartes 1988: 57). 'The clinical gaze', identified by Michel Foucault (1963), modelled science on the idea of autopsy: a corpse opened for inspection. This extreme form of objectification has been replaced by more sensitive forms of studying and by a much wider use of the senses in ethnography (Stoller 1989). The ethnographic experience cannot be taken at face value but must be studied in its sensational depth.

Itineraries, therefore, must be redeemed as valid guides to journeying in the territory of knowledge. By contrast to maps, they have a truly directive force. A map helps you situate your position, but the itinerary spells out the goal and the relevant places of reverence. It is a travellers' guide *par excellence*: it is only by knowing where you are going that you can know who you are. Identity is intimately linked to orientation in a moral space (Taylor 1989: 28ff.). This implies also that 'social actors not only acquire a sense of what is natural, they also acquire strongly motivating senses of what is desirable. They not only know, they also care' (Strauss and Quinn 1993: 3). In real life, knowledge, so often isolated as cognition in theory, is not independent of emotion. Emotions, consequently, belong to the realm of rationality (Sousa 1990).

Orientation implies agency and motivation as well as a certain awareness of place. Whenever we orientate ourselves in place, we actively constitute a space. In the words of Michel de Certeau, 'space is a practiced place' (1988: 117). Individuals move about in places, but through their movements they architecture a social space; the environment of social action is a human product (Harré 1978). For the individual, 'maps' and 'tours' alternate as relevant frames of orientation. As it happens, individuals are not only defined by their space but are also its defining consciousness (Ardener 1987: 40). In other words, people are never just victims of social forms, because social forms owe their shape partly to the fact that they are inhabited by people thinking about social forms (Hollis 1985: 232). And, as said above, thinking implies caring.

Scientists, too, architecture a particular space with its own vectors of direction towards the desirable, if these generally have been silenced. Most often the scientific space has been conceived as wholly unemotional; it has been flattened into a place. The theoretical landscapes or the territories of knowledge have been conceived more in terms of a plane projection, totalizing observations, than a discursive series of operations directed as much by implicit motives as by abstract coordinates. As 'territory', knowledge may be bounded off from the surrounding wilderness of unknowing. Kant underscores this view when he writes:

We have now not merely explored the territory of pure understanding and carefully surveyed every part of it, but have also measured its extent and assigned to everything in it its rightful place. This domain is an island, enclosed by nature itself with unalterable limits. It is the land of truth – an enchanting name! – surrounded by a wide and stormy ocean, the native home of illusion, where many a fog bank and many a swiftly melting iceberg give the deceptive appearance of farther shores.

(Kant 1991: xxx)

Such natural metaphors of understanding and truth may have had a strong motivating force within the scholarly community, which generally identifies its ambition with that of the natural sciences: discovery of unknown yet in principle perfectly knowable objects of nature. The Age of Discovery fostered the scientist as explorer of nature (Boorstein 1985); by his deeds he became a hero of his time (Frängsmyr 1984). While anthropology has for a long time aspired to a similar heroism (cf. Clifford 1988: 30), the particular kind of exploration undertaken in anthropology needs conceptual refinement in light of the ethnographic experiences recounted in this book among others. The land of truth has been discovered as fogged by its own illusions. We can no longer live by Descartes's rule that 'We should attend only to those objects of which our minds seem capable of having certain and indubitable cognition' (Descartes 1988: 1).[1] Indubitable cognition is not part of the ethnographer's luck; her certainty is established on a much wider basis of experience which again transforms the nature of the objects studied. They are somehow subjectified, and we have to understand how this does not detract from their reality. As said by Bourdieu, 'Of all the oppositions that artificially divide social science, the most fundamental, and the most ruinous, is the one set up between subjectivism and objectivism' (Bourdieu 1990: 25). The tenacity of this opposition by itself points to the importance of both, yet social scientists are surprisingly reluctant to admitting to 'touring' as well as 'mapping' particular worlds. This volume, I believe, contributes to our self-confidence in the process of getting beyond the opposition between the subjective and the objective.

The metaphor of truth as an island still suggests a distinctiveness of a particular field of knowledge to which I would subscribe, however. By their 'practising different places' and by their demonstrating the variety of textures and thematicities of social spaces, ethnographers contribute to a comparative and general knowledge about the world as a whole. Within this whole they identify global points of orientation and locally directive forces. Showing how such forces are founded in the history of argument and in discursive hierarchies rather than in relative facticity and value, anthropologists contribute to a remaking of the world by, possibly, redirecting the vectors of motivation.

The strength of the contribution is proportional to the awareness of the actual process from social experience to anthropological knowledge: 'In the social sciences, the progress of knowledge presupposes progress in our knowledge of the conditions of knowledge' (Bourdieu 1990: 1). In anthropology, the main condition of knowledge is still related to the individual fieldwork, which cannot be conceived independently of the subject; there is no experience apart from the experiencer, no knowledge without a knower. This makes it pertinent to investigate the position of the actual experiencing anthropological subject, so curiously absent in the literature as a real person in flesh and blood, if now relatively – some would say excessively – conspicuous as author (e.g. Clifford and Marcus 1986; Geertz 1988; Hastrup 1992).

The identification of the socially significant does not rest on verbal questioning alone, as we discussed in the Introduction. The feel for ethnographic relevance to a large extent is mediated by the bodily and sensory experience that may precede linguistic competence, as demonstrated by Tamara Kohn in this volume. Also, such experiences may for ever remain a repository of understanding, as shown in Judith Okely's chapter on the recollections of elderly rural people. Through particular bodily practices, abstract ideas are made corporeal and linked to certain emotions, as shown by Karin Ask in her discussion of purdah. This insight directs us towards the body as a locus of perception.

THE ABSENT BODY

The idea of the clinical gaze relates directly to the ocular and experimental view of science, modelled upon the opening and curious inspection of a dead body. One of the results was the splitting-apart of body and mind, which we have had to straddle. Realizing the impossibility of equating lived experience with dead bodies, anthropologists face a methodological problem of acknowledging the corporeal fields of people. By 'corporeal field' I refer roughly to that larger space with which every individual is inextricably linked by way of the physical, sensing and moving body (cf. Hanks 1990: 92ff.). It denotes an ego-centered field of reference. To grasp the qualities of the corporeal field, some notion of embodiment might prove useful, even if it already has a number of different connotations. Whatever the words used, we need to recognize that the apparently theoretical problem of re-uniting mind and body as the locus of action is itself constituted within a specific discourse that separated them in the first place. Therefore, we do not necessarily have a serious epistemological obstacle. What we do have is a problem of wording: like the prophet, we lack the words for, rather than the experience of, the unity of body and mind (cf. Ardener 1989; Hastrup 1989).

By contrast to a phenomenology of experience that reflects 'an experience which, by definition, does not reflect itself' (Bourdieu 1990: 25), anthropology must always question the conditions for experience and explore 'the coincidence of the objective structures and the internalized structures which provides the illusion of immediate understanding, characteristic of practical experience of the familiar universe' (ibid.: 26). In short, and as forcefully argued in this collection of papers, anthropology cannot continue to accept a radical discontinuity between theoretical and practical knowledge – or, for that matter, between mind and body. We must, therefore, track the origins of the (false) ontology and understand why it has been so tenacious before we can adequately suggest a new vocabulary for dealing with lived experience that was broken in two only in theory.

The shift in scientific theory pioneered by Galileo, and to which the Cartesian reason was intimately linked, transformed the idea of a unified Cosmos embodying the Ideas of the world, of which humans were but fractions (and representations). Instead the world became recast in mechanistic terms; moral virtue and self-mastery were transformed in the process (Taylor 1989: 144). The mechanistic approach dissociated humans from nature, as it were. This dislocation also implied a uniformation of time which dissonated with the ordinary experience of density and emptiness, as discussed by Gingrich in this volume. During the seventeenth century, reality was recast as a machine, a precise clockwork, rather than an arhythmic living body. This paved the way for the domination of nature – and of women, according to Merchant (1980: xvii).

It also redirected people's quest for self-understanding. Reflection had been inward-bound for centuries, reaching a crescendo in Augustine's 'radical reflexivity'; by contrast to earlier thinkers, Augustine adopted a first-person standpoint (Taylor 1989: 130). Knowledge or awareness became that of an agent. This is not solely a matter of musing upon one's own experience, making it an object of contemplation: 'Radical reflexivity brings to the fore a kind of presence to oneself which is inseparable from one's being the agent of that experience' (ibid.: 131). This is what makes one a being that can speak of itself in the first person, and what made the language of inwardness irresistible. 'I think' somehow became an action outside the world, inside the self.

We are now in a position to resituate thinking in the world; as testified by the chapters in this volume, notably Hervik's, reflexivity is also in the world. Not only is our historical position different from Augustine's, however; our project is also another. His project was still defined in theological terms, being one of establishing 'God' as part and parcel of the person. Self-knowledge was instrumental to knowing God; the moral resources were still located in God, if the route to the high now passed within (Taylor 1989: 139). In more general terms, it meant that moral perfection required a personal commitment to the good. 'Will' was essential in the early modern period; 'weakness of will' became the ultimate failure, however much we can now unmask it as a contradiction in terms (Davidson 1980: 21ff.).

With Descartes the moral resources became firmly placed within ourselves; outer points of orientation were evaded, and the entire inner/outer dichotomy took on a new meaning. Scientific explanation was cut loose from moral vision; the former became a question of correct representation, the latter of individual firmness of will. The very notion of 'idea' migrated from Cosmos to person; its ontic sense was translocated to an intrapsychic world. The idea became something one had 'in the mind' (Taylor 1989: 144). There, it became a means for objectifying the world, including the body. As a cultural model it had its own motivating force (cf. D'Andrade 1992). The distinction made by Descartes between *res cogitans* and *res extensa* was the basis for the model of a sharp distinction between mind and body to which we have since then become accustomed. And it is this metaphysical dualism that has ever since been reflected in the subject–object dichotomy as basic for our knowledge of the world (Bernstein 1983: 115–16).

This violates both the classic ontology and the ordinary experience of embodied understanding so vigorously demonstrated in this volume. To understand, for Descartes, involved disengagement from our own material selves, those uncontrolled sources of error and moral vice (Johnson 1987). To achieve pure knowledge one first had to achieve self-purification; self-mastery became a matter of controlling the bodily source of error. This demand for instrumental control is implicitly rejected in most of the papers in this volume; the bodily experiences in many cases were sources of revelation. Thus, they demonstrate the need for dissolving the 'Cartesian anxiety', that is, the fear of not having a fixed and stable foundation for knowledge, a grounding of reference (cf. Varela *et al.* 1992: 140). The papers also dissolve Kant's distinction between 'pure' and 'empirical' knowledge, the former being independent of experience, the latter only obtainable through it (Kant 1991: 25–6). Generally, the message of the papers is a rejection of the mind–body dualism as ontology.

There is still reason to pause and ponder over its grip upon our sense of reality, however. As convincingly demonstrated by Drew Leder (1990), the Cartesian dualism seems to resonate with important aspects of human experience after all. While it is certainly true that human experience is incarnated, as shown by Francisco Cruces and Angel Díaz de Rada in this volume, it is no less true that the body tends to disappear from our awareness of *how* we experience. This is owed to the dual nature of the body: ecstasy and recessiveness, in the terms proposed by Leder. The ecstatic body consists of the senses by which we reach out for the world and which are, therefore, prominent in shaping our experiential field, while the recessive body points to all those invisible and unknowable processes that make sensations possible at all and keep us alive as humans.

The ecstatic functions of the body, and not least the power of the gaze, are most prominent in shaping the experiential field, and are, therefore, 'natural' candidates for the Prize of Perception – first awarded by Descartes, as we saw above. The recessive qualities, by contrast, give rise to no projective field, and are therefore easily overlooked in the phenomenology of experience. This has been true also for the phenomenology of ethnography so far. In fieldwork we are heavily dependent on the ecstatic powers. We go beyond ourselves and reach out towards the new world with all our senses; we take in the differences. The other culture becomes incorporated; we consume it, literally, by way of eating. In this volume, Judith Okely's chapter in particular, but also Tamara Kohn's, demonstrate how 'in taste, the experience of world and body are perhaps most closely interwoven' (Leder 1990: 15). Metaphorically, we also internalize unknown sensations of magic and ritual anxiety, by our corporeal being in the world of others, as shown by André Gingrich.

The incorporation of culture implies a process of sedimentation (Leder 1990: 31–2). Ever larger parts of local cultural models are taken for granted. 'Culture' sediments and becomes part of the recessive or 'hidden' faculties of the self. The process of sedimentation is not the same for children or anthropologists, even though the analogy often springs to mind, as in the chapter by Ingrid Rudie in this volume discussing unprecedented experiences. For children, enculturation means a filling-up of an empty space; for anthropologists, it implies contrasting it with and revising previous understandings. In both cases, however, 'first' or 'new' experiences are maximally suggestive. And in both cases the learning implies change (Bateson 1972: 283).

The degree to which this change is embodied has been ignored, however. Sedimentation implies a degree of solidification of the world as incorporated, which will gradually make the fieldworker experience a reshaping of the body's actual ability (Leder 1990: 34). In this sense, too, culture becomes 'naturalized' in socialization and experience (cf. Quinn 1992). The notion of embodiment firmly points to the individual as the practical agent of 'culture'.

Culture is meaningful only to someone in particular. In so far as it exists, it is both in the world and in people's minds (Strauss and Quinn 1993: 28). There is a centre of knowing which has remained obscure, owing partly to the apparent naturalness of the lived space, and partly to the lack of any projective field arising from the material body itself. The naturalness of the lived space is related to 'the way our own body is, as the vehicle, the stage, and the object of experience at the same time' (Hanks 1990: 5). Through our daily activities we define and redefine a corporeal field that is so much taken for granted that it resonates with the recessive or self-concealing aspects of the living body.

The lack of projective field from the material body itself has led to an almost complete disappearance of the body from our vision of thinking. Somewhat paradoxically, this points to its absolute centrality. It is so much taken for granted that it may disappear. Only when in pain does the body become unbearably manifest and demand attention; the self must act upon a telic demand to redress the situation of absence (Leder 1990: 72). Pain, and by consequence bodily presence, becomes an emotionally loaded state, defined as temporary and unnatural. As such it is a universal human experience, even if the state it defines and loads has varying cultural expressions (Good *et al.* 1992). In other words, and as strongly suggested by recent works in medical anthropology, the 'presence' of the body is culturally mediated (Kleinman and Kleinman 1991 and 1993).[2]

What we share cross-culturally is the absence of the body. In the relatively emotionless state of reasoning, the body tends to disappear experientially; this is what makes the Cartesian epistemology a 'motivated misreading'. The dualism is based in lived experience, and then fallaciously interpreted as ontology.

THE INCARNATED FIELD

The body is never simple presence. In its ecstatic qualities it expands beyond itself and projects itself outwards; the ethnographer experiences the field through the senses. In its recessive qualities the body tends towards self-concealment; the ethnographer remains unaware of the degree to which the experience is incarnated. The almost mythological status of fieldnotes as recorded observations has obscured the pertinence of the highly emotionally loaded 'headnotes', the unwritten recollections (Ottenberg 1990). This has fostered a view of intentionality as located in a disembodied mind, and a view of agency as the outcome of cognitive rationality alone.

The 'reason' for action is not located in the mind alone, however. As John Davis has shown in this volume, an act of marriage, for instance, depends on a host of unrelated choices and scores of previous actions by others. Such a multitude of reasons cannot be accounted for in simple terms of rationality as mastery of mind. Practical mastery of the world has a more complex rationale. Ethnographers themselves often experience how, in the field (and elsewhere, of course), they are caught in a web of apparently 'irrational' behaviour. They act as if 'out of their mind', or as if they were not really 'themselves'. They hear their own voices utter absolutely unreasonable words and arguments; they even sense the unreal (Hastrup 1987a).

People, and anthropologists among them, are concurrently engaged in what philosophers call 'incontinent actions', i.e. actions that go against better knowledge, as it were (Davidson 1980: 21ff.). Incontinent actions seem to imply weakness of will; as such they have been repressed and relegated to the non-scholarly universe of anecdote and joke. Their real significance as conveyors of unprecedented insight in the workings of culture and scholarship has been overlooked. In the chapters of this volume, they have been restored to import; the experience of not being able even to understand oneself, or of acting against better (*sic*) judgment is crucial to the understanding of the limitations of reason. Reason invariably gets stuck; that is when we need emotion to break a tie (Sousa 1990: 16).

Emotions provide the solution to the problem of actions done intentionally but 'against one's better judgment', that is, the problem of weak will once again. Such actions are done for a reason, and are therefore rational, yet there were better reasons for doing something else, and the actions are therefore also irrational (ibid.). The relative saliency of the two opposed arguments or possible actions is determined by a motivational force that disconnects the 'better' judgment from the course of action, and that cannot be referred to pure reason.

The corporeal nature of knowledge as practical mastery of the world, has been stressed again and again in this volume. Pavlos Kavouras, for instance, demonstrates how moral judgment is embodied in a particular person. In general, cultural models are embodied, both in the sense that they become encoded (internalized) in bodily practices, and in the sense that they are expressed (externalized) in action rather than words. The incarnation of 'common sense', a concept which is restored to import by Marian Kempny and Wojciech Burszta in this volume, implies that the body can no longer be seen as pure object, or as a designified and passive bearer of the mind, solitarily attending to the world as subject.

In the anthropological literature the body has been largely absent as the locus of perceiving, or the ultimate point of orientation. The scientific rationality has acclaimed the mind as the sole instrument of apprehension. Yet we cannot understand the texture of the perceptual field without reference to the body (Leder 1990: 13); the body *is* the self, not just its carrier. The body is a nodal point in our attention to the world. As suggested by Merleau-Ponty, one's own body is a 'third term', always tacitly implied in any figure-ground construction (Merleau-Ponty 1962: 101). The body is the zero-point of perception, the centre from which the senses project themselves out into the world and defines the horizon of the self. As zero-point it has remained absent from view

– not unlike the ethnographer who has been a 'third person' in the cultural encounter in the field, discursively absent as locus of perception (Hastrup 1987b).

The important point is to realize that the field-world is not experienced through the fixed coordinates of a semantic space. The world is always experienced from a particular point in a social space, as particularly clearly illustrated in Thomas Widlok's discussion of the Kalahari foragers. Moreover, the point from which we experience the world is in constant motion. Ethnography starts with the tour rather than the map. Anthropologists are generally keenly aware of their shifting positions in the global culture. Their trade is based on travelling and on the incarnation of strange fields. Yet surprisingly little attention has been given to the actual travelling body; we have almost relegated the fact of travel itself to the status of metaphor, foreshadowed by 'equestrian' Montaigne as well as 'pedestrian' Rousseau (cf. Van den Abbeele 1992).

In this sense, anthropology has been deeply permeated by the European legacy of pilgrims' narratives, marked more by the implicit fear of losing one's way than by the explicit search for new horizons. This fear reached a peak in Descartes's obsession with the right way to reach truth; his work expresses an overwhelming desire for utmost certainty. The metaphors used betray Descartes's fear of losing his footing and his view of error as wanderings or aberrations from truth (Van den Abbeele 1992: 41). The *cogito* is firmly established as a topographical point. As a matter of course, ocular and travel metaphors became 'natural' vehicles of new understanding (see also Rorty 1979).

Seeing and journeying have been metaphors of directive force in anthropology too, and the worlds we have been studying have been plotted into the Cartesian coordinates. The actual substance or locus of both seeing and journeying have been strangely neglected, however. If metaphors activate inchoate pronouns (Fernandez 1986), we have to investigate the nature of the 'I' to which they are adjective. There is no seeing from 'nowhere in particular'. And there are no fixed coordinates of a semantic space that we can just objectively map. There is simply no referential practice outside a corporeal setting, in which the individual agent is situated. The shift to an ego-centric approach to referentiality is a shift from a semantic to a pragmatic view of culture, and of science. This does not exclude 'semantic' interests of course; it only integrates studies of meaning in studies of practice.

The agent of scholarship is a living person, not just a mind. This reformulates the lived body as a path of access, rather than a thing. To understand the nature of this path means to analyse the body as presence, and agency as incorporated. Apart from the obvious hard work of the ethnographer, fieldwork is quintessentially an intersubjective experience. From there we realize that 'subjective states – sensations, feelings, and emotions – cannot be found, recognized, or discovered in bodies but are attributed to them on the basis of certain observable manifestations that warrant such attribution' (Vendler 1984: 201). Attribution of feeling demands a degree of personal involvement because particular phenomena warrant attribution of feeling not because there is a scientifically established chain between experience and behaviour, but because we have learned what it means to 'be in pain', or to 'be hungry'. Thus 'the connection between subjective states and overt manifestation is to be found in one's own experience' (ibid.: 201). In other words, there is no way of understanding people except through one's own experience and power of imagination. That is why we have to incarnate the field in order to comprehend it.

THE HEGEMONY OF REASON

With self-mastery cast as an ability to control the body by means of reason, the hegemony of the latter 'is defined no longer as that of a dominant vision but rather in terms of a directing agency subordinating a functional domain' (Taylor 1989: 144). Reason must rule over passion, mind must be superordinate to body. Until recently this hegemonic relation has been almost unquestioned.

The dualism of mind and body thus implies hierarchy, an implicit scheme of evaluation: 'Descartes' ethic, just as much as his epistemology, calls for disengagement from world and body and the assumption of an instrumental stance toward them' (Taylor 1989: 155). The upshot, and one with profound consequences for the anthropological project, is a kind of rationality which is defined no longer substantively, in terms of the order of being, but procedurally, in terms of the standards by which we construct orders in science and life.

It is the 'procedural rationality', rather than the mind–body dualism itself, that we have to evince from anthropology, where it has reigned supreme for a century, since Durkheim advocated a disengaged, objective stance in the study of society, and until the most recent modes of semantic anthropology. Anthropology has grown within a field defined by Cartesian coordinates; culture and society were studied from 'above', so to speak. The objectivist road to knowledge went by a God's-eye view upon the world. To reach maturity, anthropology must work by its own lights and bring to methodological effect the fact that there is no disengaged standpoint of knowing. We cannot know except by way of our own presence and questioning. Knowledge is profoundly embodied. The previous heroes of science who gained control over the world through disengagement are replaced by human beings who achieve understanding by way of involvement. This is the rationale for scrutinizing the lived experience of the anthropologist. The third-person, objectifying perspective of the body betrays our first-person, subjective experience by way of it. There is no human life to be studied in the corpse. The threat posed by the ultimate disappearance of the body, death, may have been discursively subdued in objectivism, but lived experience is still not understood by way of it.

The capacity for understanding is not solely located in the mind, as we have seen; pure reason, as opposed to imagination, is not the locus of rationality. Human rationality is profoundly imaginative; it is a capacity for ordering representations, for making sense of unprecedented experiences, and for acting upon them in mean-ingful ways (Johnson 1987). Meaning is not a fixed relation between sentences and objective reality, as objectivism has it. 'Grasping a meaning is an *event* of understanding' (ibid.: 175); it is a dynamic, interactive and fundamentally imaginative process re-lating to previous experiences and embodied knowledge. Meaning does not exist in itself within the fixed coordinates of an abstract place; it is always meaning *for* someone in a particular social space. The 'criteria of relevance rest on and reveal our whole system of values' (Putnam 1981: 202).

The view of understanding as 'a historically and culturally em-bedded, humanly embodied, imaginatively structured event' (Johnson 1987: 175) breaks the hegemony of reason viewed as a hierarchical relationship between mind and body.

ANTHROPOLOGICAL KNOWLEDGE INC.

The desire for fixed standards in science is challenged by the frightening indeterminacy of experience. By insisting on social experience as the starting-point for anthropological reflection, anthropology gives this challenge a profound epistemological potential, which we are only beginning to explore. The exploration takes off in a view of science which derives as much from Romanticism as from Enlightenment notions of rationality.[3]

To understand the interplay between social processes and cultural knowledge, the model set by Enlightenment (natural) science is of limited value. The search for the One Truth in the Many is at odds with the relativist experience of anthropology. This relativism, too often reduced to caricature in criticisms of anthropology, is conceptual rather than ontological (Davidson 1984: 227ff.). The empirical equivalence of alternative reference schemes, abundantly demonstrated by anthropology, does not imply that all kinds of knowledge are equally valid. The fact that there is no uniform objective reality does not mean that there are *no* objective realities at all (Shweder 1991: 29). These realities are studied by anthropologists in a project resembling Romanticism as much as Enlightenment: imagination is restored to value as a quintessential quality of reason. In the words of Richard Shweder, the project of Romanticism is 'to dignify subjective experience, not to deny reality; to appreciate imagination, not to disregard reason; to honor our differences, not to underestimate our common humanity' (ibid.: 11).

Within this view of the anthropological practice, there are no facts without value, no reason without emotion, and no knowledge without experience. This implies a view of truth and objectivity as based in rational acceptability (Putnam 1981 and 1990); and in agreement within a scholarly community of potential dissenters (Rorty 1989 and 1991). Acceptability, again, is (generally) obtained not by force, but by a degree of coherence with experience. This is part of the answer to the question put by Mark Johnson: 'How is it that knowledge and objectivity are possible given the irreducibly imaginative and embodied character of human understanding and rationality?' (Johnson 1987: 196).

In this volume we have seen not only how knowledge is possible; we have also seen how the particular conditions of knowledge in anthropology as founded in fieldwork contribute to a sense of shared experience among anthropologists. This is what incorporates us into a field of knowledge which embraces the individual projects and transcends them all. Incorporated knowledge may be put into action and thus reflect back upon and change social experience. This is the substantial rationale for continuing to practise anthropology.

NOTES

1 This is Rule Two in Descartes's *Rules for the Direction of our Native Intelligence*, originally composed in 1628. My references to Descartes in this chapter are from *Descartes: Selected Philosophical Writings* (1988).
2 In the works referred to here, pain is generally studied from the perspective of the individual. As such they are fine illustrations not only of the 'body in the world', but also, and no less significantly, of the fact that pain strikes one alone. It 'is marked by an interiority that another cannot share' (Leder 1990: 74). In this, pain contrasts with pleasure, which is most often shared.
3 These notions are used in a very broad sense as indicators of two different, yet most often somewhat entangled, perspectives on the world.

REFERENCES

Ardener, Edwin (1987) 'Remote areas: some theoretical considerations', in Anthony Jackson, ed., *Anthropology at Home* (ASA Monographs 25), London: Routledge.
—— (1989) *The Voice of Prophecy and Other Essays*, ed. Malcolm Chapman, Oxford: Blackwell.
Bateson, Gregory (1972) *Steps to an Ecology of Mind*, New York: Ballantine.
Bernstein, Richard J. (1983) *Beyond Objectivism and Relativism*, Oxford: Blackwell.
Boorstein, Daniel (1985) *The Discoverers: A History of Man's Search to Know his World and Himself*, New York: Vintage.
Bourdieu, Pierre (1990) *The Logic of Practice*, Cambridge: Polity Press.
Certeau, Michel de (1988) *The Practice of Everyday Life*, Berkeley: University of California Press.
Clifford, James (1988) *The Predicament of Culture*, Cambridge, Mass.: Harvard University Press.
Clifford, James, and Marcus, George, eds (1986) *Writing Culture: The Poetics and Politics of Ethnography*, Berkeley: University of California Press.
D'Andrade, Roy (1992) 'Schemas and motivation', in Roy D'Andrade and Claudia Strauss, eds, *Human Motives and Cultural Models*, Cambridge: Cambridge University Press.
Davidson, Donald (1980) *Essays on Actions and Events*, Oxford: Clarendon Press.
—— (1984) *Inquiries into Truth and Interpretation*, Oxford: Clarendon Press.
Descartes, René (1988) *Selected Philosophical Writings*, introd. John Cottingham, Cambridge: Cambridge University Press.

Fabian, Johannes (1983) *Time and the Other*, New York: Columbia University Press.

Fernandez, James (1986) *Persuasions and Performances: The Play of Tropes in Culture*, Bloomington: University of Indiana Press.

Foucault, Michel (1963) *Naissance de la clinique*, Paris: Plon.

Frängsmyr, Tore (1984) *Vetenskapsmannen som Hjälte*, Stockholm: Norstedt.

Geertz, Clifford (1988) *Works and Lives: The Anthropologist as Author*, Stanford, Calif.: Stanford University Press.

Good, Mary-Jo Delvecchio, Brodwin, Paul E., Good, Byron J., and Kleinman, Arthur, eds (1992) *Pain as Human Experience: An Anthropological Perspective*, Berkeley: University of California Press.

Hanks, William F. (1990) *Referential Practice: Language and Lived Space among the Maya*, Chicago: University of Chicago Press.

Harré, Rom (1978) 'Architectonic man: on the structuring of lived experience', in R.H. Brown and S.M. Lyman, eds, *Structure, Consciousness and History*, Cambridge: Cambridge University Press.

Hastrup, Kirsten (1986) 'Veracity and visibility: the problem of authenticity in anthropology', *Folk* 28: 5–17.

—— (1987a) 'The challenge of the unreal, or how anthropology comes to terms with life', *Culture and History* 1: 50–62.

—— (1987b) 'Fieldwork among friends', in Anthony Jackson, ed., *Anthropology at Home* (ASA Monographs 25), London: Routledge.

—— (1987c) 'The reality of anthropology', *Ethnos* 52: 287–300.

—— (1989) 'The prophetic condition', postscript to Edwin Ardener, *The Voice of Prophecy and Other Essays*, ed. Malcolm Chapman, Oxford: Blackwell.

—— (1992) 'Writing ethnography: state of the art', in Judith Okely and Helen Callaway, eds, *Anthropology and Autobiography* (ASA Monographs 27), London: Routledge.

—— (1993) 'Hunger and the hardness of facts', *Man* 28, 4: 727–39.

Hollis, Martin (1985) 'Of masks and men', in M. Carrithers, S. Collins and S. Lukes, eds, *The Category of the Person: Anthropology, Philosophy, History*, Cambridge: Cambridge University Press.

Johnson, Mark (1987) *The Body in the Mind: The Bodily Basis of Meaning, Imagination, and Reason*, Chicago: Chicago University Press.

Kant, Immanuel (1991) *Critique of Pure Reason* (1781), trans. J.M.D. Meiklejohn; introd. A.D. Lindsay (Everyman's Library), London: Dent.

Kleinman, Arthur and Kleinman, Joan (1991) 'Suffering and its professional transformation: toward an ethnography of interpersonal experience', *Culture, Medicine, and Psychiatry* 15: 275–301.

—— (1993) 'Remembering the cultural revolution: alienating pains and the pain of alienation/transformation', paper originally presented to the Association for Asian Studies Annual Meeting, New Orleans 1991.

Leder, Drew (1990) *The Absent Body*, Chicago: University of Chicago Press.

Merchant, Carolyn (1980) *The Death of Nature: Women, Ecology and the Scientific Revolution*, San Francisco, Calif.: Harper & Row.

Merleau-Ponty, Maurice (1962) *Phenomenology of Perception*, trans. Colin Smith, London: Routledge & Kegan Paul.

Ottenberg, Simon (1990) 'Thirty years of fieldnotes: changing relationships to the text', in Roger Sanjek, ed., *Fieldnotes: The Makings of Anthropology*, Ithaca, NY: Cornell University Press.

Putnam, Hilary (1981) *Reason, Truth and History*, Cambridge: Cambridge University Press.

—— (1990) *Realism with a Human Face*, Cambridge, Mass.: Harvard University Press.

Quinn, Naomi (1992) 'The motivational force of self-understanding', in Roy D'Andrade and Claudia Strauss, eds, *Human Motives and Cultural Models*, Cambridge: Cambridge University Press.

Rorty, Richard (1979) *Philosophy and the Mirror of Nature*, Oxford: Blackwell.

—— (1989) *Contingency, Irony and Solidarity*, Cambridge: Cambridge University Press.

—— (1991) *Objectivity, Relativism, and Truth*, Cambridge: Cambridge University Press.

Salmond, Anne (1982) 'Theoretical landscapes', in David Parkin, ed., *Semantic Anthropology* (ASA Monographs 22), London: Academic Press.

Shweder, Richard A. (1991) *Thinking through Cultures*, Cambridge, Mass.: Harvard University Press.

Sousa, R. de (1990) *The Rationality of Emotion*, Cambridge, Mass.: MIT Press.

Stoller, Paul (1989) *The Taste of Ethnographic Things: The Senses in Anthropology*, Philadelphia: University of Pennsylvania Press.

Strauss, Claudia, and Quinn, Naomi (1993) 'A cognitive/cultural anthropology', in Robert Borofsky, ed., *Assessing Developments in Anthropology*, New York: McGraw-Hill.

Taylor, Charles (1989) *Sources of the Self: The Making of the Modern Identity*, Cambridge: Cambridge University Press.

Van den Abbeele, Georges (1992) *Travel as Metaphor from Montaigne to Rousseau*, Minneapolis: University of Minnesota Press.

Varela, Francisco J., Thompson, Evan, and Rosch, Eleanor, eds (1992) *The Embodied Mind: Cognitive Science and Human Experience*, Cambridge, Mass.: MIT Press.

Vendler, Zeno (1984) 'Understanding others', in Richard A. Shweder and Robert A. LeVine, eds, *Culture Theory*, Cambridge: Cambridge University Press.

Name index

Subject index

action 30, 41, 106–11, 232–30; *see also* body; meaning; motivation
ageing: in rural France 3, 45–63
animal taxonomy, native 132
anthropology of anthropology 124
archaeological methods 46
archives, Libyan 201–9, 212
authority, ethnographic 4–5, 49, 80, 93
authority relations: in Pakistan 70–1, 74, 76–7
autobiography 1, 2; Kalitsa's 146; *see also* self

Barsawa 180–7
bereavement 21
body 76–7, 83, 90, 92, 103; absence of 7–8, 227–32; body/mind dualism 228, 229–30, 233, 235–6; incarnated field 231–35; mastery of *see* purdah
Boers 188
Botswana *see* Kalahari debate
Brazil 24
Bushmen 180–97

caste conflict: in Nepal 22–4
categorization 84, 97; and relationship between anthropological language and social practice 104, 105, 107, 108, 110, 117
cattle-lending and herding *see* Kalahari debate

ceremonies: in Karpathos 146, 150–2, 153–4; *see also* ritual
clothes: use of, in purdah 66, 71–3, 75
cognition 76, 77, 113–14, 121, 124, 128, 132–6; *see also* categorization; knowledge
cognitive anthropology: interdisciplinary research in 180, 181, 192–4
cognitive science 83, 193
common sense 9–10, 121–36, 233
communication 25, 114, 115; analogic and digital 31, 41–2, *see also* language
community: and moral judgment in Greece 139–61; *see also* space
comprehension: Weber and 106
computers: use in research 201, 206–20
congruence 90, 96
contextualization 28
cultural models 6–7; and shared reasoning in fieldwork 83–6, 87, 88–9, 96, 97
culture 2, 231; invention of 28–43; relation to language 15, 16, 24, 28

dance 41–2
death: in Brazil 24
discourse 95, 96, 111, 125
distance: creation of 35, 38, 39, 41, 92, 180